God's First King

God's First King
The Story of Saul

SHAUL BAR

CASCADE Books • Eugene, Oregon

GOD'S FIRST KING
The Story of Saul

Copyright © 2013 Shaul Bar. All rights reserved. Except for brief quotations in critical publications or reviews, no part of this book may be reproduced in any manner without prior written permission from the publisher. Write: Permissions, Wipf and Stock Publishers, 199 W. 8th Ave., Suite 3, Eugene, OR 97401.

Cascade Books
An Imprint of Wipf and Stock Publishers
199 W. 8th Ave., Suite 3
Eugene, OR 97401

www.wipfandstock.com

ISBN 13: 978-1-62032-491-2

Cataloguing-in-Publication data:

Bar, Shaul.

God's first king : the story of Saul / Shaul Bar.

xviii + 152 pp. ; 23 cm. Includes bibliographical references and index.

ISBN 13: 978-1-62032-491-2

1. Saul, King of Israel. 2. Bible. O.T. 1 Samuel—Criticism, interpretation, etc. I. Title.

BS580 S3 B37 2013

Manufactured in the USA

Chapter 6 "Saul and the Witch of En-dor" is used by permission from my earlier book: *I Deal Death and Give Life* (Piscataway, NJ: Gorgias Press, 2010) 290–98.

Dedicated to the memory of
Shifra Lerner
Moshe (Monjek) Raz
Shuli Finkelstein Roth
Forever in our hearts

Contents

Acknowledgments · ix
Abbreviations · xi
Introduction · xiii

1 **The Search for a King** · 1
   Appoint a King for Us
   Samuel's Denunciation of Kingship
   The Lost Donkeys of Kish
   Saul's Anointing

2 **Saul's Wars** · 22
   The Rebellion against the Philistines
   The Battle at the Valley of Elah
   The War against the Amalekites
   The Wars in Trans-Jordan

3 **Saul versus David** · 46
   The Rise to Power
   The Unknown David
   Saul's Hostility
   Killing David
   Relinquishing David
   Pursuer and Pursued

4 **Feuds in the King's Court!** · 68
   Jonathan
   Saul and His Courtiers
   Saul and His Daughters
   Military Heroes
   Saul and Samuel

5 Saul a State Builder · 92
Servants in the King's Court
Taxation
Army
Capital
Cultic Center

6 Saul and the Witch of En-dor · 110

7 The Last Battle · 117
The Death of Saul
Ish-bosheth
The Return of Michal
The Murders of Abner and Ish-bosheth
Mephibosheth and Saul's Remaining Descendants

8 Conclusion · 140

Bibliography · 143
Index · 153

Acknowledgments

To start with, I would like to thank my colleague Stephen Benin at the University of Memphis who read an early draft of the manuscript and offered many perceptive comments and insights. Other friends read subsequent drafts of the manuscript, particularly Bob Turner, Circulation Librarian at Harding School of Theology. The Renaissance man, Dr. Steve Wachtel, read part of it and offered his wisdom. Dr. Dan Bahat, former Chief Archeologist of Jerusalem, made suggestions about archaeological matters. Anna S. Chernak read the manuscript and offered valuable advice and continuous encouragement.

I want to express appreciation for the resources and to the staff of the Harding School of Theology in Memphis, where Librarian Don Meredith led me to materials, Associate Librarian Sheila Owen helped me with research, and Evelyn Meredith supported my research with great cheerfulness. I am grateful as well to J. Andrew Sowers for preparing the index and to Clint Burnett, now a student at Boston University School of Theology, for helping with the preparation of the manuscript for publication.

Special thanks to the Hebrew Union College Library in New York, where Head Librarian Dr. Philip Miller provided me with all the necessary help and wisdom, and Librarian Tina Weiss helped me with research.

Finally, a special thanks to Dr. K. C. Hanson, editor in chief at Wipf & Stock, for his devotion and expertise in transforming my manuscript into this book.

Shaul Bar
Memphis, Tennessee
June 2012

Abbreviations

AASOR Annual of the American Schools of Oriental Research
AB Anchor Bible
ABD *The Anchor Bible Dictionary.* 6 vols. Edited by D. N. Freedman. New York: Doubleday, 1992
AJBA *Australian Journal of Biblical Archeology*
ANEP *The Ancient Near East in Pictures Relating to the Old Testament.* Edited by J. B. Pritchard. Princeton: Princeton University Press, 1954, 1968
ANET *Ancient Near Eastern Texts Relating to the Old Testament.* 3rd ed. Edited by J. B. Pritchard. Princeton: Princeton University Press, 1969
BA *Biblical Archaeologist*
BAR *Biblical Archaeologist Reader*
BASOR *Bulletin of the American Schools of Oriental Research*
BDB F. Brown, S. R. Driver, and C. A. Briggs, *Hebrew and English Lexicon of the Old Testament.* Oxford: Clarendon, 1907
BethM *Beth Miqra*
BHH *Biblisch-historisches Hanwörterbuch.* 3 vols. Edited by B. Reicke and L. Rost. Göttingen, 1962–1966
Bib *Biblica*
BN *Biblische Notizen*
BZAW Beihefte zur Zeitschrift für die alttestamentliche Wissenschaft
CS *The Context of Scripture.* Vol 1. *Canonical Composition from Biblical World.* Edited by W. W. Hallo. Leiden: Brill, 1997. Vol. 2: *Monumental Inscription from the Biblical World.* Leiden: Brill, 2000

Abbreviations

EMiqr	*Entsiqlopedia Miqrait – Encyclopaedia Biblica.* 8 vols. Jerusalem, 1950–1982
FAT	Forschungen zum Alten Testament
FRLANT	Forschungen zur Religion und Literatur des Alten und Neuen Testaments
HALOT	*The Hebrew and Aramaic Lexicon of the Old Testament.* Edited by L. Koehler and W. Baumgartner. Translated by M. E. J. Richardson. 4 vols. Leiden: Brill, 1994–2000
HSM	Harvard Semitic Monographs
IEJ	*Israel Exploration Journal*
JBL	*Journal of Biblical Literature*
JPOS	*Journal of the Palestine Oriental Society*
JSOT	*Journal for the Study of the Old Testament*
JSOTSup	Journal for the Study of the Old Testament Supplement Series
JSS	*Journal of Semitic Studies*
KTU	*Die keilalphabetischen Texte aus Ugarit,* I, ed. M. Dietrich, O. Loretz, and J. Sanmartin. AOAT 24. Neukirchen-Vluyn, 1976
NCB	New Century Bible
OTWSA	Die Ou-Testamentiese Werkgemeenskap in Suid-Afrika
PEQ	*Palestine Exploration Quarterly*
RB	*Revue Biblique*
RS	Ras Shamra text
Syria	*Syria: Revue d'art oriental et d'archéologie*
TA	Tel Aviv
Tarb	Tarbiz
TDOT	*Theological Dictionary of the Old Testament.* 14 vols. Edited by G. J. Botterweck and H. Ringgren. Translated by Geoffrey W. Bromiley et al. Grand Rapids: Eerdmans, 1974–2004
UT	Ugaritic text
UT	C. H. Gordon. *Ugaritic Textbook.* Analecta Orientalia 38. Rome: Pontificium Institutum Biblicum, 1965
VAB	Vorderasiatische Bibliothek. 7 vols. Leipzig, 1907–1916
VT	*Vetus Testamentum*

Introduction

SAUL, SON OF KISH, from the tribe of Benjamin, was the first king of Israel (1029–1005 BCE). His life was full of drama and tribulations, and ended tragically. The books of Samuel and Chronicles are the main sources of information about Saul. The biblical prophetic books and Psalms barely mention him, and sometimes even ignore him as they do in Pss 78:59–72; 89:20–39. Saul's life is related mainly in 1 Samuel 9–15; the text is neither homogeneous nor cohesive, and evidently derived from earlier sources. These sources tend to describe Saul's reign as an introduction to the career of David, and a source that modifies the part played by Samuel. According to the Talmud, Samuel wrote the book that bears his name, and he wrote Judges and Ruth as well. The Talmud asks: "But it is written in it, *Now Samuel was dead?*—It was completed by Gad the seer and Nathan the Prophet."[1] The two books of Samuel were originally one book in the Hebrew canon. They have been divided in Hebrew manuscripts and printed editions since 1448. The death of Saul is a logical ending to First Samuel. Second Samuel continues with the story of David; but David's story extends into the first two chapters of 1 Kings.

In modern scholarship, 1 Samuel is part of the so-called Deuteronomistic History. This includes the books of Deuteronomy, Joshua, Judges, 1–2 Samuel, and 1–2 Kings. These books tell the history of Israel from the time of Moses to the destruction of the kingdom of Judah in 586 BCE. They are believed to comprise a single work because they share the elements of structure, writing style, and theological outlook. The books examine the history of Israel according to the laws set forth in Deuteronomy. The main doctrines of Deuteronomy are: centralized worship in Jerusalem, obedience to the Deuteronomistic law, and abstinence from apostasy. Victory and defeat accordingly result from obedience or disobedience to the law.

1. *B. Bat.* 15a.

Introduction

Hence it is more theological history than pure history. However, examination of the book of Samuel reveals a limited influence of the Deuteronomistic redaction. According to McCarter, the most striking aspect of the Deuteronomistic redaction of the books of Samuel is its sparseness.[2] The strict Deuteronomistic structure that is found in the books of Judges and Kings is not evident in Samuel.

The book of Samuel is a blend of historiography, literary poetics, and ethical and theological perceptions. There is little agreement among scholars about the original formation of the material in Samuel.[3] Analysis of the book points to the presence of three major blocks. The first block (chapters 1–7) tells the story of the prophet Samuel, who is the dominant figure. Chapter 8 is transitional and introduces the monarchy. The second block (chapters 9–15) tells the "Story of Saul" where Saul is the protagonist. The third block (chapters 16–31) contains the "Story of Saul and David," and describes the feuds between the two rivals. We will show that an author sympathetic to David at the time, probably wrote the third block when David needed to justify his claim to the throne in response to claims of Saul's family.

The book of Samuel portrays Saul as a colorful personality with excesses—the classical hero of a tragedy. Moreover, Saul's excellent virtues qualified him for the monarchy. He had courage and military power, and he was chosen to reign.[4] His prowess was evident in his first battle against the Ammonites. He went with his sons to his last battle against the Philistines, even when he knew the outcome of the war. He fell on his sword, and died on the battlefield as befits a classical hero. Saul was also modest and shy and it is not surprising that he rebuked Samuel for making him king. Later, when people were looking for him he was not found, since he was hiding among the equipment.

The first detail we learn about Saul is that he was unusually handsome.[5] We also read that he was shy and modest implying that he tried to humble himself. Evidently, there is a contradiction between his physical description and his behavior, which points to his irreconcilable character.

---

2. McCarter, *I Samuel*, 15. For a similar conclusion see: Weiser, *Old Testament*, 168; Haran, *Biblical Collection*, 285–87.

3. For a summary on the different views of the composition of the book of Samuel see Garsiel, "Book of Samuel, " 1–42.

4. *Mid. Sam.* 11:78–79.

5. 1 Sam 9:2; *Ber.* 48b

Introduction

Only later, after the spirit of God seizes him, will he appear to the people with resolved enthusiasm and with boldness.

The rabbis emphasized Saul's modesty, according to Midrash Tanḥuma the casting of lots was initiated because Saul doubted whether he was worthy to be elected.[6] The Midrash puts words in Saul's mouth: "I am not worthy of kingship." They identified the man of Benjamin who came to Shiloh from the battlefield (1 Sam 4:12) with Saul: "R. Levi said: sixty miles Saul marched on the same day. He was in the battle line, and (there he) heard that the tablets (of the law) were carried off. He went and snatched them from Goliath's hand, and (then) he came (to Shilo)."[7] This points to Saul's bravery and to the fact that he fought for God long before he was chosen to be king. The Midrash also stresses Saul's obedience to Jewish Law (*halakha*) since he ordered that sacrificial commandments and laws be kept (1 Sam 14:32–35).[8]

The sages, who were intrigued by his personality, changed their interpretation concerning his sin in the war against Amalek so that the sin is portrayed favorably. Therefore, Saul refused to see the women, children, and cattle as sinners who deserved death. Thus, "A *bat kol* (Heavenly voice) emanated and said to him: 'Do not be overly righteous.'"[9] Moreover, the sages thought so highly of Saul that they listed him among their eight princes: Jesse (the father of king David); Saul himself; the prophets Samuel, Elijah, Amos, and Zephaniah; the righteous King Zedekiah; and the Messiah.[10]

In contrast to the positive portrayal of Saul in the Bible and the midrashim, there are passages which portray him differently: a man who chases demons, a man obsessed with pursuit of David, and a man who is paranoid. Thus he struggles constantly with his own family members as well as his circle of friends. He feuds with the prophet Samuel. He is ruthless and merciless. He kills the priests of Nob and massacres the Gibeonites. From the battle at Michmas till the last day of his life, fear is his constant companion—fear of the people, fear of his son Jonathan, fear of David, fear of the Benjaminites, and fear of the Philistines, the people of Nob, and the Gibeonites. Even on the eve of his last battle against the Philistines, "When Saul saw the Philistine force, his heart trembled with fear" (1 Sam 28:5).

6. *Tanḥ. B Lev.* 2b:4
7. *Midr. Sam.* 11:1; *Midr. Pss* 7:2
8. *Midr. Sam.* 7:2; *b. Zebaḥ.* 120a
9. *Yoma* 23b.
10. *Succah* 52b.

Introduction

When Samuel rose from the grave and delivered his message to him, Saul was terrified (v. 20). Evidently these fears were not baseless but reflective of actual threats. Fear also caused him to indulge in self-pity: "May you be blessed of the Lord for the compassion you have shown me!" (1 Sam 23:21). This self-pity was so obvious that in his pursuit of David he was transformed from pursuer to pursued.

The ambivalent attitude towards Saul is also found among the sages, who, as mentioned above, praised Saul on one hand, but criticized him harshly on the other. In reference to Ps 7:1: "Shiggaion of David which he sang to the Lord, concerning Cush, a Benjaminite," they said that Saul was unusual in the aspect of his deeds.[11] The sages believed that power changes people and affects their attitude: "Because when Samuel came to anoint Saul as a king, Saul ran away (from the kingship). But once he had ascended (the throne) and Samuel told him to step down from it in favor of David, (Saul) tried to kill David."[12]

Many important works have appeared in recent years concerning Saul and the establishment of the Israelite monarchy, including: Birch, *The Rise of the Israelite Monarchy: The Growth and Development of I Samuel 7–15*; Edelman, *King Saul and the Historiography of Judah*; Edelman, *Saulide Israel: A Literary and Historical Investigation*; Garsiel, *The First Book of Samuel: A Literary Study of Comparative Structures, Analogies and Parallels*; Brooks, *Saul and the Monarchy: A New Look*; and Ehrlich and White, eds., *Saul in Story and Tradition*. In addition, there are two important commentaries on the book of Samuel by Hertzberg, *I & II Samuel* and McCarter, *I Samuel* and *II Samuel*. All of them are limited to particular aspects of this topic. By contrast, we shall attempt to look at the subject from additional perspectives including those of the Talmud and Midrashim and the Jewish medieval commentators. The Babylonian Talmud contains a vast amount of *aggadot*—stories. The Midrash includes anthologies and compilations of homilies including biblical exegesis and public sermons. The various sects and currents in Judaism left their mark on it; and almost everything that Jews thought during a period of more than a thousand years can be found there. Though the interpretative methods of the medieval commentators vary, we still find that they compromise between the literal and the Midrashic interpretation of the biblical text. In addition, they pursue philological-contextual interpretation with a view to reason and science.

11. *Moed Katan* 16b.
12. *Menachot* 109b.

Introduction

In this book, our main goal is to rediscover Saul, to have a better understanding of his achievements and failures as the first king of Israel. In chapter 1, we examine the establishment of the Israelite monarchy and we look for the reasons behind its formation. Did fear of the Philistines require a political change? Or were other reasons more important, reasons such as social and political motives for the demand. Why did Samuel reject the idea of monarchy, and why do we read that Saul was anointed as king three times: the first time in secrecy, the second time in Mizpah before all the people, and the third time in Gilgal?

In chapter 2 we scrutinize Saul's wars. According to the biblical narrative, Saul waged war against the Moabites, Ammonites, Edomites, the Philistines, and the kings of Zobah (1 Sam 14:47-48). In addition, Saul fought three major wars which are described in detail: the war against the Ammonites (chapter 11), the war against the Philistines where three major battles are described (chapters 13-14; 17; 28-31), as well as battles with the Philistines on a smaller scale (chapters 18:27, 30; 19:8; 23:1, 27). The third major battle was the war against the Amalekites portrayed in chapter 15. In this chapter, we analyze Saul's wars from a literary and historical perspective. We will try to find the historical truth behind Saul's wars. Thus, we discuss the questions why Saul fought those particular enemies, and what exactly he wanted to achieve.

In chapter 3 we contrast the two major heroes in the book of Samuel—Saul and David. We examine the images that the narrator creates for our heroes. We review them as they are described in the book of Samuel, and we evaluate the reasons for this description. We compare the coronations of Saul and David. We examine the stories dealing with Saul's hostility towards David. Saul tried to kill David on several occasions. We look at the narrator's depiction of David. Was he totally different from Saul? We trust that our comparison will provide a basis for understanding why the kingship was taken from Saul and transferred to David.

In chapter 4 we will monitor the feuds in the king's court. Saul is portrayed as fighting and distrusting the people in his inner circle. Even among his own family, there is constant tension, and suspicion between Saul, his son Jonathan, and his daughters, who side with David against their father. In addition, we describe Saul's relations with his courtiers and warriors, and we evaluate the reasons for their support of David. We also look at the relations between Saul and the prophet Samuel, who rejected Saul as the king of Israel, but nevertheless grieved over him in the

Introduction

end. This study will provide a deeper understanding of Saul's character. It will shed a different light on his personality and ultimately help us to understand his seemingly bizarre behavior.

In chapter 5 we survey Saul's achievements. Since Saul was the first king of Israel, the inevitable question is, what changes did he introduce? Did Saul create a new administrative system? Kings in the ancient world relied on their army to rule. Did Saul establish a standing army? Did he impose taxes in order to govern? Kings in the ancient world were known for grandiose building projects—capital cities, religious centers, and fortresses. Did Saul have any part in this? These questions will help us discover if the new king achieved his goal to change Israel from a loose federation of tribes into a unified monarchy.

In chapter 6 we look at the story of Saul and the witch of Endor. In his distress, Saul seeks a medium to bring up the spirit of the dead prophet Samuel, because the Lord has failed to answer him, whether by dreams, by the *Urim ve-Tummim*, or through prophets. What did Saul see and what rites did the medium employ to raise Samuel? The Midrash reports that "she did what she did, and she said what she said, and raised him." Why was Samuel angry with Saul: "Why have you disturbed me (*hirgaztani*) and brought me up?" (1 Sam 28:15). Finally how did Saul and the witch react to Samuel's message?

Chapter 7 deals with the downfall of the house of Saul. There are three different versions of Saul's death on Mount Gilboa during his last battle. What is the reason for the inclusion of these accounts? How do they differ from each other, and what message are they trying to convey? Saul's death did not end the long feud between the House of Saul and the House of David. With Saul's death we find that Abner crowned Ish-bosheth as Saul's successor, while the men of Judah anointed David over the House of Judah. The war between the House of Saul and the House of David continued. What lay behind these wars? Ish-bosheth and Abner were both murdered. Was David responsible, and also behind the death of Saul, as some suggest? According to the biblical narrative, David handed Saul's seven descendants to the Gibeonites because of alleged bloodguilt. Was this bloodguilt the main reason for his action, or were there some other hidden motives for David's act? Finally, what prompted David to restore lands to Mephibosheth and offer him a seat at the royal table? We consider these and other questions at length.

We trust that this study will afford a provocative and useful insight into the character of Saul, the first king of Israel.

1

The Search For a King

IN ANCIENT NEAR EASTERN civilizations it was believed that kingship came down from heaven. It was a divine institution, and some kings were even considered to be the offspring of gods, or at least semi-divine in nature. Not so in the Hebrew Bible, which records that a human was chosen king; this was none other than Saul. The book of Samuel is the only source from the ancient world that gives us a detailed description of how the monarchy was established. Indeed, the Israelites urged Samuel to appoint a king over them. The elders demanded a king who would govern and rule them. This is described not as a myth or a legend that existed among other nations, but as an accurate tradition reflecting a historical process. Therefore, we will investigate what suddenly prompted the Israelites to ask Samuel to appoint a king over them.

Until this request, Israel was a theocracy, and their heavenly king endowed earthly judges with charismatic powers to fight and deliver them from their enemies. So what prompted Israel's demand for a king? Was it fear of the Philistines? Or were there social and political motives for the request? In two major speeches, "the rights of the king" (1 Sam 8:1–22), and in his farewell speech to the people of Israel (1 Samuel 12), after he had already anointed Saul as a king, the prophet Samuel rejects harshly the idea of kingship. This rejection is puzzling since God already told Abraham: "I will make you exceedingly fertile, and make nations of you; and *kings* shall come forth from you" (Gen 17:6). More so, there is no prohibition against human kingship in the laws of Deuteronomy. Thus, in what era were these anti-monarchial views composed, and by whom? What was the main reason for Samuel's objections to kingship? Was there any personal agenda

God's First King

behind his rejection of kingship? In addition, Saul's coronation appears in three versions. These different versions have provoked much debate among modern scholars, and what stands behind each version requires analysis. Why are they related in different places and in different ways? Are there links between the different traditions?

APPOINT A KING FOR US

Samuel's old age and his sons' corruption led the elders of Israel to implore Samuel to appoint a king to judge them (1 Sam 8:5). Surprisingly, in the Hebrew Bible old age is not always a sign of grace and wisdom, but sometimes is the reason for failure by the biblical hero. Therefore, Isaac's old age facilitated Rebecca and Jacob's deception, and helped appropriate the birth right from Esau (Genesis 27). Eli, in his old age, did not rebuke his sons for their sins (1 Sam 2:22; 3:2, 13). King David, in old age, did not scold Adonijah for his boasting (1 Kgs 1:6); and the aged King Solomon married foreign women and worshiped other gods (1 Kgs 11:4).

Another reason the elders mentioned was the behavior of Samuel's sons. They are described as being bent on gain, accepting bribes, and subverting justice. These transgressions are associated with judges and people with power; personality types the biblical narrators criticize. In Deuteronomy (10:17; 16:19; 27:25) and Exodus (23:6, 8) they appear as transgressions against God's laws. The wicked lives led by Samuel's sons are analogous to Hophni and Phinehas, the sons of Eli, who were known for their sinful lives (1 Sam 2:12–17). Evidently, the criticism of Samuel's sons initiated a crisis and caused tension between Samuel and the elders. This tension is noted as: "Samuel was displeased" (1 Sam 8:6).

At first glance, it is not clear whether the appointment of Samuel's sons as judges was to replace him or to relieve him of judicial responsibilities at a remote site.[1] It was not customary for a judge to appoint his own sons as judges since judgeship was not hereditary. By appointing his sons, Samuel broke the customary practice of God appointing a new judge. Samuel probably tried to create "a hereditary succession" to replace the house of Eli.[2] Therefore, after the destruction of Shiloh he did not ask the people to rebuild Shiloh, but built an altar in his hometown of Ramah

---

1. Josephus mentions a tradition that has one son in Bethel and the other in Beer-sheba (Josephus, *Ant.* 6.32).

2. Hertzberg, *I & II Samuel*, 71.

(1 Sam 7:17). Moreover, he called the people to fast, pray, and sacrifice at Mizpah. He did not even mention the presence of the Ark of the Covenant housed in Kiriath-jearim.[3] It appears that Samuel sought to establish his own dynasty, but the people opposed this attempt. According to R. P. Gordon, Samuel conducted his own "little dynastic experiment."[4] The people of Israel did not want to confront Samuel directly, so they raised concerns about his age and his sons' behavior. Their opposition was directed against the dynastic idea.

The elders believed that the current system was insufficient to handle the Philistine threat. Therefore, the elders do not request a new righteous judge, but asked instead for a king to judge them like all the other nations.[5] This request is repeated after Samuel describes "the rights of the king" (1 Sam 8:11–17). Samuel attempts to persuade the people to abandon the idea of human kingship. Despite Samuel's harsh criticism of human kingship, the people refuse to listen and repeated their demand for a king (8:19; 10:19; 12:12). In 8:20, the people demand that the king will "go out before us and fight our battles." Ackroyd points out that this verse refers to functions of kingship that emphasize "order and security."[6] The people of Israel thought and believed that kingship would bring military advantages; the king would lead them and fight their battles. The Israelites constantly battled with the Philistines, who had oppressed them at the end of the period of the judges and during Eli's tenure as priest. After the defeat at Aphek, the Philistines controlled a large part of the territory of Ephraim. Their army controlled and occupied part of the land of Israel; they set prefects to control those areas. Recent archaeological data show that late in the eleventh century many villages were destroyed and abandoned and others grew in size and became regional centers.[7] Inhabitants of these villages moved to larger and more protected sites. The Philistine threat induced this process. The war with the Philistines was long and continued throughout Saul's lifetime. During Samuel's era, the Philistines were repelled from Ekron to Gath in the south (7:11–14). This victory was short-lived. Later, during Saul's monarchy, after the victory over Goliath, the Israelites chased the Philistines from Gath

3. Ne'eman, "המלכת שאול," 97.

4. R. P. Gordon, *1 & 2 Samuel*, 109.

5. The verb *špṭ* can mean either "to govern" or "to judge." For a detail discussion of the word *špṭ* in West Semitic languages, see Ishida, *History and Historical*, 41–44.

6. Ackroyd, *First Book of Samuel*, 73.

7. Faust, "Settlement Patterns," 14–38.

to Ekron (17:52). Evidently, the temporary leadership that existed since the time of the judges could not deal effectively with the Philistine threat. Therefore, strong leadership was necessary, and a drastic change inevitable. But, was there more than just a threat from the Philistines?

The threat from the Philistines in the west was not the only problem faced by Israel. At the same time, the Ammonites posed a threat on the east side of the Jordan River. The Ammonites had oppressed the Israelites since the time of Jephthah. The victory against the Ammonites was brief (Judg 11:29–34; 12:1–7). There is probably historical truth to the story of the rise of Nahash, the king of the Ammonites (1 Sam 12:12). Most likely, the Israelite tribes in the Transjordan asked for a king in order to face the threat from the Ammonites. Their proximity to the Ammonites, coupled with the fact that Ammon and Moab were monarchies, contributed to their fears. Additionally, 1 Samuel reads: "But when you saw that Nahash, the king of the Ammonites, had come against you, you said, 'No! A king shall rule over us'" (12:12). This is the first example of a demand for a king to fight the Ammonites.

The demand for a king for military reasons is a repeated motif in the other parts of the narrative. In the story of Saul's coronation, God chooses Saul to deliver the Israelites from the hands of the Philistines (9:16). In his speech after the victory against the Ammonites, Samuel describes the idyllic kingship. When the Israelites see that Nahash, king of the Ammonites, was advancing they say to Samuel: "No! A king shall rule over us" (12:12). The demand for a king and desire to be like other nations is ironic. God calls the Israelites his own people; however, they aspire to be like all the other nations. God was their King; nevertheless they want a human king.

Moral and Economic Changes

There was also a moral dimension to the request for a king. Starting at the period of the judges, there are repeated statements about lack of justice that prevailed among the Israelites because there was no king. In Judges 17–21 we find the common refrain: "In those days there was no king in Israel; everyone did as he pleased." This formula unifies diverse stories in Judges by demonstrating the chaos that existed in the absence of a king.[8] The author describes murders, wars, strife among brothers, rapes, and cultic sins. This kind of reality also existed on the eve of the monarchial period. It was the

---

8. Greenspahn, "Egyptian Parallel," 129–30.

The Search For a King

lack of justice and prevailing anarchy that also contributed to the demand for a king. Interestingly, an almost identical formula appears in Egyptian literature from the same period. Papyrus Harris I, most likely dating from the reign of Ramesses IV (ca. 1150 BCE), includes a retrospective history of the interval before the pharaoh Sethnakht's accession, which is described as a time of lawlessness: "The land of Egypt was abandoned, every man a law unto himself. They had no leader (for) many years previously, until other times, when the land of Egypt had officials and city rulers, one (man) slew his fellow, great and humble."[9] After this period, the document describes another time consisting of "empty years" in which the Syrian Irsu set himself up as a prince of Egypt, followed by an account of Sethnakht being chosen by the gods, saying, "He (re)established order (in) the entire land, which had languished: he slew the rebels who had been in Egypt; he cleansed the Great throne of Egypt."[10]

Another possible explanation for the formation of the monarchy in Israel lies in social and economic changes that occurred in Israelite society. The boost in population and growth in agriculture needed to be accommodated.[11] It was the technological advancements, such as agricultural terracing and plastered cisterns for holding rainwater, coupled with the new iron technology that enabled the expansion of settlements and the creation of agricultural surplus. These new independent settlements with their flourishing agriculture attracted the Philistine aggression, which led to the formation of kingship. Gottwald mentions the Philistines as the main reason for the establishment of the monarchy, nevertheless he also claims that the use of iron and plastered water cisterns allowed the expansion of agriculture in the hill country, and thus led to population growth. The production of surpluses required complex management beyond the family unit; this led to social changes.[12]

By the end of the eleventh century the population in the central hill country more than doubled, and other regions of the highlands followed this pattern.[13] The growth in population increased the growth in agricultural productivity, which transformed the Israelite social structure. Population

---

9. Peden, *Egyptian Historical*, 213.

10. Ibid.

11. Frick, *Formation of State*, 26, 66, 138, 191–204.

12. Gottwald, *Tribes of Yahweh*, 655 58.

13. Finkelstein, "Emergence . . . Socio-Political Aspects," 21; Finkelstein, "Emergence . . . Socio-Economic Aspects," 59.

God's First King

growth within the current social structure of the Israelite society, where only the oldest son received double the inheritance, deprived many young men from relying solely on farming for a livelihood. The land in the highlands was very limited, thus many young, unmarried males looked for other economic opportunities. Yet, the establishment of the monarchy created new opportunities; it offered the young people a "safety valve," enabling careers in the military, government, or priesthood.[14] It is believed that David, who was the youngest in his family, was forced to leave home because there wasn't much inheritance left for him when he became of age. David left home because he was looking for a new resource for his livelihood. He found it in the military activity in the service of Saul and later as the leader of his own outlaw band of mercenaries.[15]

SAMUEL'S DENUNCIATION OF KINGSHIP

In contrast to the elders' demand for a king, Samuel the prophet vehemently rejected the idea of human kingship. Modern scholars disagree strongly concerning the reason behind Samuel's denunciation of kingship, and the timing of its composition. Wellhausen believed that the stories describing Samuel's anti-monarchial views were composed in the Second Temple period. Theocratic views were prevalent among the priests and sages who governed during that period. The disappointment arising from the destruction of the temple buttressed this ideology, which viewed human kingship as a sin. The ideal was a religious community, which, through the study of the Torah and the fulfillment of God's commandments, would receive God's mercy and salvation.[16]

Budde held that the anti-monarchial stories were composed in the second half of the eighth century BCE, marked by the decline of the northern kingdom and its eventual destruction. To support his view, he points to the prophecies of Hosea that describe disappointment with human kingship (Hos 3:4–5; 8:4, 10; 13:10–11).[17] Nevertheless, the same prophet embraced messianic expectations, prophesying that in the end days the Israelites: "Will seek the Lord their God and David their King" (3:5).

14. Stager, "Archaeology," 25–27.
15. McKenzie, *King David*, 22.
16. Wellhausen, *Prolegomena*, 255–56; Wellhausen, *Israelitische*, 51, 197, 280; Wellhausen, *Die Composition*, 240.
17. Budde, *Die Bücher Samuel*, 184.

The Search For a King

The opposition to kingship did not emerge in a later period, for it had already existed much earlier among the Israelite tribes. The verses in Samuel that object to kingship do not reflect a later period; they do describe the reality that existed during Saul's period. Those passages were probably composed at the beginning of Saul's reign.[18]

Opposition to human kingship is an early phenomenon and appears in the book of Judges with the story of Gideon.[19] When the men of Israel say to Gideon: "Rule over us—you, your son, and your grandson as well," Gideon replied: "I will not rule over you myself, nor shall my son rule over you; the Lord alone shall rule over you" (Judg 8:22–23). Rejection of human kingship is also found in the fable of Jotham (Judg 9:8–15). The fable parodies human kingship, with its origin in the "plants legend" found in Sumerian literature.[20] In the fables of Gideon and Jotham, the rejection of human kingship is a theme. The stories possess literary traits of an earlier period and do not have traits of later composition, such as Deuteronomistic terminology. One senses that people did not want to give up their individual freedom and liberties.[21]

It was Samuel, not God, who was unhappy with the people's request.[22] Samuel's main objection was the fear that the Israelite kingship would be similar to "the other nations," but as noted already, Samuel had a different agenda; he tried to establish his own prophetic dynasty.[23]

Samuel outlined the rights of the king (1 Sam 8:11–18) to express his objection to human kingship. The whole section is directed against the demand for a human king. Samuel included the following reasons for his objections:

1. The demand for a human king displays distrust in God and his ability to save his people.

2. The request for a king is similar to worshiping other gods.

---

18. Kaufmann, *Toledot ha-'emunah*, 371–73 (Hebrew).

19. In contrast according to Garsiel, the rejection of the monarchy originated from the opposition to change in the existing rules reflected in 1 Sam 8:7–8; 8:11–18, "the law of the king," and in 1 Sam 10:17–19; 12. He believes that "the law of the king" was written during or after Solomon's reign. See Garsiel, "Dispute," 325–27.

20. Lambert, *Babylonian Wisdom*, 151–59.

21. Tsevat, "Emergence," 67.

22. Givati, "משפט המלך ומשפט המלוכה," 220–27.

23. Ibid., 224.

God's First King

3. Human kings will appropriate all the people's possessions, control their lives, and revoke their liberties.

4. Since humans and not God choose the king, God will not answer their pleas or deliver them of their distress (v. 18).[24]

This is one-sided; Samuel avoids mentioning the positive elements of kingship such as establishing justice, providing leadership, and maintaining security. The people of Israel were aware of Samuel's motives and told him: "Let our king rule over us and go out at our head and fight our battles" (1 Sam 8:20).[25]

The rejection of human kingship is also repeated in Samuel's farewell speech (1 Samuel 12). The speech is presented as a dialogue between Samuel and the people where Samuel is the protagonist. It has three major sections: (1) The prophet is compared to the king; (2) the power of the prophet is demonstrated; and (3) the future of the prophet is foretold.[26] In the speech, the king is portrayed as a person who does things for his own self-interest, not as a leader, judge, and warrior. To strengthen this, the king is described as a person who will take (*laqaḥ*) everything from the people and enslave them.[27] Yet, Samuel takes nothing from the people. The king described in Samuel's speech is antithetical to the judges who previously delivered the Israelites from oppression. The implication is clear; this kind of leader is neither needed nor desirable. In comparing the old and the new, the prophet glorifies the past while criticizing the future king.

Samuel viewed himself as God's instrument on earth, and saw human kingship as a threat to his authority and status. It was a direct threat to establishing his dynasty. The demand was also a threat against the authority of the priests in the holy places like Mizpah, Bethel, and Gilgal. A human king meant a decline in priestly power and influence. Evidently, Samuel's fears were justified and from the time that Saul was elected, Samuel's stature declined steadily. He had no role in the establishment of the army (1 Sam 13:2), or the recruitment of people in the war against the Philistines. Moreover, Saul assumed cultic leadership of making sacrifice, a function

---

24. Elat, *Samuel*, 60 (Hebrew).
25. Garsiel, "Dispute," 341.
26. McCarter, *I Samuel*, 218.
27. Weiser, *Samuel*, 40. There are some similarities here to Moses's speech. Korah, Dathan, and Abiram challenged Moses leadership. In his response, Moses said: "I have not taken the ass of any one of them, nor have I wronged any one of them," (Num 16:15). For Hittite parallels see Hoffner, "Crossing," 184.

The Search For a King

formerly held by Samuel. Another blow to his status was the return of the priests of the house of Eli, who became priests in the service of the king. Indeed, from here on, the priests came increasingly to serve the kings of Israel. Not surprisingly Samuel opposed the idea of kingship, realizing that kingship meant a diminution in his power. Samuel's speeches reflect the early monarchial period foreshadowing the future of constant battles over power and influence between the prophets and the kings of Israel.

THE LOST DONKEYS OF KISH

The story of Saul searching for the lost donkeys of his father, and then founding the kingship has been termed by scholars as a *Legende*.[28] The story describes ancient events directed by God. In other words: God chooses the king and the prophet anoints the king. But the Bible does not elucidate why God picked Saul. Similarly, when God chose Abraham no detail of his past life is given, his first seventy-five years are ignored. The same pattern occurred with Gideon, Samson, and David; no explanations for their selection are provided. This evidently troubled the sages, who tried to clarify the rationale for the selection of Saul. According to them, Saul was known for his bravery in the battle of Ebenezer, where he snatched the tablets from the hand of the Philistine warrior Goliath and brought them to Shiloh.[29]

Scholars point to several layers in the account, which includes the story of the lost donkeys and the anointing of Saul. However, they disagree on the subject of which verses to assign to each story.[30] Recently, several studies point to a single account that has been revised and expanded during the process of transmission.[31] The earliest part of the tale belonged to the folkloristic story, describing Saul searching for his father's donkeys.[32] While searching, he encounters a seer or a man of God who indicates his future greatness. The story of Samuel anointing Saul as a prince was inserted into this story.[33]

---

28. Wildberger, "Sage," 1641–44; Fohrer, "Die Sage," 60.

29. *Midr. Sam.* 11.1; *Midr. Pss. Soḥer Tov* 32.

30. Birch, "Development," 55–68; Miller, "Saul," 157–61; Mettinger, *King and Messiah*, 80–98; Klein, *1 Samuel*, 84.

31. Schunck, *Benjamin*, 86–89; Schmidt, *Menschlicher*, 58–102.

32. Klein, *1 Samuel*, 84.

33. Ibid.

God's First King

The editor who inserted this section was influenced by a "call form," which is found in stories about Moses, Gideon, and several prophets.[34]

Saul first appears as a young man sent by his father to search for lost donkeys. The Bible describes him as "an excellent young man; no one among the Israelites was handsomer than he; he was a head taller than any of the people" (1 Sam 9:2). The Hebrew term *baḥur* suggests that he was a young man about to enter adult life. In other words, Saul had reached his maturity and was ready to assume adult responsibilities. Richter suggests that the term means one who can fight in war, receive inheritance, and was of marriageable age.[35]

The second detail about Saul was his physical attraction. The rabbis stress his physical stature, noting he was one of the biblical personalities who were created in God's likeness.[36] Describing an Israelite hero as attractive is a biblical staple, e.g., Joseph (Gen 39:6), Moses (Exod 2:2), David (1 Sam 16:12), Absalom (2 Sam 14:25), and Esther (Esth 2:7). Eissfeldt claimed that God chose Saul because of his height, "he was taller than all the rest of the people from his shoulder upward" (1 Sam 10:22).[37] This is unlikely since God tells Samuel: "For it is not as a man sees that God sees: a man looks into the face, but God looks into the heart" (16:7).[38]

Saul's father, Kish, loses some donkeys. He enlists Saul to help him find the lost animals. In ancient times nobility rode donkeys, and in Zech

---

34. Birch thus points to the existence of the "call form" that includes the following elements: divine confrontation, (9:15), an introductory word (9:16–17), commission, (10:1), objection (9:21), reassurance (10:7b), and sign (10:1b 5–7a). Habel points out that there is a different order in the Saul episode from the standard "call form." He explains this discrepancy by asserting that the call was attached to the pre-existing story of the search for the donkeys. In addition, he points to the function of Samuel who serves as the human mediator of the call. None of this is attested in the Bible. In contrast to Habel, Richter sees parallels between the call of Saul to the calls of Gideon and Moses. He points to the following elements: 1. I have seen the affliction, 9:16, Exod 3:7; 2. Their cry has come to me, 9:16, Exod 3:9; 3. The Sending, 9:16, Judg 6:14–15; Exod 3:10, 15; 4.The anointing as prince, 9:16; 10:1; 5. Savior formula 9:16, Judg 6:14–15; 6. Objection, 9:21, Judg 6:15, Exod 3:11; 4:1, 10; 7. The formula God is with you, 10:7b, Judg 6:16, Exod 3:12; 4:12. 8. Giving of the spirit, 10:6, Judg 6:34. See Richter, *Die sogenannten*, 50; Birch, "Development," 55–68; Klein, *1 Samuel*, 84; Habel, "Form and Significance," 297–323.

35. Richter, *Berufungsberichte*, 30.

36. *Soṭah* 10a.

37. Eissfeldt, *Die Komposition*, 7.

38. In the Koran (2:248), the name that was given to Saul was *Ṭalut*, which is an allusion to his exceptional height. This name was probably influenced by the name given to Goliath, *Jalut*.

The Search For a King

9:9 the messiah rides an ass. Mules are mentioned with the elevation of Solomon as a king (1 Kgs 1:33–35, 38–40). Hence, loss of the donkeys denotes poverty and inability to function as a leader.[39] C. H. Gordon compares Saul with King Agamemnon, whom Nestor encountered wandering at night, and he asks if he is looking for one of his mules or comrades (*Iliad* 10:84).[40]

The search for the lost donkeys leads Saul and his servant across the hill country of Ephraim. Failing to find them, Saul becomes discouraged and resolves to turn back. At this point, the servant urges Saul to seek the help and advice of the man of God who will inform them correctly about their journey. The Hebrew word used for advise is *yaggid* from the verb *higgid* (inform/ make known), which is related etymologically to *nāgîd*, the title that Samuel subsequently bestows on Saul in 10:1. Ironically, Saul asks the man of God to tell him *higgid* about the lost donkeys, but he informs him that he will be king *nagid* of Israel.

It was customary to pay the man of God for advice; hence, Saul was dispirited because of his inability to compensate the man of God with a gift. Paul calls it an "interview fee." Indeed, we read about Jeroboam's wife who accepted gifts when she visited Ahijah (1 Kgs 14:3); gifts for Elijah (2 Kgs 4:42); and prophetic fees in Amos 7:12 and Mic 3:5.[41] Gifts were vital in establishing good relations, and were part of social interaction in the ancient world. After a long journey, a traveler was especially expected to return bearing many gifts.[42] As mentioned above, Saul was dejected because he bore no gift for the prophet.[43] Later, coincidentally, we read that Saul's servant found a quarter of a shekel of silver to give to the prophet. The servant is the dominant character here. First, he urged Saul to consult the prophet after he abandoned his search for the donkeys. Then, after Saul was disheartened for not having a gift, it is the servant again who rescued him with a quarter shekel of silver.

---

39. Stoebe, *Das erste Buch Samuelis*, 202.
40. C. H. Gordon, *Before the Bible*, 229.
41. Paul, "I Samuel 9:7," 542–44.
42. C. H. Gordon, *Before the Bible*, 272–73; Homer, *Od.* 11:355–61.
43. The word for gift here is *tešurah*—a hapax legomenon. It probably comes from the verb *šwr*, to see. Thus *tešurah* is a "gift of greetings." Interestingly, the man of God is called *ro'eh*, which was an old name for the word prophet. *Ro'eh* means seer, and is a participial form of the Hebrew verb "to see." Thus, there is a link between the gift and the prophet. For more information, see Cohen, *Biblical Hapax Legomena*, 24.

God's First King

The Meetings

The narrative records a meeting between Saul and the maidens at the well, even before Saul meets with Samuel. This resembles previous meetings at wells, including Abraham's servant meeting Rebecca, Jacob meeting Rachel, as well as Moses meeting Ziporah. All these meetings result in marriages; but in this meeting, the girls direct Saul to Samuel, who would anoint Saul as king. The girls knew about the prophet's arrival, where he was staying, and about the sacrifice. They were heralds who directed Saul to his destination. Similarly, when Joseph sought his brothers, he encountered a man in the field who had seen them and knew their final destination. In both episodes one senses God's guiding hand, acting behind the scene and directing events. The sages point out that Saul asked the girls a brief question, "Is the seer here?" while the girls replied at length. The Gemara comments: "Because women are talkers, another answer: But Shmuel said: They delayed in order to gaze upon Saul's handsomeness. As it is written about Saul: *from his shoulders up, he was taller than any of the people.*"[44]

Saul did not anticipate the meeting, but Samuel knew about it in advance (9:15–16). God revealed Saul's arrival to Samuel, and instructed him to anoint Saul. Likewise, in the New Testament, God told John the Baptist that Jesus is the Messiah and he will baptize him (John 1:29–34). Ironically, when Saul met Samuel, and he says "tell me" (*haggidah-na*), the reader already knows that Samuel has to designate him as *nagid*/king. Therefore, when Saul says to Samuel "tell me" (*haggidah-na li*), it might mean "designate me."

Samuel asked Saul to dine with him, at which time he will tell him everything that is on his mind. The narrator does not tell us that Saul asked about the donkeys per se, but we learn that they have been found. In addition, Samuel told Saul: "And to whom do the riches of Israel belong if not to you and to your father's house" (9:20). Saul understood it as a reference to kingship. The people of Israel knew that Samuel was looking for a king. Therefore Saul said: "'Am I not a Benjaminite?,' i.e., from the smallest tribe of Israel and from the humblest clan of all the tribe of Benjamin? Then why have you spoken to me this way?" Saul claims he is unworthy, a typical response by people called for a mission by God, as did Moses (Exod 3:11) and Gideon (Judg 6:15).[45]

---

44. *Ber.* 48b

45. R. P. Gordon, *1 & 2 Samuel*, 115.

The Search For a King

Saul is God's anointed; therefore Samuel brought him to a sacrificial meal, placing him at the head of thirty guests. The number thirty is typological, and appears often in Judges and Samuel.[46] The LXX and Josephus have seventy guests.[47] Seventy is an artificial number identifying the guests with the institution of the "elders of Israel" that the Torah numbers seventy (Exod 24:1; Num 11:16, 24). Additionally, Adonijah held a banquet-sacrifice when he planned to succeed his father David as a king, while Absalom invited two hundred people to a banquet-sacrifice as part of his plan to become king (2 Sam 23:13, 18).

Saul sat at the head of the table as a form of introduction. Saul was introduced to those who would be his subjects. Similarly when Moses introduced Joshua as his successor, it reads: "Have him stand before Eleazar the priest and before the whole community, and commission him in their sight" (Num 27:19). At the meal, Saul received the "thigh of consecration"—that part of the sacrificial animal reserved for the priests and their families.[48] He is the only king who received the "thigh of consecration," and is treated as a priest as he is given the priestly share of the sacrifice (1 Sam 10:4). Leviticus (8:32) states that only Aaron and his sons are allowed to eat from this sacrifice, and what was not eaten had to be destroyed. C. H. Gordon points out that all guests were not equal in rank, which was indicated by the amount and quality of their serving. He terms it a "proportionate feast" with parallels in the *Odyssey* (8.98; 11.185).[49] By giving Saul the "thigh of consecration," Samuel indicated Saul's future role.

The encounter between Saul and Samuel contains several motifs found in other prophetic stories. Samuel appears as a prophet; he knows what will happen to Saul on his return journey and whom he will meet (1 Sam 10:2, 3-4, 5-6, 10-11).[50] Samuel prophesied that Saul would meet a band of prophets and prophesy along with them (1 Sam 10:5-6). Thus, like prophets, Saul becomes God's messenger. Another element typical to the prophetic stories that we alluded to was the giving of a suitable gift for his consultation to the prophet (1 Sam 9:7-8; 1 Kgs 14:3; 13:7; 2 Kgs 5:15; 8:8-9).

---

46. Judg 10:4; 12:9; 14:11-13, 19; 20:31, 39; 1 Sam 19:21.

47. Josephus, *Ant.* 6.52.

48. Milgrom, "Alleged Wave Offering," 33-38.

49. C. H. Gordon, *Before the Bible*, 241.

50. Similarly, Elijah directed Ahab on his journey from Carmel to Jezreel (1 Kgs 18:45-46). Elisha prophesied to Kings Jehoram and Jehoshaphat what would take place in their military campaign to Moab (2 Kgs 3:19, 25).

God's First King

SAUL'S ANOINTING

Ramah

At the break of day, Samuel secretly anointed Saul. The servant is dispatched. Saul is left alone with Samuel. In the biblical literature, a divine call is depicted as a private experience. Samuel anointed David among his brothers (17:3-5, 13); Jehu was anointed by one of the disciples of the prophet Elisha (2 Kgs 9:10); Ahijah the Shilonite told Jeroboam that he would become the king when they were outside of Jerusalem (1 Kgs 11:29). On the other hand, the Bible reveals that the coronation ceremonies of Solomon (1 Kgs 1:32-39) and Joash of Judah (2 Kgs 11:12, 14) were public. The high priest, dignitaries, and representatives of the people participated. The high priest did the anointing while the people shouted praises.[51]

When Saul was anointed, he was not termed king (*melek*), but is given the title *nāgîd*. This has led some scholars to believe that Samuel and the tribal leaders never intended to elevate Saul to the kingship.[52] However, the term *nāgîd* means a person chosen by God for kingship.

Samuel anointed Saul, which consisted in rubbing or smearing with oil. This act, it was believed, transferred the sanctity of the national god to the king. Anointing symbolized a covenant between God and the king, indicating that God would protect the king, and it bestowed legitimacy.

The sages believed that kings who formed a new dynasty, or renewed an interrupted dynasty, or kings with a disputed coronation, were anointed:

> They anoint kings only on account of civil strife. Why did they anoint Solomon? Because of the strife of Adonijah. And Jehu? Because of Joram. And Joash? Because of Athaliah. And Jehoahaz? Because of Jehhoiakim his brother, who was two years older than he. A king requires anointing, [but] a son of a king does not require anointing. A high priest, son of a high priest, even up to the tenth generation, [nonetheless] requires anointing.[53]

Thus the question arises: why was there a need to hide the anointing of the first king of Israel since he did not usurp the office? According to Elat, the story of Saul's secret anointing contains no historical truth.[54] Its origin lies

---

51. 1 Sam 10:24; 1 Kgs 1:39; 2 Kgs 9:13; 11:12.

52. Alt, *Kleine Schriften*, 2:324; Noth, *Geschichte Israels*, 156 n. 2; Bright, *History of Israel*, 185.

53. *T. Sanh.* 4:11.

54. Elat, *Samuel*, 97.

in a literary motif reflecting the social and political realities of Israel where prophets like Ahijah, Elijah, and Elisha fought against sinful kings. They anointed a person they believed was chosen by God, in place of a sinful king. It was the prophetic circles who, from the time of David and Solomon, acted and continued subsequently in the northern kingdom. This prophetic circle introduced Samuel as the father of their circle, who anointed the first king.[55] Yet, we must stress that Saul did not replace a sinful king.

The anointing of Saul was done secretly and privately because there are two stages of the election depicted here. The first stage entailed divine designation before the proper enthronement ritual. Many times, the chosen person was young, weak, and felt unworthy. A private ceremony could encourage him and instill confidence in his ability to carry out his task successfully. The two-stage election is manifest with Jeremiah who says that he was selected from the womb, and later when he was young, was sent on a mission (Jer 1:5–6).[56] Parallels exist in Egyptian and Mesopotamian traditions. Thut-Mose III claimed that the god Amon said that he would be upon his throne while he was still nestling. Later it was Re who established his throne.[57] Thutmose IV claimed that Re told him in a dream that he shall bequeath the kingdom to him long before he ascended to the throne.[58] Mesopotamian literature tells of kings like Assur-rêsh-ishi, Asshurbanipal, and Nabonidus, who claimed to be designated in the womb.[59]

In the biblical story, the first stage takes place in Ramah, where Saul is designated as future king. In Mizpah, where Saul is crowned before the whole nation, the second act occurs. Saul's anointing also includes a message from Samuel: Saul would liberate the Israelites from their enemies. Samuel gives Saul signs that God has anointed him as a king of Israel. These *three* signs would occur in three different locations. The first will take place at Rachel's tomb, where he will meet two people who will tell him *three* things: the donkeys were found, his father had given up on finding the donkeys, and his father is worried about him.

The second will take place at the Oak of Tabor where he will meet *three* people. One will carry *three* kids, one will carry *three* bags of bread, and one

55. Ibid.
56. Halpern, *Constitution*, 127–28.
57. "Divine Nomination" *ANET*, 446–47.
58. "Divine Oracle," *ANET*, 449.
59. For Assur-rêsh-ishi and Ashurbanipal, see Luckenbill, *Ancient Records*, 209, 765. For Nabonidus see Langdon, *Die neubabylonischen*, 218, 1:4–5.

God's First King

will carry a jug of wine. They will greet him and offer him two wave offerings of bread, which he will accept. The bread is intended for God, but Saul is instructed to accept it.[60] It is possible that the second sign is a fulfillment of the royal tribute that was mentioned by Samuel (9:20). Indeed, Wiseman points out that the bread was to be accepted "since such 'greetings' and gifts were part of the customary diplomatic acknowledgment of a king's new position and authority."[61]

The third encounter will occur at the Hill of God where the Philistine prefect was located. Saul will encounter a band of prophets who will have timbrels, flutes, and harps in front of them, and they will be prophesying with musical instruments.

Samuel predicted that the encounter with the band of prophets would change Saul, as "The spirit of God will rush upon" him, and he would prophesy (1 Sam 10:6). This is a typical expression in the stories of Samson and Saul where the hero is empowered by God's spirit to perform heroic actions (Judg 14:6, 19; 15:14; 1 Sam 11:6). Saul started to prophesy by musical inspiration the same way Elijah prophesied by music (2 Kgs 3:15). As the spirit rushes upon him he changed (1 Sam 10:9). And when the spirit departs, while David was playing the lyre (1 Sam 16:14, 23), an evil spirit seizes Saul (1 Sam 18:10).

The Coronation at Mizpah

Contrasting the private secretive anointing of Saul, the coronation at Mizpah was public. Saul was anointed by Samuel first as *nāgîd*, now he is elected a king. As Herzberg pointed out, Saul's rise to power was narrated in different ways in different places. However, he acknowledges the general agreement that God directs the events and uses Samuel as his instrument.[62]

Here, Saul is chosen king by a "lot." The Hebrew Bible maintains that a lottery was used to determine an unknown offender. In the Achan story, a lot was cast to find the person who did not follow the laws of the ban (Josh 7:1). Later a lot was cast to find out who broke Saul's vow (1 Sam 14:24–29). In each case the reader knows who will be caught. It is not clear why a lot was cast to identify the king of Israel since Samuel had already anointed

---

60. Afterwards, David, to Saul's displeasure, will accept bread from the priest of Nob (1 Sam 21:7).

61. Wiseman, "Is it Peace?," 318.

62. Hertzberg, *I & II Samuel*, 87.

The Search For a King

Saul. Moreover, the fact that a lot was cast to find the king of Israel gives the impression that Saul might be guilty of something. The feeling that things will turn deleteriously arises. According to McCarter "there is a clear, if subtle, implication that he is an offending party by the virtue of the election itself."[63] The word "lot" is not used, but is inferred. Instead the writer uses the word *hiqrib* "present," which also means sacrifice.

Since Saul was not found, Samuel again asked Yahweh. There is a play on words: the verb *šaʾal* "ask, inquire," and the name Saul (*šāʾûl*). Saul was hiding the entire time the casting of lots took place. This motif of hiding also appears in the New Testament. In the Gospel of John we read that Jesus runs to the mountains when they came to crown him (John 6:15).[64] It does not say why Saul was hiding. Was it modesty or shyness? The Talmud commenting on this passage asserts that Saul was a model of humility. This detail is significant in understanding the different stages in Saul's coronation. Saul's hiding proves that there is a link between Saul's secret anointing and the anointing in Mizpah. Why does Saul hide? How did he know that he would be chosen? Evidently, one tradition holds that there were two stages of Saul's anointing. Therefore, he concealed the matter of the kingdom from his uncle (1 Sam 10:17); and he hid because he already had been anointed by Samuel, suggesting that he knew he would be chosen by lot.

When Samuel brought Saul forth from his hiding place, the narrator repeats some of the details mentioned previously in the anointing story. Once again we are told that he was taller than the rest of all the people, yet this will be repudiated later in the story (1 Sam 16:7).[65] Further repeated details are that Saul was the son of Kish from the tribe of Benjamin, and that he was modest and shy. Modesty is a quality associated with Moses (Num 12:3), Gideon (Judg 6:15), David (1 Sam 18:23; 2 Sam 7:18–21), and Solomon (1 Kgs 3:7). In Saul's anointing and coronation ceremonies, his modesty is stressed. It is mentioned in connection with Saul's appearance (1 Sam 9:21), when Saul was elected by lot (10:22), when Saul concealed the kingship from his uncle (10:16), and lastly when Saul already was the king of Israel (15:17).

Saul was presented as Yahweh's chosen one. This reflects the belief that the king is God's elected one and the elected one of the people. Samuel

---

63. McCarter, *I Samuel*, 196.

64. Daube, *New Testament*, 19

65. Note the story of Athtar in the Baal myth, where we read: "sits on Mighty Baʻlu's seat. (But) his feet do not reach the footstool; his head does not reach the top (of the seat)." Thus, because he was short, he was rejected as king. See Pardee, "The Baʻlu Myth," 269.

God's First King

quickly tells the people of Israel: "And now here is the king you have chosen! Yahweh has appointed a king over you" (12:13). Likewise, we read that Hushai justified his support for Absalom saying: "No, the one chosen by the Lord, by these people, and by all the men of Israel" (2 Sam 16:18). The belief that the king is the one chosen by God and the people is also known from ancient Near Eastern texts. In the Hebrew Bible the preeminently chosen one of Yahweh is David; but at the early stages of the monarchy, Saul was seen as the chosen one. By shouting, "Long live the king!" the people of Israel recognized Saul as king. This phrase is repeated throughout the historical books of the Bible to express the approval of the king (1 Kgs 1:25, 34, 39; 2 Kgs 11:12). R. P. Gordon points out that: "for the first time since his introduction in 9:1f. Saul is called 'king'; significantly, it is the people who acclaim him so."[66]

In spite of Saul's election by God and his recognition by the people, some people did not accept Saul as a king. The Bible mentions two groups, stalwart men and worthless men. The former refers to soldiers or warriors, and connotes loyalty. They were part of the army that Saul gathered (1 Sam 14:52). The second group refers to disloyal traitors. They expressed their contempt to the new king by words and actions. They asked, "How can this fellow save us?" (v. 27). They spurned him and tendered no gifts. No evidence exists for giving a gift following a new king's election; nevertheless the biblical narrator stressed that fact. Gift giving by a vassal to a king was considered a sign of recognition and loyalty to the king.[67] The same people's contempt towards Saul will be mentioned after his victory over the Ammonites.

Saul Proclaimed King at Gilgal

After the victory over the Ammonites, Samuel asked the people to join him in renewing the kingship at Gilgal (1 Sam 11:14). The people went to Gilgal and, in the presence of Yahweh, crowned Saul as their king. There they sacrificed to Yahweh, and Saul and all Israel rejoiced. Medieval commentators such as Rashi (Rabbi Solomon ben Isaac, 1040–1105) and Radak (Rabbi David ben Joseph Kimḥi, 1160–1235) raised the question: why was a third coronation needed in Gilgal? They claimed there was disagreement about Saul. Many people rejected him believing he could not save them (10:27; 11:12). After he proved his military ability a need arose to renew his kingship.

66. R. P. Gordon, *1 & 2 Samuel*, 121.
67. 1 Kgs 5:1; 2 Kgs 3:4; 17:3–4.

The Search For a King

Modern scholars also debated the existence of the three different versions of Saul's coronation. It was pointed out that the three versions are problematic and difficult to reconstruct what really took place.[68] According to McKenzie, the three stories came from three different sources that were available to the Dtr. Instead of choosing one of them, the Dtr merged the three stories by a series of editorial additions.[69] Mettinger says that Saul's rescue of Jabesh-gilead is the most reliable tradition describing the events that led to Saul's coronation. This tradition is unfamiliar with the casting of lots at Mizpah, and so he believes that 1 Sam 11:1–15 is an independent tradition and never had any connection with the Mizpah version.[70]

Edelman does not accept the view that Saul's rescue of Jabesh-gilead led to his coronation. According to her, Saul's ability to lead his people in a battle after defeating the Ammonites is historically implausible. This battle took place only after Saul became a king with a strong army.[71]

Perhaps the confusion and disagreement among scholars for why a third ceremony was needed at Gilgal derives from their failure to discern the meaning of the Hebrew word *uneḥaddeš*. The word is usually translated to *renew* or *restore*. In other words, the people wanted to renew Saul's kingship.[72] But examination of the Hebrew word shows that it has a second meaning, which means to strengthen. According to 2 Chr 24:5, 12, King Jehoash decided to renovate the temple. There we read that the word *leḥaddēš* is parallel to *leḥazzek*, which means to strengthen.[73] Thus, the ceremony that is described at Gilgal strengthened Saul's rule. One purpose was to strengthen his kingship by bringing the Israelite tribes in the Trans-Jordan under the authority of the new king. Having freed the Israelite tribes from the oppression of the Ammonites, it was the right time to make Saul king.[74]

---

68. Bright, *History of Israel*, 182–83; Jagersma, *History of Israel*, 88–89.

69. McKenzie, *King David*, 29.

70. Mettinger, *King and Messiah*, 83–84.

71. Edelman follows Halpern, who pointed to a three-part designation; the search for a candidate, his anointing that showed divine approval, and public acclamation, expressed by the phrase "Long live the king." She believes that those three stages were followed by a testing stage. However, the rescue of Jabesh-gilead could not have been the catalyst triggering the foundation of the monarchy. See Edelman, "Saul," 993; Edelman, "Saul's Rescue," 195; Halpern, *Constitution*, 127, 130, 134.

72. BDB, 293–94; HALOT, 1:294.

73. Elat, *Samuel*, 124.

74. Interestingly, the author of 1 Chr 29:22 uses the word *šēnît* meaning again and not *leḥaddēš* to describe Solomon's second coronation.

God's First King

The location of the coronation in Gilgal was not accidental. It was east of Jericho and close to the Jordan crossing; thus it was convenient to the tribes from west and east to meet and strengthen the king's rule. There is also a possibility that this location was chosen because of a pre-existing altar that symbolized the connection between the tribes of the Trans-Jordan and the tribes of the west (Joshua 23). The place was called Gelilot (Josh 18:17) and an altar was built there, therefore it is probably Gilgal. In contrast to the past two ceremonies, here at Gilgal, we are told that Saul and all the men of Israel celebrated exuberantly.[75] Klein balanced the statement of celebration with critical comments about kingship from the book of Hosea: "They have made kings, but not by my sanction," (8:4), and "All their misfortune [began] at Gilgal, for there I disowned them" (9:15).[76] This is not surprising, since the text echoes Samuel's prior rejection of kingship. The arrival of kingship would signal a decline of prophetic power.

Following the victory against the Ammonites and before the celebrations at Gilgal we read that the people of Israel had already accepted Saul. Evidently, his victory removed any doubt about his leadership abilities. Thus, when the people of Israel asked Samuel, "Who was it who said, 'Saul shall not reign over us?'" (11:12). They turned to Samuel who was still perceived as a judge, and demanded these people be put to death. But Saul interfered and declared that no one should be slain. Here Saul appropriated the authority to judge from Samuel, after this episode, Samuel's decline began. By taking the authority to judge, Saul became like the other kings of the ancient Near East who judged their people.

The proclamation of Saul's kingship was done by all the people. Interestingly Samuel's name is not mentioned as taking part in the celebration. The people sacrificed peace offerings, part offered to God while the rest was eaten by the worshipers. Despite the absence of the covenant terminology in v. 15, the ceremony focused on the ratification of a covenant between the king and the people before Yahweh.[77] There is some evidence for the use of sacrificial rites in connection with the proclamation of kingship (1 Kgs 1:19). This was the second public coronation of Saul. As pointed out there were people who did not accept Saul's kingship. Thus, the coronation

---

75. Another place we read that Saul rejoiced is after the victory against Goliath. But this is indirectly described by Jonathan (19:5).

76. Klein, *1 Samuel*, 109.

77. Alt, "Formation," 195.

in Gilgal came to strengthen his claim as undisputed king of Israel, and to incorporate the tribes from the Trans-Jordan into his new monarchy.

In conclusion, Saul was anointed privately and secretly at Ramah as *nāgîd*, which means a person chosen by God for kingship. He was designated by God to deal with the threat that the Israelites were facing. This was the first stage where God selected a young man for promotion. The second time, at Mizpah, Saul was designated as king following the casting of lots, which indicates divine selection. This was done in the presence of the tribes and their representatives. According to the biblical account, there was dissatisfaction by some of the people with Saul's kingship (1 Sam 10:27; 11:12). Thus, following the victory against the Ammonites, a third ceremony took place where Saul was declared king. This third ceremony had one purpose: to strengthen Saul's rule by incorporating the Israelite tribes from the Trans-Jordan. It signified his undisputed authority as king over Israel and over the Israelite tribes in Trans-Jordan. The main reason for the election of Saul was the Philistine threat. The temporary leadership that existed since the period of the judges could not deal effectively with the Philistine threat, or with the Ammonites who oppressed the Israelites in Trans-Jordan. Evidently, there were other reasons that required a change, a moral decline as well as social and economic development in Israelite society. The increased population and expanded agrarian productivity were catalysts in transforming the Israelite social structure. The old system could not respond to the emerging new reality; only a new monarchial system that offered young people new opportunities could respond. In two major speeches "the rights of the king" (1 Sam 8:1–22) and his farewell speech to the people of Israel (1 Samuel 12), Samuel rejected the idea of kingship. This is because he tried to establish his own prophetic dynasty, and human kingship meant decline of his power and status, and posed a threat to his authority. Samuel's speeches projects future battles over power and authority between the prophets and the kings of Israel.

2
Saul's Wars

IN THE BOOK OF Judges, God gave up the Israelites to their enemies on *all sides,* and they could no longer hold their own against their *enemies* (Judg 2:14). Consequently, God sent judges to deliver the Israelites from their enemies. Not a single Judge delivered the Israelites from *all* their enemies. Instead, God sent different Judges to fight against Israel's enemies. Yet in the book of Samuel, a new picture emerges: "After Saul had secured his kingship over Israel, he waged war on every side against all his enemies: against the Moabites, Ammonites, Edomites, the Philistines, and the kings of Zobah; and wherever he turned he worsted [them]. He was triumphant, defeating the Amalekites and saving Israel from those who plundered it" (1 Sam 14:47–48).

In addition, Saul fought three major wars: the war against the Ammonites (chapter 11); the war against the Philistines that includes three major battles (chapters 13–14; 17; 28–31); and battles with the Philistines on a smaller scale (18:27, 30; 19:8; 23:1, 27). The third major battle was the war against the Amalekites described in chapter 15. It was no coincidence that Saul fought against all the enemies from all sides. Saul was the first king of Israel; his kingship signifies a transition from the period of the Judges to the monarchical era. Unlike a Judge who fought a single battle, Saul, as king of Israel, fought many battles against the enemies of Israel. This was one of the distinctions between a King and a Judge. The first part of this chapter will examine Saul's wars with the Philistines and the Amalekites. The second part will look into his wars in the Trans-Jordan. This chapter will analyze Saul's war from a literary and historical perspective, attempting to distinguish between the fictional embellishment and the historical truth that is behind Saul's wars. In addition,

Saul's Wars

we will try to find out why Saul fought against those particular enemies and what he tried to achieve in those battles.

THE REBELLION AGAINST THE PHILISTINES

Geba

Jonathan attacked the Philistine garrison in Geba which was an act of rebellion, initiating the war between the Philistines and Israelites that would last throughout Saul's life. The intention was to remove the Philistine presence from the hill country, and thus unite the Israelites. Surprisingly, the reader is not told who Jonathan is. There is no hint that he was the king's son, and this information is revealed only in the last verse of chapter 13. Here the narrator used the technique of delay. It is possible that the narrator did not provide the reader with Jonathan's background because he was famous.[1] However, it is more likely that the narrator omitted the information in light of the relationship between Saul and his son, Jonathan. It appears as if the narrator wanted, at an early stage of the story, to disassociate Jonathan from his father Saul. In addition, Jonathan's surprise attack was attributed not to Jonathan but to Saul (v. 4). Saul was praised instead of Jonathan, but this was due to his being the king. Likewise, the conquest of Hebron was attributed to Joshua, in spite of the fact that it was Caleb who conquered the city (Josh 11:21; 14:14).

Following Jonathan's successful attack against the Philistine prefect, Saul sounded the trumpet throughout the land with the message: "Let the Hebrews pay attention." It is quite strange that an Israelite would use such a designation for his fellow Israelites. Scholars have pointed out the connection between the term Hebrew and *'apiru*. Some believe that the term *'apiru* refers to mercenaries. Gottwald suggested that Saul was appealing to a "third force" to listen, they were the *'apiru* warriors who served in the Philistine army. Saul summoned the *'apiru* to come and to fight alongside the Israelites.[2] Evidently, they were a band of armed Israelites who gave their services to the Philistines, but returned to the Israelite side when the battle turned against the Philistines.

Upon receiving the news about the assassination of their prefect, the Philistines reacted quickly by gathering their huge army—including three

---

1. For different interpretation see Long, *Reign and Rejection*, 75–77.
2. Gottwald, *Tribes of Yahweh*, 423.

thousand chariots and six thousand cavalry—compared to Sisera who had only nine hundred chariots (Judg 4:3). It deserves mention that the terrain in the surrounding area of Michmas was not fit for a large force of chariots. The large number of the Philistine battalion is indicated by the phrase "troops as numerous as sand" (Josh 11:4; Judg 7:12; 2 Sam 17:11). Meanwhile, we read that the Israelites were terrified, some of them were hiding. This was perhaps due to the fact that the troops with Saul and Jonathan did not have enough weapons to fight, thus: "no sword or spear was to be found in possession of any of the troops with Saul and Jonathan; only Saul and Jonathan had them" (1 Sam 13:22). At the same time, the Hebrews crossed the Jordan to the territory of Gad and Gilead.[3] Afterward, in 14:21 we read that the Hebrews came to the aid of Saul. Thus one wonders if the Hebrews mentioned in 13:3, 7 and 14:21 are the same people. The first group of Hebrews deserted the Philistine camp and escaped to the territory of Gad and Gilead. Subsequent to the Philistines losing the battle, a second group of Hebrews deserted the Philistine camp and joined Saul in his battle against the Philistines.

Following the feud between Saul and Samuel (see chapter 4), Saul returned from Gilgal to Geba of Benjamin. Meanwhile, the Philistines camped at Michmas, reversing their positions from the beginning of the campaign. Three squadrons emerged from the Philistine camp. The Philistines used the same strategy here that Saul used against the Ammonites; they divided their army into three. Their mission was to destroy the settlements in the east, north, and west. A similar view is found in Josephus's account of the event, where he describes the Philistines as dividing their army into three companies.[4] The Philistines divided their forces into three in order to accelerate the downfall of Saul. That left their main camp without ample defenses, which helped Saul defeat the Philistines. Kallai speculated that the Philistines were sending raiding parties in order to obtain supplies for their army. He maintained that the Philistine plan was not to confront the Israelites, but rather to rob and to intimidate the Israelites.[5]

Michmas

Chapter 14 continues to describe the battle between Saul and the Philistines. The main Philistine forces went to Michmas. They remained there,

3. Ibid., 424.
4. Josephus, *Ant.* 6.105.
5. Kallai, "Wars of Saul," 135–36.

while, at the same time Saul was at the outskirts of Geba with six hundred troops. Geba is situated only a mile or two from Michmas. A deep ravine that turns into a wadi, called *eṣ-Ṣuwēnīṭ*, separates the two camps. The Philistine army camped north of the ravine while the Israelites encamped to the south. This wadi was an important pass from the Jordan Valley into the Ephraimite hills. Jonathan and his weapon bearer launched an attack on the Philistine post. This post was strategically accessed via a pass through the Wadi, naturally defended by rocks or a ford on both sides. On his side, these rocks were called Seneh and the other side was called Bozez. This attack was made without Saul's knowledge or his troops. Jonathan attacked the Philistine garrison only after receiving a sign from God. This is similar to Gideon's attack of the Midianite camp after receiving only a sign. In the raid, Jonathan and his armsbearer killed twenty people, which indicates that this post was small. Jonathan led the attack, and his weapon bearer would finish off those who had fallen behind. This unexpected attack caused turmoil and terror in the Philistine camp that was felt in the field and the raiding parties. According to Josephus, the raid took place while the Philistines were sleeping:

> So they fell upon them as they were asleep, and slew about twenty of them, and thereby filled them with disorder and surprise, insomuch that some of them threw away their entire armor and fled; but the greatest part, not knowing one another, because they were of different nations, suspected one another to be enemies, (for they did not imagine there were only two of the Hebrews that came up,) and so they fought one against another; and some of them died in the battle, and some, as they were fleeing away, were thrown down from the rock headlong.[6]

This episode is similar to chapter 13. Both chapters 13 and 14 describe surprise attacks by Jonathan. In chapter 13, Jonathan attacked the Philistine garrison at Geba and in chapter 14 he attacked the Philistine garrison at Michmas. In both, Jonathan fights his father's battles, replacing his father as a leader. Jonathan uses guerrilla tactics with small forces, surprising the enemy from different locations. Edelman reads 13:3 differently. According to her, it is a "literary fiction" since Jonathan was too young to take part in the war with the Philistines. Na'aman believes that chapters 13 and 14 have one purpose, which is the denigration of Saul.[7] He points to the fact that Saul was

---

6. Josephus, *Ant.* 6.6.2.
7. Na'aman, "Pre-Deuteronomistic," 646.

rejected by Yahweh. He is at Gibeah without taking any initiative while his son Jonathan attacks the Philistines at Michmas. Even though at the end, Saul leads his men to a victory, all the glory goes to Jonathan. Na'aman explains this negative portrayal of Saul claiming that it was the Deuteronomistic editor who portrayed Saul as a man who deserted his God and did not wait to receive divine help to join Jonathan in chasing the Philistines.[8] In addition, he made the army take an oath to fast, and thus he failed to see the negative effect of this on the army. Brooks adds to Na'aman's hypothesis, asserting that the same author or editor also inserted the story of the conflict between Samuel and Saul. The aim was to downplay Saul's success. According to her, if we remove the incident of this conflict and the references that attribute the victory to God, we might receive a better historical portrayal of the events.[9]

Jonathan's attacks against the Philistine camps in Geba and Michmas were part of the rebellion against the Philistines. The first attack signaled the beginning of the bitter war against the Philistines that lasted all of Saul's life. This attack was committed with Saul's knowledge and approval. Since his election, the people of Israel were waiting to attack the Philistines, and one of the reasons Saul was elected was to confront the Philistine threat. Indeed, already in v. 2, before the attack, we learn that Saul built a force of 3,000 men from Israel and the remainder of the troops was sent home. Why did Saul dispatch the rest? We are not told, but Saul probably wanted to conceal his real intentions and to surprise the Philistines when he sent the troops home. Jonathan's attacks against the Philistines came to challenge their rule. The attacks on Geba and Michmas had one purpose: to remove them from the territory of Benjamin. Saul was aware of his military weakness, so he employed guerrilla tactics and small forces. Following Jonathan's attack at Geba, Saul retreated to Gilgal where he expected to receive support from the Giladites whom he saved before. Realizing afterwards that the Philistines could attack him there and given that the landscape topography favored them; he retreated back to Geba, which Jonathan controlled. Saul acted quickly because the Philistine forces were divided at that time into three columns. He wanted to attack the small force that was left in Michmas. Evidently, the Philistine commanders realized the situation: "Now the Philistine garrison had marched out to the pass of Michmas" (1 Sam 13:23). Saul lost the element of surprise, but this was reversed by Jonathan's surprise attack.

8. Na'aman, "Beth-aven," 17.
9. Brooks, *Saul*, 107–8.

Saul's Wars

Jonathan's second attack was not premeditated. Jonathan and his attendant were scouting and gathering information about the enemy. They realized that they had an opportunity to defeat the Philistines. It was Driver who suggested that, based on the corrupt Hebrew text and the LXX, Jonathan and his armsbearer used arrows and stones.[10] They probably used the cover of the rocky crag, and attacked the Philistines from behind it with arrows and slings. The Benjaminites were known to use these types of weapons with accuracy. Following the initial attack, Jonathan and his arms-bearer entered the Philistine camp and killed those who were already injured. Josephus explains that the mayhem resulted from miscommunications between the soldiers who came from different nations. This explanation sounds logical. This mayhem in the Philistine camp was noticed by Saul's scouts. After realizing that Jonathan and his armsbearer were missing, Saul connected it to the chaos in the Philistine camp and attacked. The victory was total; even the men of Israel who were hiding in the hill country of Ephraim pursued them in a battle. According to the LXX, the battle against the Philistines also took place in some cities of Ephraim. Saul not only defeated the Philistines in Michmas, but chased them to Aijalon, the modern Yalu, some twenty miles to the west of Michmas to the edge of the hill country. The battle of Michmas was decisive; it removed the Philistine presence from the territory of Benjamin. The hill country was now dominated by Israel. It was one in a long series of battles against the Philistines that came to end their oppression, and free the rest of the land of Israel. The military strategy, the site identifications, and the topographical descriptions all show that the story reflects historical events, even though in some cases due to the theological view, the story was exaggerated.[11]

From a literary standpoint this is similar to the story of Gideon's war against the Midianites, which represents the period of the Judges.[12] The language that describes the calling of people to war, the strength of the enemy, the fear that fell upon the people, and the description of them hiding in caves, dugouts, and pits—all these elements appear in both stories. In both, Gideon and Saul lead a small contingent to battle the enemy. Gideon led three hundred; Saul led six hundred. Both stories describe spying on the enemy camp. On the one hand, Gideon and his lad went at night to the Midianite's camp; on the other hand, it was Jonathan and his weapons-bearer who went to the

---

10. Driver, *Notes*, 108–9.
11. Kallai, "Wars of Saul," 134–38; Garsiel, "Battle of Michmas," 15–50.
12. Garsiel, *First Book of Samuel*, 87–93.

God's First King

Philistine camp. In both stories, the enemy soldiers gave the sign for victory. In both, it was the few who caused chaos and confusion in the enemy camp that led the enemy soldiers to kill each other (Judg 7:22; 1 Sam 14:20). In both tales, the people of Ephraim joined the chase after the enemy. Both have the same message; God has the power to deliver the victory of the few over the many; everything is in God's hands and comes from God. Jonathan's portrayal is akin to Gideon. Like Gideon he asked God for a sign, and fought with few against the many. Saul, on the other hand, failed because he did not query God. He did not trust the small number of his soldiers, and when their numbers dwindled, he committed a sin.

THE BATTLE AT THE VALLEY OF ELAH

For forty days, a representative from the Philistine camp named Goliath, came out to challenge the Israelites to choose a man to fight him. This single battle would determine the outcome of the war, and the losers would become the slaves of the victors. There are many examples from the ancient Near East and classical sources that describe a battle between two representatives. The Iliad records the battles between Paris and Menelaus, as well as the famous encounter between Hector and Achilles. From the ancient Near East, we read about Marduk who killed Tiamat. De Vaux interpreted the battle of twelve servants of Ishbosheth and twelve servants of David as an extension of the single warrior battle (2 Sam 2:12–17).[13]

David's appearance on the field of battle is portrayed as opportunistic and ambitious. He shows interest in the threefold reward that king Saul has promised to the one who will kill the Philistine: the king will enrich the man, he will give him his daughter, and his father's house will be exempt from taxes.[14] Giving such rewards for victory in war was a known custom in the ancient world. Caleb announced that he would give his daughter Achsah in marriage to the man who would capture Kiriath-sepher (Judg 1:12).[15] The reward was announced several times. David probably heard

---

13. De Vaux, *Bible*, 130.

14. Rainey pointed to the Akkadian adjective *zaki* that describes an emancipated slave (RS 16.250:21–22) or a soldier who, because of his bravery, was granted freedom by the king from service to the palace (RS 16.269:14–16). According to Rainey, this is very similar to the offer made by Saul. See Rainey, "Institutions," 104; McCarter, *I Samuel*, 304; Wiseman, "Alalakh," 126.

15. See also 2 Sam 5:8; 1 Chr 11:6.

about the reward, entered into a conversation with the men, and declared his intention to accept Goliath's challenge.

David's words of defiance about the uncircumcised Philistine were brought to Saul's attention. As a result, he was summoned before the king. Saul appears hesitant and frightened in his conversation with David. It is David who encourages the king of Israel: "Let no man's courage fail him." Instead of "no man's," the LXX reads "not my lord's." Van der Kooij explains it as a secondary "exegetical rendering."[16] David encourages the king to overcome his fear. Not wanting to insult the king, he used the phrase "no man." Moreover, he speaks to the king with respect and refers to himself as "your slave."

David is the protagonist and initiates the conversation. Ironically, he, and not the king, speaks first, as might be expected. Although both Saul and David are anointed, David speaks first. Brueggemann believes that: "through this technique the narrator demonstrates David's primacy over Saul."[17] David speaks to the point, and offers to fight Goliath. However, Saul's hesitation and fear surface again when he refuses to grant David his wish. Saul cites David's youth and inexperience for his initial refusal. David, on the other hand, shows persistence and power of persuasion. He points to his experience as a shepherd, protecting the flock from a lion or a bear. More than anything, David points out that it was God who saved him from the lion and the bear, and he will deliver him from the Philistines. It is David who mentions Yahweh for the first time. Neither the people nor Saul mentioned him. No doubt the narrator wanted to stress this since David's perception of the battle is a theological one.[18] David's confidence and belief in God is similar to Jonathan's in the previous battle against the Philistines at Michmas. Saul, on the other hand, is portrayed as frightened, and he ordered the priest to stop inquiring of God (1 Sam 14:19). In times of pressure, Saul does not properly consult God, and in this episode he did not even try to. He utters the name of God "and may the Lord be with you" (1 Sam 17:37); but this is a form of blessing. Evidently, the narrator wanted to exacerbate the differences between Saul and David.

David's belief in God is emphasized as he approaches Goliath. The conversation between David and Goliath is remotely reminiscent of the speeches of the Homeric heroes before battle.[19] David repeats his belief that the same

---

16. Van der Kooij, "Story of David," 124.
17. Brueggemann, *First and Second Samuel*, 129.
18. Ibid., 130
19. Hertzberg, *I & II Samuel*, 152.

God's First King

God who was the subject of Goliath's defiance will deliver him into his hands. The victory will be achieved through God, not by military means. God will battle Goliath through a human agent: a shepherd boy with a sling and a few stones. The significance is that David is God's instrument. David came to rescue Israel and to defeat the Philistines, but by doing so, he announces: "All the earth shall know that there is a God in Israel" (1 Sam 17:46).

The MT describes Goliath the Philistine champion as being 9'9" tall. The LXX, Josephus (*Ant.* 6.171), and 4QSam^a read 6'9". It appears that decreasing his height was deliberate since it felt his size was exaggerated. He wore a helmet and he was dressed in plated cuirass, which was believed to weigh about 126 pounds. He had bronze greaves on his legs, and a bronze scimitar between his shoulders. The shaft of his spear is compared to a weaver's beam. Yadin renders this a javelin and says that a weaver's beam refers to the shape and nature of Goliath's javelin not to its size.[20] The iron spear weighed 15 or 16 pounds. A shield-bearer preceded him. This is similar to the weapon used by Homeric heroes in the *Iliad* and in the *Odyssey*.[21] It is possible that mentioning the bronze is archaic, since by that time the Philistines' weapons were iron. Indeed this description does not match the portrayal of Philistine warriors in the Egyptians reliefs. This description shows how well he was prepared and armed. Needless to say, it was a frightening vision. This description of Goliath shows how imposing he was, and how God acted through David.[22] Evidently the function of this description was literary rather than historical.

Saul dressed David in a garment with a bronze helmet and he bore Saul's sword. This equipment, even though it was light, was too much for David. He tried to walk once or twice but told Saul he could not walk. David never tried previously to use this kind of gear; thus, it was unwise to give it to him before such an important battle. Also, the gear was insufficient for attacking Goliath, who was dressed in armor from head to toe. So they removed them, and David took his stick and five smooth stones, which he put in his pouch, and went out with the sling in his hand. According to this text, the sling was a shepherd's weapon, but armies in the ancient world used it also. Assyrian slingers, wearing copper helmets and coats of mail are depicted on

---

20. Yadin, "Goliath's Javelin," 58–69. In contrast to Yadin, Finkelstein has argued that Goliath's panoply indicates that the story should be dated to a later stage of the Iron Age in the seventh century BCE. We have to stress, however, that Goliath's description was literary rather than historical. See Finkelstein, "The Philistines in the Bible," 142–48.

21. *Il*. 6.318; 7.41; *Od*. 18.378.

22. Galling, "Goliath," 150–69.

Saul's Wars

Sennacherib's palace at Nineveh.[23] The Benjaminites were known for using this weapon with astonishing accuracy (Judg 20:16; 1 Chr 12:2; 2 Chr 26:14).

Removing the gear from David gave him an advantage. David could now move more easily, while Goliath was limited in movement by his armor. Indeed, it says that David ran out quickly to meet him. Josephus makes a similar observation: "Still, the Philistine, the load of his armor impeding a more rapid advance, gradually approached David."[24] David hit Goliath in the forehead with a stone. The LXX adds, "through the helmet" (v. 49). The LXX translators were thinking of the Greek helmets with nose guards. However, the author of the Hebrew text was thinking of the helmet that was used by the Assyrians that did not have a nose guard. The stone killed Goliath, so David, with no sword in his hand, took Goliath's own sword and decapitated him. Verses 5–7 do not say that Goliath had a sword nor did David, thus the general term for sword refers to the Philistine's *kidon*, a scimitar.[25] Interestingly, in Psalm 151 LXX addition to the book of Psalms, it says that David killed Goliath with his own sword and does not mention the sling at all. The authors were familiar with the LXX but not with the additions to the MT. Evidently those additions came to enhance the image of David who killed Goliath first with a sling.

According to this text, David killed Goliath. However, reading 2 Sam 21:19 suggests that Elhanan slew Goliath. It has been suggested by an Aramaic Targum, and later by Bright, that Elhanan and David were the same person. The name David afterwards was his name on the throne.[26] This, however, is unlikely since 1 Chr 20:5 says that Elhanan killed Goliath's brother. It appears that the author of the book of Chronicles tried to resolve the contradiction in Samuel. But still, if David killed Goliath, why is it not stated in the book of Chronicles? This book was written several hundred years after the Davidic dynasty. Why hide from the reader such a heroic deed performed by David? Instead, the heroic act is attributed to Elhanan, whom the sages claimed was David. Examination of the list of David's warriors, however, reveals that one of his warriors was "Elhanan son of Dodo [from] Bethlehem" (2 Sam 23:24). In other words, Elhanan was a member of the royal family. This fact is repeated in the book of Chronicles (1 Chr 11:26). Thus, it is possible that the author of 1 Samuel 17 attributed the

23. Douglas and Hillyer, eds., *Illustrated Bible Dictionary*, 115.
24. Josephus, *Ant.* 6.9.4
25. McCarter, *I Samuel*, 294.
26. Bright, *History of Israel*, 188.

God's First King

great victory to David instead of Elhanan who killed Goliath for the simple fact that in ancient times, heroic actions of the king's warriors were attributed to the king. Indeed as the reader might recall, Jonathan's victory in Geba was attributed to his father, King Saul (1 Sam 13:3–4).

A shepherd boy who overcomes the giant is believed to occur in fairy tales. The same is true with rewards promised by the king to the man who will defeat the giant.[27] In addition, theological elements were added to the story where the defeat of the Philistines does not point to the superiority of the shepherd's slingshot over battle armor, but to David's faith. David will fight and win: "All the earth shall know that there is a God in Israel. And this whole assembly shall know that the Lord can give victory without sword or spear. For the battle is the Lord's and He will deliver you into our hands" (1 Sam 17:46–47). The contrast is no longer a folktale, but it is a confrontation between two people of different faiths.

In spite of the literary and theological elements that were added to the story, examination of the battlefield shows that this story has a basis in history. As mentioned previously, the sling was a shepherd's weapon, but armies in the ancient world used it as well. David's mobility, his ability to conceal his weapon and to attack from a distance gave him an advantage over the Philistine. According to McKenzie, it is possible that at an earlier stage of his career David defeated a formidable Philistine opponent.[28]

Moreover, the geographic details of the battle between the Israelites and the Philistines in the Valley of Elah reflect knowledge of the terrain. This valley was strategically important to the two parties. Important routes from the Shephelah to Judah traversed this valley. Thus, the battle was to seize control over this important valley, thereby winning the allegiance of Judah.

After the Philistines saw that their hero Goliath was dead, they fled just as the Israelites had fled upon hearing the taunts of the Philistines (v. 24). The men of Israel and Judah pursued them past Shaaraim to Gath, the hometown of Goliath, and to Ekron. Shaaraim has not yet been identified, but it is mentioned in a list of towns in the northern Shephelah district (Josh 15:33–36). Driver suggested that Shaaraim "was presumably some place down the valley between Sochoh and Tell eṣ-Ṣâfiyeh. Its actual site can, however, only be conjectured."[29] Na'aman concurs with Driver and

27. Rofé, "Battle of David," 117–51.
28. McKenzie, *King David*, 77.
29. Driver, *Notes*, 147.

suggests that the site must be sought near Naḥal Elah, an important road that led from Socoh and Azekah to Gath.[30] It was the last Judahite site on the way to Gath, thus received the name Shaaraim "the gate" to Philistia. According to 1 Sam 17:52, Saul and his warriors continued their pursuit westward along the Shaaraim road towards the gates of Gath and Ekron. In his pursuit of the fleeing Philistines, Saul restored the same territory that was previously added by Samuel (7:14).

THE WAR AGAINST THE AMALEKITES

In contrast to his previous battles against the Philistines, Saul did not initiate the campaign against the Amalekites. It was the will of God, and his servant Samuel, who ordered Saul to utterly destroy the Amalekites. The Amalekites were to be put under a ban, meaning they and their animals were to be completely exterminated. This war was retribution for the Amalekites, who fought the Israelites during their journey in the wilderness where they attacked Israel from the rear at Rephidim (Exod 17:8). The book of Exodus reads: "The Lord will have war with Amalek from generation to generation" (17:16). More so, it became a command for Israel in Deut 25:19: "You shall blot out the memory of Amalek from under heaven." The purpose was to prevent syncretism: "lest they teach you to follow all the detestable things they do in worshiping their gods, and you sin against the Lord your God" (20:18).

The Amalekites, who were a semi-nomadic tribe, raided the Negev region, making war against them inevitable. Interestingly, there is no reference to them in external sources. In the Bible, they are symbolic of the oppression of Israel.

Saul mustered his army of 210,000 infantry, which is more in the realm of folktale, which was enormous when compared to the previous chapter where Saul had an army of only six hundred to three thousand (13:2, 15). However, several years passed since the victory against the Philistines, therefore the army may have grown. The narrator probably mentioned this number to demonstrate Saul's military superiority, which dismisses potential excuses for not carrying out God's command. As in the battle of Jabesh, Judah's army is mentioned separately (11:8). Yet, the fact that it is mentioned at all shows that they saw themselves as part of the new

---

30. Na'aman, "Shaaraim," 4.

kingdom. It is necessary to remember that the Amalekites were near Judah's borders and raided its territory.

Before the battle, Saul warned the Kenites, thus giving them time to escape. There may have been a non-aggression treaty between the Israelites and the Kenites. Saul reminded the Kenites of their obligation to be friendly to the Israelites, and to respect the covenant between them. However, there is no clear evidence of this.[31] It is more likely that Saul spared the Kenites because they dealt kindly with the Israelites when they emerged from slavery in Egypt. Saul refers to Jethro the Kenite (Exodus 18), and also hints at Jael the wife of Heber the Kenite who killed Sisera (Judges 4–5). Here, in contrast to the Amalekites, the Kenites are spared because of the merits of their forefathers.

The war against the Amalekites is described very briefly; neither tactics nor strategy are elaborated. The narrator evidently was more concerned with the result of the war, and particularly what followed. Saul destroyed the Amalekites, but did not follow Samuel's instructions totally.[32] Saul captured Agag, the king of the Amalekites, alive and spared his life, as well as the best of the sheep, the oxen, the second born, the lambs, and all else that was of value. On the other hand, he destroyed what was despised and worthless (1 Sam 15:9). Saul failed another crucial test here, and had to accept the consequences of his actions. Sparing the cattle and all the goods can be understandable (human greed); why he spared Agag is not clear. According to Josephus, Saul spared his life because of his beauty and his stature; he thought that it was worthy to be saved.[33] Pseudo-Philo, in a description derogatory to Saul, says that Saul spared Agag because the later had promised to show him hidden treasures.[34] Smith mentions several reasons including: "pride, hope of ransom, an ill-timed emotion of pity, respect of persons."[35] There is some similarity between the previous chapter and this chapter; in both we read about a ban. In the chapter 14, the people of Israel redeem Jonathan from death (1 Sam 14:44–45), they demanded that Saul spare the life of his son. In chapter 15, again they demand and pressure King Saul

---

31. Fensham, "Did a Treaty," 51–54.

32. An echo to Saul's victory can be found in the Balaam oracle "their king shall rise above Agag" (Num 24:7). Interestingly, the LXX and Samaritan read Gog, thereby giving the oracle eschatological flavor.

33. Josephus, *Ant.* 6.7.2.

34. *L.A.B.* 58.2.

35. Smith, *Books of Samuel*, 134.

Saul's Wars

to break the ban. In both episodes, Saul yielded to the people's demand instead of forcing his will as a king on his subjects.

God rejected Saul as a king, which is expressed by the word 'regret.' The word is repeated again at the end of the chapter the "Lord regretted that He had made Saul king over Israel" (15:35). This is anthropopathism, or ascribing human emotions to God.[36] God rejected Saul because he did not implement God's commands. It is remarkable that Samuel, who fought against the idea of monarchy, now tries to save the king. He asked mercy for Saul all night long. Nevertheless, he carries out God's words and confronts Saul.

The question yet remains: besides God's command, what motivated Saul to start a campaign against the Amalekites? The Amalekites lived mainly in Sinai and the Negev; but there is mention of them in Ephraim (Judg 12:15) and in the valley of Jezreel (Judg 6:33). They raided Israelite territories during the time of the Judges (Judg 3:13; 5:14; 6:3, 33; 7:12; 10:12; 12:5). David also fought against them (1 Sam 27:8; 30; 2 Sam 8:12). Since the Amalekites occupied the territory south of Judah, they use to raid Judah. Military actions were needed to protect the tribe of Judah from them.[37] This was a good opportunity that provided additional motivation for Saul to expand his rule and influence outside of the central hill country.

The Amalekite stronghold, Ir Amalek, which Saul attacks, was identified with the site Tel Masos in the Beersheba basin.[38] Further archaeological excavation shows that the place was a regional trade center in the Iron I period.[39] The conflict between Amalek and Israel centered on control of the Arabian trade. Saul wanted to control the lucrative trade routes in the south. The Amalekites were aware of the growing power of Saul's monarchy and the threat it posed to their trade monopoly. Saul had good reason for destroying the Amalekites. By fighting them, Saul removed a major threat against the tribe of Judah, and additionally he gained control of the Arabian trade. Following the Amalekites defeat, Saul built fortified settlements in

---

36. Similarly the word is used in the book of Genesis when God regretted that he created man (Gen 6:6–7).

37. Edelman on the other hand raised the possibility based on Judg 12:15; 5:4; 2 Sam 1:2–26, that Saul's campaign took place in the hills of south Samaria. If this is the case, why did Saul have to muster his troops at Telam if it is identical with Telem mentioned in Josh 15:24? Since it is mentioned after Ziph, that suggests a location somewhere in the Negev.

38. Kochavi, "Rescue," 27.

39. Finkelstein, "Arabian Trade," 247–52.

God's First King

the south to protect Israel against future Amalekite raids, which evidently occurred at Hatira, Refed, Har-Boqer, and Atar Haroah.[40]

Saul demonstrated political savvy; the defeat of the Amalekites insured a monopoly of the Arabian trade for him. Also, by protecting the tribe of Judah, he incorporated an important tribe into the emerging monarchy. Indeed, the people of Judah, Maon, Carmel, and Ziph became loyal to Saul after this campaign (1 Sam 26:1; 23:13; 25:2-11) and hostile to David, their own tribesman; they even tried to hand him over to Saul. This was Saul's only total victory in war; he even captured the Amalekite king. Therefore, when the narrator describes Saul's other wars, he uses the word "he waged war" but with the war against the Amalekites he uses the word "destroyed" (1 Sam 14:48; 15:7).

THE WARS IN TRANS-JORDAN

Ammonites

In the war against the Ammonites, Saul demonstrated his ability to save Israel. The Israelite tribes, the Gadites and Reubenites, were being oppressed by the Ammonites. They approached Nahash, the king of the Ammonites, to enact a treaty whereby Jabesh would become a vassal city to the Ammonite king. In exchange, Nahash would assure them good treatment and protection. Nahash agreed, on the condition that he would gouge out the right eye of each of them. This punishment is attested to in the Ugaritic literature, where it is classified as a curse.[41] The Bible describes the gouging out of two eyes so the prisoner will be an obedient slave, as presented in the case of Samson (Judg 16:21) and in the story of King Zedekiah, who was blinded by the Babylonians (2 Kgs 25:7). According to a text from Qumran (4QSam^a) and also a Greek text that is preserved in Josephus's writings, Nahash gouged out only the right eye.[42]

The text from Qumran was restored by Cross and reads as follows:

> 6. [And Na]hash, king of the Ammonites, sorely oppressed the children of Gad and the children of Reuben, and he gouged out a[ll] their 7. right eyes and struck ter[ror and dread] in Israel.

---

40. Herzog, "Beer-sheba," 22; Meshel, "Ḥorvat Ritma-an," 110–35. In contrast, Cohen dates the settlements to the time of David and Solomon ("Fortress King," 56–70).

41. C. H. Gordon and Rendsburg, *Bible*, 184.

42. Josephus, *Ant.* 6.68–71.

There was not left one among the children of Israel bey[ond] 8. [Jordan who] se right eye was no[t go]ouged out by Naha[sh king] of the children of [A]mmon ; except seven thousand men 9. [fled from] the children of Ammon and entered [J]abesh-Gilead./ About a month later, Nahash the Ammonite went up and besieged Jabesh-[Gilead]/ and all the men of Jabesh said to Nahash 10. [the Ammonite, "Make] with [us a covenant and we shall become your subjects." Nahash [the Ammonite said t]o [th]em, ["After this fashion will"] I make [a covenant with you][43]

According to the Qumran text, Nahash, king of the Ammonites, gouged out the right eye of all the Israelites except for the seven thousand men who escaped to Jabesh-gilead. Nahash went to Jabesh-gilead to punish its citizens for harboring his enemies. How much historical validity is contained in the Qumran passage is a matter of dispute among scholars, since there is a possibility that the text is a late haggadic expansion. Rofé, for example, maintained that despite being supported by another ancient authority, this text must be treated as secondary.[44] However, Ulrich says that it is possible that 4QSam^a "correctly preserves an entire narrative lost from all other biblical mss."[45] Another possibility is that there was more than one version. The sense, however, has been that the biblical narrator was more concerned with the delivery of the Israelites than the oppression of Nahash, king of the Ammonites.

Not clear, however, is what stands behind the conflict between Nahash and the tribes of Gad and Reuben. Further, why did Nahash gouge out the eyes of every male Israelite in the Trans-Jordan? Thus, it was Oded who raised the possibility that the reason for the quarrel between the two sides stemmed from territorial conflict.[46] The kings of Ammon saw the territory that was held by Gad and Reuben as theirs, an occupied territory indeed, an echo to the ensuing conflict between these sides can be found in Judg 10:6–9, 11. As for the severe punishment of gouging out the right eye, Josephus noted: "for he cut out the right eyes of all who either surrendered to him under oath or captured by right of war. This he did with intent—since the left eye was covered by the buckler to render them utterly unserviceable."[47]

43. Cross, "Ammonite Oppression," 149–50.
44. Rofé, "נחש מלך בני," 456–62.
45. Ulrich, Qumran Text, 169.
46. Oded, "עמון," 254–71.
47. Josephus, Ant. 6:69.

God's First King

In other words, the shield covered the left eye, so gouging out the right eye made fighting impossible.

In response to Nahash's conditions, the elders of Jabesh requested seven days in order to send messengers throughout the territory of Israel to find someone to deliver them. The seven days may be a literary convention found elsewhere (Joshua 6 and the Keret epic).[48] According to Fleming, as in Joshua 6, "seven day intervals belong to the sacred time of military campaign undertaken by divine command."[49] The usage of the term *mōšia* "deliverer" recalls stories in Judges when God sent judges to deliver the Israelites (Judg 3:9, 15).[50] However, why Nahash agreed to the Jabeshites request to send throughout all the land of Israel for a savior is not clear. Klein raised the possibility that "this concession was a sign of his arrogance or of his feeling of absolute military superiority"[51] Tsumura believes that Nahash knew about the state federation among the Israelite cities and he wanted to bring reproach upon all Israel, thus he was willing to wait for seven days.[52]

The people of Jabesh-gilead sent messengers to the tribe of Benjamin since familial ties related them.[53] More so, they probably heard about Saul's coronation, so they sent messengers directly to him. However, because they wanted to surprise him, they did not tell this to Nahash, and therefore, the narrator indicates that they sent messengers throughout Israel. The messengers did not demand actions from Saul. Saul acts on his own initiative. This account develops a charismatic type of leadership into kingship, which resembles the charismatic judges portrayed in the book of Judges. The king is the direct successor to the heroes of the past. His powers are divinely inspired.

The story of Saul's deliverance was written by a sympathetic author who glorified Saul's actions. However, even in this sympathetic description, there is a warning sign for the future. In order to summon the help of the Israelites, Saul dismembered an ox, and sent the parts throughout the territory of Israel. He threatened the Israelites that if they did not respond to his call they would suffer the same fate as the ox. Dismembering an animal to muster troops has its origin in covenant-making treaties (Genesis 15).[54] Saul orders and

---

48. Fleming, "Seven-Days Siege," 228.
49. Ibid., 213.
50. Sawyer, "What Was a *Mošia'*?," 475–86.
51. Klein, *1 Samuel*, 106.
52. Tsumura, *First Book of Samuel*, 305–6.
53. Melamed, "Benjamin and Gilead," 121–25 (Hebrew).
54. Wallis, Paralelle, and Polzin, "'HWQY'," 227–40.

Saul's Wars

threatens the people of Israel to join him to fight. In the context of holy war, blowing the horn was the way to muster troops (Judg 3:27; 6:34; 1 Sam 13:3).

This episode recalls the story of the Levite and his concubine at Gibeah (Judges 19). There the Levite dismembered the body of his concubine into twelve pieces and sent them throughout Israel to show that: "Such a thing has never been seen or done, not since the day the Israelites came up out of Egypt" (Judg 19:30). Following this incident, the Israelite tribes went and fought against the Benjaminites, and after several battles, the Benjaminites were defeated. The people of Jabesh-gilead did not join the Israelites in those battles, thus the Israelites fought against them.

The similarities are obvious. Saul's dismembering of the ox and sending its parts throughout Israel parallels what the Levite did with the body of his concubine. The messengers arrived to Gibeah, which is probably Givat Benjamin, the same place where the heinous crime was committed. Saul went to rescue the people of Jabesh-gilead; yet, the people of Jabesh-gilead did not help the tribes of Israel in their war against the tribe of Benjamin. This parallel diminishes the favorable portrayal of Saul, since we are also reminded about the inequity of the tribe of Benjamin, the people of Gibeah, and also the people of Jabesh-gilead. While, according to Polzin, everything in vv. 1–11: "contributes toward a conscious and deliberate *ignoring* of the monarchic status of Saul in favor of depicting him as someone who, like the judges of old, leads Israel to victory under God's inspiration."[55]

In spite of negative nuances, however, it is at this juncture that Saul acts like a king for the first time. He summons the tribes and musters three hundred thousand people from Israel, and thirty thousand of Judah. He also sent a message to assure the people of Jabesh-gilead of their deliverance. According to Josephus, Saul's promise to the people of Jabesh-gilead before he summoned the tribes was: "to come to their aid on the third day and to conquer the enemy before the sun rose, so that the ascending sun might see them victorious and released them from their fears."[56]

Saul also appears as a military tactician because he created the impression that the people of Jabesh would surrender on the following day. At the same time, he quickly moved with his army, and arrived by dawn at Jabesh. Saul divided his army into three groups and surrounded the Ammonite camp. He attacked the enemy at an early hour of the day. This recalls a few similar military strategies that were used by Gideon in his attack on the Midianite

---

55. Polzin, "On Taking Renewal Seriously," 502.
56. Josephus, *Ant.* 6.76.

God's First King

camp (Judg 7:16, 20); Abimelech's attack on Shechem (Judg 9:43); and this same strategy was used afterwards by the Philistines (1 Sam 13:17–18). Josephus claims that Saul: "not satisfied with merely having rescued Jabesh, made an expedition against the territory of the Ammonites, subdued it all, and having taken much booty, returned home a famous man."[57]

Saul was portrayed as a shy person and hesitant in his coronation at Mizpah. Here he appears as a strong leader who mustered his people by threat, and as a military leader who defeated the Ammonites quickly and decisively. In some ways, his depiction is similar to the judges who preceded him, but here, for the first time, he forces his will on the whole people of Israel and Judah. He rushed to save the tribes in the Trans-Jordan and delivered them from oppression. He is also kind towards people who refused his leadership and despised him. This stands in glaring contrast to King David and King Solomon, who did not show any mercy towards their opponents and killed them. It is not by accident that Samuel is missing from most of the story, since it is a transitional one in which Saul is the main character. Saul is the undisputed king of Israel and assumes his duties as a king. When Saul's coronation was renewed at Gilgal, it was done by the whole people from both sides of the Jordan River without Samuel.

Saul's home was at Gibeah, not far away from the Philistine garrison at Michmas, and according to 1 Sam 10:5 and 13:3 there was a garrison in Gibeah. Thus, if there was a war between Saul and the Philistines, how could Saul leave Gibeah?[58] We believe that at this stage the relations with the Philistines were peaceful and Saul's actions were useful for the Philistines since Saul, at that time, was a ruler under the Philistines.[59] According to Edelman, Saul's ability to lead his fellow Benjaminites in the successful battle against the Ammonite army as depicted is historically implausible. Such a battle, she believes, took place later after Saul became established as king when he had a strong and trained army that was able to succeed.[60] The narrative unit of 1 Sam 11:1–11 is an artificially constructed tale of the so-called major Judges. More so, she believes that Saul's victories in 1 Sam 14:47–48 is the core tradition upon which chapter 11 has been based.[61]

---

57. Josephus, *Ant*. 6.80.
58. Stoebe, *Das erste Buch Samuelis*, 207, 241.
59. Kreuzer, "Saul," 49.
60. Edelman, "Saul," 993; Edelman, "Saul's Rescue," 204.
61. Ibid., 207.

Saul's Wars

However, it seems that the story took place at the beginning of Saul's kingship. Jonathan, Saul's son who participated in his father's wars (13:2–3; 31:2) is strangely not mentioned in the war against the Ammonites. This is due to the simple fact he had not reached puberty, and was too young. A period of time passed between the war against the Ammonites and the rebellion against the Philistines. The war against the Ammonites took place between 1029 and 1005 BCE. At the start of that century, the Ammonites started to exert their influence and power, therefore, not surprisingly, Jephthah had to battle them. However, in the third quarter of the century they started to oppress the people of Gilead and reached the city of Jabesh-gilead. Saul rushed to the aid of the people of Jabesh-gilead because they were related by blood to the people of Jabesh and the tribe of Benjamin. According to the book of Judges, four hundred virgins from Jabesh were given to the men of Benjamin (Judg 21:12–14). There is no doubt that Saul came to the rescue of the people of Jabesh-gilead. Later, they showed their loyalty to Saul and his sons, after their death (1 Sam 31:11). According to the biblical account, when the men of Jabesh-gilead heard what the Philistines had done to Saul, they went and removed Saul's corpse and his sons' corpses from the wall of Beth-shan. According to 1 Sam 31:12–13, the people of Jabesh-gilead burned the corpses before they buried the bones. Evidently, in this case, the bodies were cremated to prevent the Philistines from abusing their corpses.[62] More so, the ties and the bonds between the people of Jabesh and the tribe of Benjamin were strong; therefore, not surprisingly, Saul's son Ishbosheth was crowned as a king at Gilead. In his battle against the Ammonites, Saul achieved two major victories. First, he liberated the people of Jabesh-gilead from the oppression of the Ammonites. Second, he incorporated the Gileadites into his young kingdom.

Saul's Wars against Moab, Ammon, Edom, and Zobah

A summary of Saul's battles against the nations whom he fought follows Saul's war with the Philistines (1 Sam 14:47–48). It was pointed out that there is linguistic linkage to the Dtr, and interestingly as the Dtr included summaries

---

62. While according to Josephus: "So the people of Jabesh wept all in general, and buried their bodies in the best place of their country, which was named Aroura; and they observed a public mourning for them seven days, with their wives and children, beating their breasts, and lamenting the king and his sons, without either tasting meat or drink" (*Ant.* 6.14.8).

God's First King

of David's wars in 2 Sam 8:2, 3–5, 12–14, he included them here as well.[63] According to the list, Saul fought against Moab, Ammon, Edom, and the kings of Zobah. There is no evidence, however, that Saul fought against these nations. Evidently, the order of the list is geographical—mentioning the nations of the Trans-Jordan such as Moab, Ammon, Edom, and Zoba, and after them—the nations located on the other side of the Jordan River, the Philistines and Amalekites. It is not significant that Moab appears in the list before Ammon because this order is also found in the list of David's wars, and in Jeremiah 48–49. Scholars believe that the names of these nations were taken from the list of nations against whom David fought in 2 Samuel 8.[64] Klein points out that this probably resulted from a comparison with the list of David's battles.[65] It is believed by scholars that the Deuteronomistic historian wanted to stress the point that despite losing his kingship (chapters 15–16), Saul remained just as adequate a savior as David.[66]

As was mentioned, there is no testimony besides this verse that Saul fought against the Moabites. However, David had familial ties with the Moabites. First Samuel 22:3–4 tells that the Moabite king allowed David, his father and mother, and his people to stay in Moab. This hospitality was probably motivated by political calculations; the king of Moab wanted to weaken the monarchy of Saul, and therefore he collaborated with David, Saul's archenemy. Thus, it is indeed possible that Saul fought against the Moabites in order to extend the eastern borders of his kingdom, and to defeat the coalition between Moab and David, which threatened his rule.

The war against the Ammonites probably continued the battle to save the people of Jabesh-gilead, signifying the beginning of Saul's wars in the Trans-Jordan to strengthen his rule (1 Sam 12:12). Like his ties with the Moabites, David also had ties with the Ammonites "David said, 'I will keep faith with Hanun son of Nahash, just as his father kept faith with me" (2 Sam 10:2). Evidently, Nahash allied himself with David during the reign of Saul in order to offset the threats against his nation. Saul, in his battle against the Ammonites, started his campaign in the Trans-Jordan to extend the border of his kingdom, and to eliminate the threats from the east, from David and from the Ammonites.

---

63. Klein, *1 Samuel*, 141.
64. Indeed, the Lucianic recension of the LXX adds Beth-rehob to our list.
65. Klein, *1 Samuel*, 141.
66. Ibid.

Saul's Wars

As for the war against the Edomites, it was part of Saul's wars in the Trans-Jordan that included the wars against Moab and Ammon. Edom was missing from the wars mentioned in the book of Judges (10:6, 11, 12). The mention of Edom signals the arrival of a new power close to the Israelite border. Family ties between the Amalekites and the Edomites already existed. The Amalekites were descendants of Timna, the concubine of Eliphaz, the son of Esau (Gen 36:12). The Edomites probably exerted influence on the Amalekites and controlled them where they lived in the Negev. Thus, a war with the Edomites came to remove a threat from the eastern border and also a threat from the Negev.

Brooks raises the possibility that since the Amalekites were connected with Edom, the narrator meant to write Amalek, not Edom. However, she points out that the campaign against Amalek was in the Negev, whereas Edom was in the opposite direction, to the east.[67] Moreover, the following verse (v. 48) mentions that Saul fought against the Amalekites, thus creating a duplication. Brooks raises another possibility, that the campaign against Edom was motivated by economic factors.[68] Indeed, as she points out, the King's Highway passed through the territory of Edom, this was a very significant route for trade. The same explanation can be offered regarding Moab and Zobah. During this period, people were looking for territories to settle to ensure their livelihood. As was mentioned in chapter one, archaeological surveys pointed to the expansion in the number of settlements, and to the increased population during that period. Therefore, it is more than likely, that Saul, the new king of Israel, tried to ensure better economic conditions for his people by conquering new territories.

The other enemies that Saul fought in the Trans-Jordan were the kings of Zobah. Raviv does not accept the historicity of this, since the kingdom of Aram Zobah was established after Saul.[69] Budde also does not accept the mention of Zobah, asking if Saul had time to fight the Aramean, since he was constantly fighting the Philistines. The LXX changes to King Zobah, in singular instead of the plural of the MT version. The mention of kings of Zobah reflects the historical reality of King Saul's era when the Kingdom of Zobah was loosely connected with different kings ruling at the same time. It was only afterwards, during the Davidic era, that one king exerted his authority over the Arameans.

67. Brooks, *Saul*, 114.
68. Ibid.
69. Reviv, *From Clan to Monarchy*, 110.

God's First King

Another piece of information that might point to Saul fighting against Zobah can be found in 2 Sam 8:3, which reads: "David defeated Hadadezer son of Rehob, king of Zobah, who was then on his way to restore his power at the river Euphrates" (RSV). There is uncertainty about the expression *lᵉhāšîb yādô* "to restore his authority" or literally "his hand," which means to restore his monument as the JPS, NEB, and NJV translate. The first interpretation is correct. Indeed, Rashi interpreted this as retrieving the territories that he conquered to expand its border. Similarly, the expression is also found in Ezek 38:12 *lᵉhāšîb yādᵉkā*, where it denotes extending one's power for Gog. In Isa 1:25, *vᵉšîbâ yadî 'āláyîk* "I will turn my hands against you" is an idiom for taking a stronger measure against. But the question still remains: since when did Israel control this territory? The fact that David went to restore the territorial situation leaves us with the possibility that during the time of Saul those territories were conquered.

To the general statement about Saul's war, one should remember a verse from Chronicles, which describes the sons of Reuben: "And in the days of Saul they made war on the Hagarites, who fell by their hand; and they occupied their tents throughout all the region east of Gilead" (1 Chr 5:10). The Hagarites were a semi-nomadic people who lived in the Trans-Jordan. Verse 19 tells us their names Jetur, Naphish, and Nodab. The first two names are similar to the names of the two sons of Ishmael (Gen 25:15), and the name Hagarites derives from their matriarch, Hagar. Though, according to Ps 83:7, the Hagarites were allied with Edom, Ishmael, and Moab. The war against the Hagarites describes the expansion eastward. Verses 18–22 describes a war by the sons of Reuben and Gad and the half-tribe of Manasseh against the Hagarites. According to Midrash *Bereshit Rabbah*, it appears that this is the same war as described in v. 10.[70] It is not clear who fought this war, the sons of Reuben? maybe Saul's army? This war resulted in the Reubenites settling in their tents throughout all the land east of Gilead. In other words, the Israelite tribes were expanding their territories beyond Joshua's instructions. This is also obvious from the description of the wars that were waged by the sons of Simon in 1 Chr 4:34–44.

In conclusion, Saul was the first king who fought for the welfare of all the Israelite tribes. In his wars, he tried to achieve three major objectives: to remove the presence of the enemies from Israelite territories, to protect Israelite territory, and to unite the Israelite tribes around his kingdom. In the east, in the Trans-Jordan, he fought against the Ammonites, as well as

---

70. *Ber. Rabb.* 98:15.

Saul's Wars

the Moabites, Edomites, and the kings of Zobah. By fighting in the east, he expanded the border of his young monarchy to the Trans-Jordan and eliminated the threat that came from the alliance between David, the Ammonites, and Moabites. In addition, he incorporated the Israelite tribes of the Trans-Jordan into his kingdom. In the south, he fought against the Amalekites who raided the territory of Judah. His victory over them added the tribe of Judah to his realm. In addition, by defeating the Amalekites, he insured a monopoly on the Arabian trade. But the main foe was the Philistines against whom he fought three major battles and many skirmishes (for the last battle see chapter 7). Saul's aim was to break the Philistine's oppression by liberating large territories of Israel from their dominion. The first battles against the Philistines took place at Geba and Michmas, and as a result, Saul removed the Philistine presence in the hill country.

The second major battle at Elah signals the liberation of the land of Judah, namely the Bethlehem mountain area from Philistine domination. Additionally, after the battle, the men of Israel and Judah pursued the Philistines from the battle field past Shaaraim to Gath and Ekron. Saul's second major historical battle restored the same territory to his young monarchy as was restored before him by Samuel (7:14). It liberated the land of Judah from the Philistines and linked Saul's kingdom to Hebron and the northern Negev. It cemented his ties with the tribe of Judah who fought with him against the Philistines. Saul's victories created a new reality in the central and southern part of the land of Israel and in the Trans-Jordan. Saul tried to create a new reality in the valley of Jezreel and Galilee but evidently lost his last battle there. In spite of exaggerations and the insertions of theological views and the legendary style of the narrations, a close study showed that the stories contain information of realistic geographical and strategic aspects that support the belief that they reflect true events. The stories were composed at the time of the united monarchy when the author had access to finding sources and knowledge of the land.

3

Saul versus David

SAUL AND DAVID, THE first two kings of Israel, are the protagonists of the book of Samuel. From the moment David arrives on the scene, the reader cannot but compare him to Saul. A technique employed by the biblical narrator to describe his heroes is to compare and contrast them. Using this technique the narrator points to the virtues and weaknesses of his hero. Characters can be revealed through their actions, lack of actions, appearances, gestures, and comments. In the narrative, characters are revealed both by statements made by them or by other characters, in addition to descriptions given by the third-person narrator.[1] In this chapter we will look at the image the narrator creates for our heroes. We will describe them as they appear in the book of Samuel, and look for reasons for this description. This comparison will ultimately yield a better understanding of why the kingship was transferred from Saul to David.

THE RISE TO POWER

There is a great similarity in the stories depicting Saul's and David's rise to power. Therefore, the story of David's anointing is very similar to Saul's anointing. In both stories a sacrificial meal precedes the anointment, which Samuel organizes. Saul was placed at the head of the table that included thirty invitees, and was given a priestly portion. The following day he was secretly anointed.

1. Alter, *The Art of Biblical Narrative*, 117.

Similarly, Samuel invited David's family, along with the elders of the city of Bethlehem, to a sacrificial feast. David had not been mentioned by name before this, according to Smith "this is probably intentional, to heighten the effect."[2] During the anointing, the text says that only the brothers were present. However, this is doubtful as David was anointed in secret like Saul. We know this from Eliab's rebuke of David, when he arrived in the valley of Elah (1 Sam 17:28–29). Eliab evidently was not aware of his brother's new status. Samuel probably anointed David in secret.[3]

Neither Saul nor David was present at the time of their election. Saul was in hiding and had to be brought to his coronation (10:22–23). David was tending sheep and brought to his anointing (16:11–12). Saul and David are depicted as insignificant and unworthy. Saul said: "But I am only a Benjaminite, from the smallest (*miqaṭane*) of the tribes of Israel, and my clan is the least of all the clans of the tribe of Benjamin!" (9:21). While David is described as the "youngest" (*haqaṭan*, 16:11), in both stories a young man directs the events unintentionally. In the first case, the young man is leading Saul to meet Samuel, who later anoints him. In the second tale, a young man advises Saul to bring David to his house. Saul asked for a person who can play the harp, but the young man brought a person who has many attributes such as: "stalwart fellow and warrior, sensible in speech, and handsome in appearance, and the Lord is with him" (16:18). At first glance, it appears that David's characteristics are irrelevant and did not answer Saul's request for a musician. However, these characteristics are mentioned here to give the reader a broader perspective of David, and will be displayed again in the conflict between Saul and David.

Rofé attaches a late date to the stories about the hero's beginning. According to him, the story of David's anointing is a late composition and has no organic connection with the narrative. The story belongs to the genre of the hero's setting out, and it is relatively late. To strengthen his argument he points to the fact that the story is not even mentioned once in the book of Samuel, even though legitimization was important to David. Moreover, there is no mention of it in the book of Chronicles. The first reference to it can be found in the late Apocryphal Psalm 151, also found in Cave 11

---

2. Smith, *Books of Samuel*, 145.

3. In v. 13 the letter should be *mem* instead of the letter *beit*—(*beqerev*) *mem* (*miqrev*). Thus the text should read: Samuel took David *from among* his brothers and anointed him (1 Sam 16:13). This is not in the Vaticanus text of the Septuagint, which omits the verses describing David's arrival at the battlefield to meet his brothers (1 Sam 17:12–31), including Eliab's rebuke. It is possible that we have here a different tradition.

God's First King

at Qumran.[4] Thus it appears that David's secret anointing is a late story designed to confer legitimacy on David's kingship.[5]

The moment that David was anointed, the divine spirit rested upon him and departed from Saul because David had replaced him as God's anointed. There could be only one king with transcendent powers. David had them, but Saul was still the legal ruler. Saul was the king for a number of years but without any legitimization. In contrast to David, an evil spirit from the Lord seized Saul and terrified him. Saul was not aware when the spirit departed from him, we read similarly about Samson: "For he did not know that the Lord had departed from him" (Judg 16:20). The evil spirit that is mentioned here is similar to the evil spirit that was sent by God between Abimelech and the citizens of Shechem (Judg 9:23). Some say that Saul suffered from mental illness and paranoia but according to Hertzberg: "Saul's suffering is described theologically, not psychopathetically or psychologically."[6] However, we believe the evil spirit was probably visions and dreams sent by God: "You frighten me with dreams, and terrify me with visions" (Job 7:14).

David's arrival at Saul's court resembles the signs that Saul received after his anointing. On that occasion, Samuel told him that asses were found and that he would meet three people making pilgrimage to God at Bethel. One will carry three kids, another will carry three loaves of bread, and the third will carry a jar of wine. Later, he will encounter a band of prophets proceeded by lyres, timbrels, flutes, and harps. In the section that describes Jesse sending David to Saul, we read that he took an ass and sent him with bread, a skin of wine, and a kid (1 Sam 16:20). Afterward, when the evil spirit came upon Saul, David took a lyre and played.

Ironically, at the first encounter between Saul and David, we find that Saul loved David very much, and he became his weapon-bearer. The Targum and Radak translate weaponbearer, while Abarbanel prefers "utensil bearer." David would bring any musical instrument Saul desired to hear or play, or any utensil, such as the shepherds make when they are in the fields with their flocks. Thompson has suggests that the verb "love" has some political nuance here, because of a certain ambiguity.[7] The verb denotes genuine affection between humans, but can also have political implications.

4. Rofé, *Prophetical Stories*, 46 n16.
5. For further study see Stoebe, *Das erste Buch Samuelis*, 302–3.
6. Hertzberg, *I & II Samuel*, 141; Smith, *Books of Samuel*, 148.
7. Thompson, "Significance," 334–38.

Saul recognized David and made a legal commitment to him, in other words he "loved" him and appointed him, as a trusted servant, to be his weaponbearer. Another subtle feature in the story is that by making David his weaponbearer Saul gave him his own weapon that foreshadows events. Then, before fighting Goliath, Saul gives David his own garment, bronze helmet, and sword (17:38–39). Similarly, Jonathan will give David his uniform, his sword, his bow, and his belt (18:4).

The fact that Saul sent messengers to Jesse to ask for his son indicates modesty and humility (1 Sam 16:19). Saul did not assert his right as king— "he will take your sons" (8:11). Saul's warm feelings towards David are repeated when he again sends messengers to Jesse to allow David to remain with him. He says that he is pleased with him (1 Sam 16:22). He also treats Jesse with respect when he turned to him, the participle *na'* is added to the imperative softening the command. Sending messengers to Judah showed that Saul's kingdom already extended its authority beyond the territory of Benjamin.

Initially, David was brought to Saul's court to serve as a musician. In pagan religions, the lyre was used for exorcism, but there is no sign of that here. Music was believed to possess magical powers to keep away demons and evil spirits. The use of music as a remedy in ancient times is well attested, and is used for therapy today. According to Radak, the power of relieving Saul's melancholia was a divine gift. Saul's first encounter with prophecy was with a group of prophets who were inspired by music and were sent into prophetic ecstasy; he was seized by ecstasy and turned into another man. Here, in contrast, Saul needed music to relieve him from the evil spirit.

THE UNKNOWN DAVID

Commentators were puzzled by Saul's question to his army commander Abner—"Whose son is that boy, Abner?" (1 Sam 17:55)—when he saw David go out against Goliath. Did Saul not recognize him? The previous chapter says: "And he became his weapon-bearer" (16:21). David also played the lyre for Saul who sent a messenger to his father: "Let David remain in my service, for I am pleased with him" (16:22). If Saul did not know him, why did Saul not verify who David was when he suggested he fight Goliath? Why did Saul send a boy whom he did not know on such an important mission that would determine his fate and the nations as well: "but if I best him and

God's First King

kill him, you shall be our slaves and serve us" (17:9).[8] Some scholars believe that the contradictions exist because the story of David and Goliath was an independent story that was inserted by the Dtr into the History of David's rise, even though the two documents did not agree. The LXX preserves the original version, which includes only vv. 1–11, 32–49, 51–54. Evidently, the LXX omits this whole section. According to Halpern, it appears as though the Greek text was harmonizing an apparent contradiction.[9] With the passing of time, stories tend to grow and this is what happened here. The other verses (12–31, 50, 55–58) were added to the Masoretic Text after the translation of the LXX thus increasing the legendary elements of the story. Yet, there are scholars who try to solve this apparent problem by claiming that Saul did not recognize David because a "bad spirit" seized him at that time. While his army commander, Abner, probably recognized David, but did not want to embarrass the king; he acted as though he did not know David. However, it should be stressed that Saul did recognize David later on, and remembered his success even though the "bad spirit" was upon him (18:10–12).

Another interpretation is that Saul did recognize David but did not remember his father's name, his lineage, and therefore, asked him: "Whose son are you, my boy?" (17:58). It is possible that Saul investigated David's lineage, since he promised the victor his daughter.[10] However, David's lineage was mentioned previously in chapter 16:18, where his father and the name of his city are mentioned.

Some try to explain these difficulties by pointing to a different chronological order. David's victory over Goliath occurred when he was an unknown youth. He was not among the warriors; he arrived at the battlefield by chance, and his brother rebuked him. After staying at home for a while, one of Saul's servants remembered and recommended him to the king as a stalwart fellow, warrior, and skilled in music. Therefore, after he returned from defeating Goliath, Saul and Abner did not know him well and asked about his identity.

The biblical narrator did not organize the story chronologically because of literary objectives. One of them was the need to describe how after the anointment of David, the spirit of God left Saul and gripped David. As a

---

8. Some scholars believe that the Hebrew text is a combination of two stories; one of them was incorporated after the third century. But this is incorrect; see Tov, "Composition"; Rofé, "Battle of David."

9. Halpern, *David's Secret Demons*, 7.

10. Bar-Efrat, *I Samuel*, 234–35 (Hebrew); Tsumura, *First Book of Samuel*, 470.

Saul versus David

result, David was brought to the king's court to play music for him. However, this hypothesis is unsatisfactory. At the end of chapter 17 and 18:1–5, David is brought to Saul's court due to his heroic action. This is followed by a pact between Jonathan and David who became a commander and successful warrior in Saul's army. There is no hint in the text that David returned home, and then, when a musician was needed, was brought back to Saul's court.

Scholars see two different sources or two different traditions describing David's arrival at Saul's court.[11] According to one tradition, David was brought to Saul's court as a musician; Saul liked him and made him his arms bearer (16:19–23).[12] According to the second tradition, when David defeated Goliath only then did he stay at the king's court. The redactor placed those two traditions next to each other. However, one might ask: why didn't the editor notice the difficulties with this, and why did he not try to harmonize them?

The rabbis on the other hand, took a different approach. According to them, Saul recognized David and the long conversation between the two testified to his love for David.[13] However, Saul's fear and concern that he might lose his kingship to a more worthy man troubled him (15:28). This caused him to think that this hero might be David. He probably felt, "The heart alone knows its bitterness" (Prov 14:10).

When Saul inquired, "Whose son is this lad?" he was seeking to identify not David's father, but his lineage. Saul knew that David was from the tribe of Judah, and Saul knew that Jacob had predicted that kings would descend from Judah (Gen 49:8–10). He wanted to know from which of Judah's sons he descended, Peretz or Zerach: "If he descends from Peretz, he will be a king. Since a king may break through (*poreitz*) other people's fences to make a path for himself, and no one may protest against him. If, however, he descends from Zerach, he will merely be prestigious."[14]

Rashi asked: what signs of royalty did Saul recognize in David that made him apprehensive and interested in his lineage? "For it is written: And Saul dressed David with his [battle] garments (*madav*). The term *madav* alludes that they fit to [David] size (*mideto*). And it is written about Saul: from his

11. Scholars who defend this solution assign 16:14–23 to the J or early source and 17:1—18:4 to the E or late source, see Gray, *Critical Introduction*, 71; Pfeiffer, *Introduction*, 347, 361; Budde, *Die Bücher Samuel*, xiv.

12. Willis calls 16:14–23 an "anticipatory redactional joint." See Willis, "Function of Comprehensive."

13. *Midr. Sam.* 22:1.

14. *Yebmot* 76b.

God's First King

shoulders up, he was taller than any of the people. Since his garments fit David miraculously, Saul inquired whether David was destined for kingship."[15]

To Saul's question "whose son is this lad," Abner swore that he did not know the identity of the boy. Saul ordered him to inquire "find out." Abner does not ask David whose son he is; he brings the boy to King Saul, so that he himself will ask. Abner refers to Saul with the honorary title King; the narrator also uses the same title. While Saul was speaking to David he referred to him as "my boy," the feeling is that he did it on purpose, wanting to diminish his success, he does not mention David's great victory against Goliath and the reward that he deserved. The love that Saul showed towards David disappeared and jealousy replaced it. It was probably the head of the slain Philistine that David held in his hand that caused this resentment. David, on the other hand, stood before King Saul as victorious. He addressed the king with honor and humility and styled himself, *your servant*.

SAUL'S HOSTILITY

Saul brought David to his court after the battle with Goliath. Unlike the past Saul wished to keep him at court. Saul had asked Jesse if his son David would remain in his court (16:22), but this request was denied (17:15). Saul's act recalls "the right of the king" to take sons and daughters (1 Sam 8:11–20). The account is parallel to the description of David's in chapter 16, where David appeared before the king as a musician and was made his arms bearer. Here, David is again in the king's court and Saul gave him a military commission that he carries out successfully. According to Edelman, Saul knew about David's anointment by Samuel, and to secure the blessings that David would bring to Israel, Saul made him part of his household.[16] Being part of his staff also made it easier for Saul to watch David to prevent any possible threats. Ironically, David, not Saul fought the battles, as if to proclaim that he was king. Saul even gave him command over an elite unit. The people and Saul's inner circle recognized David's high status. According to Abravanel, in spite of his superior position over them, they did not envy him. His elevated status and success added to his popularity. The Targum uses *maṣliaḥ*, the same word used to describe Joseph's success in Potiphar's house that led to his elevated status and eventually his downfall, similar to David's career in Saul's court.

15. Ibid.
16. Edelman, *King Saul*, 136.

Saul versus David

The women's victory song that greeted the army following the victory against the Philistines, roused the jealousy of Saul: "Saul has slain his thousands; David, his tens of thousands" (1 Sam 18:7). It was customary in the ancient world to greet the army or a hero after a victory. Miriam, Moses's sister, after the victory at the Sea of the Reeds, came out with a timbrel and all the women sang after her (Exod 15:20); similarly, Jephthah's daughter came with a timbrel and danced (Judg 11:34). This custom existed among the surrounding nations: "Tell it not in Gath, Do not proclaim it in the street of Ashkelon, Lest the daughters of the Philistines rejoice, Lest the daughter of the uncircumcised exult" (2 Sam 1:20). The homecoming victory song celebrated the equal triumph of Saul and David. It is inconceivable that women would sing a song to the king where he is not the most important figure.[17] More so, when they came to greet Saul they added the title king to his name so as to say that they came to honor him as their king. Thousands and ten thousands are used synonymously in Deut 32:30; Ps 91:7; and in the Ugaritic text.[18] The women's aim was not to compare Saul and David, rather to glorify both of them equally. According to Klein, it could be paraphrased as: "Our two heroes have killed many, many people!" Still the rhyme suggested a contrast between Saul and David; therefore the listener might think that the numbers are also compared.[19]

Saul heard the song jealously; from his perspective, even the idea of equality was unacceptable. Indeed, Freedman notes: "the very fact that David was accorded equal treatment with the king in the song would be sufficient to arouse the suspicions of any monarch, and especially of one insecure in his position and jealous of his prerogatives."[20] Saul's displeasure is articulated by two expressions "he was very chagrined" and "the matter displeased him." The second expression blatantly exposes the contrast with the people's attitude towards David's success "and he was pleasing in the eyes of all the people" (v. 5). While the women mentioned Saul before David, here he changed the order, mentioning David first as hinting that David was looked upon as worthier than he was. By saying "all that he lacks is the kingship," Saul expressed his jealousy and fear that David was the worthier man Samuel spoke about. Rashi comments: "He needs nothing else but the kingdom." Radak, in his interpretation, says that David was

17. Hertzberg, *I & II Samuel*, 156.
18. *UT* 51:I:27–29, "He pours silver by thousands, gold he pours by ten thousands."
19. Klein, *1 Samuel*, 189.
20. Freedman, "Review of Patterns," 201.

given everything; the only thing missing was that the women did not call him king. It was from that day, that Saul kept an eye on David. The Hebrew verb, *'oyen* comes from *'ayin*, "eye." The verb is a hapax, however, it is known in Ugaritic *'yn* "to behold."[21] It also appears in the Talmud in Piel meaning "look carefully."[22] Rashi, Radak, and Targum Jonathan render: "was lurking for David," i.e., he was seeking an opportunity to kill him when he would be off his guard.

Saul's hostility towards David was so intense and great that he attempted to kill him. First Samuel 18:11–12 likens this event to another attempt made by Saul in 19:9–10 to kill David. Some scholars think this is a duplication of the later episode, indeed, in the LXX^B our verses are missing.[23] A close reading of the conflict between Saul and David, however, reveals that they are continuously feuding. Saul tried to kill David in different ways, several times, and it was the narrator's technique in telling a similar story to stress this. Here, in our episode, Saul tried to kill David twice and failed. It is not completely clear if Saul threw the spear or simply raised it in the air. The LXX, Targum Jonathan, and Abravanel read that he raised the spear and was thinking to pin David to the wall. But the Hebrew verb *wayyaṭel* has the meaning "to throw" it is Hiphil from the root *ṭwl* (Jonah 1:1–5). More so, the fact that David eluded him twice, favors this interpretation. David displays his athletic abilities here, a swiftness similar to his speed in the battle with Goliath.

The verb *hikkah* a key word in the previous chapter (1 Sam 17:9, 25, 27, 35, 36, 46, 57) appears here: "Saul has slain (*hikkah*) his thousands; David, his tens of thousands." The rage and anger on hearing this caused Saul to take his spear and say: "to pin (*'akkeh*) David to the wall." Saul failed to kill David but ironically David defeats the Philistines again: "and killed (*wayyak*) two hundred Philistines" (v. 27).

Saul's violent attack on David is filled with irony. David was playing the lyre to cheer the king; instead, it caused him anger. David tries to alleviate Saul's pain—when the bad spirit seized him—then Saul tried to kill David. David was holding the lyre and Saul a spear. Later Saul said: "Let not my hand strike him: let the hand of the Philistines strike him" (18:17).

---

21. *UT*, 19.1846.

22. Jastrow, *Dictionary of the Targumim*, 1053–54. In Phoenician the verb *'yn* could even mean, "look at (with the Evil Eye)." See Caquot and du Buisson, "La second tablette," 391–406. In post-biblical Hebrew *'ayin* often meant 'the Evil Eye." But this seems unlikely in our text.

23. Klein, *1 Samuel*, 188.

Saul versus David

Saul's royal power is symbolized by holding the spear, a symbol of war and strife, while David holds the lyre, an instrument of calm.[24]

Saul's failure to kill David made him afraid. Before, Saul was hostile and jealous of David. Now he is fearful. The motif of fear will be repeated three times in this chapter (vv. 12, 15, 29). The first time we are told that Saul was afraid, the second time, that he dreaded him, and the third time, Saul grew still more afraid, Saul's enmity toward David increases.[25] This fear of David will play a major role in the ensuing events and feeds Saul's desire to kill David. Indeed, Saul will give a direct command to murder David (19:1).

Saul realized that God had turned away from him and was with David, a fact that is mentioned twice (vv. 12, 28). Not only was God with David, even all of Israel, as well as Judah, loved David (v. 16), as did Saul's courtiers (v. 5). More than that, Saul's own family loved David. His son Jonathan (v. 1) and his daughter Michal (vv. 20, 28) loved him. The fact the God was with David brought him success, and is repeated three times in the chapter (vv. 5, 14–15), echoing the Joseph story, where the text explicitly says that God was with Joseph. It was Garsiel who pointed to the analogy between David and Joseph. According to him, the author of Samuel wanted to provide David with Joseph's halo, thus he made the linkage.[26]

Since his plan to kill David failed, Saul devised a different plan. First, he removed David from his inner circle; he wanted him out of sight. This was done out of fear of David, but at the same time he appointed David chief of a thousand. Here, the narrator leaves the reader in the dark and does not explain the reason for David's new appointment and promotion. It is only later that the reader learns of Saul's real intent and motivation. Saul wanted to get rid of David; he wanted to make David die at the hand of the Philistines, and this is mentioned three times in the narrative (vv. 17, 21, 25). As Edelman puts it: "shifting responsibility for thwarting of Yahweh's plan on to Yahweh's own enemies and so avoiding any threat to his own life."[27]

The second part of Saul's plan was to give his oldest daughter, Merab, to David in marriage. Saul set a trap, however, by adding the condition that David would have to fight the Philistines. Ironically, David acted similarly

---

24. Edelman, *King Saul*, 134.

25. Driver, *Notes*, 155.

26. Joseph was considered as the youngest just as David. Both were shepherds, and are described as good looking. They are sent by their father to see their brothers. Both lived in a strange country Joseph in Egypt David in Philistia. For further comparison see Garsiel, *First Book of Samuel*, 121.

27. Edelman, *King Saul*, 139.

God's First King

many years later by sending Uriah the Hittite to die in battle. David succeeded, and Uriah died, while Saul failed. Yet, every time that David battled the Philistines he was successful.

Marriage to the king's daughter had already been promised to whomever defeated Goliath. Saul, however, created a new condition. Evidently, Saul did not have any intention to give his daughter to David, as he was planning to kill him and Merab was only the bait. Strangely, Merab was already betrothed to Adriel the Meholathite. It is possible that Merab, without her father's knowledge and consent, had accepted a marriage proposal from Adriel. Alternatively, Saul hated David so much that he could not bear the thought of giving his eldest daughter to him. Instead, he gave her to someone else. Moreover, Adriel is mentioned in 2 Sam 21:8 as Adriel the son of Barzillai. Adriel was from Abel-meholah, which was located in the Trans-Jordan. Saul it appears wanted to strengthen the ties between his kingdom and the settlements in the Trans-Jordan. This episode is missing from LXX^B, however, its inclusion in the MT is crucial from a literary point of view. It prepares the reader for the next section that tells the reader about Michal, David's wife.[28] Alternatively, it is possible that Saul offered Merab to David, he refused, and only then Michal, the younger daughter, was offered and he accepted.

At first, David refused to marry the king's daughter, replying to Saul with humility. He says, "Who am I, and what is my life" (v. 18); as to say "I am a humble person and my life is of little value." He also mentioned his family origin by using the word *ḥayyi*. The word appears in Arabic (*ḥy*) and it refers to "a group of families united by blood ties." Those families acted together and formed a unity. According to this explanation, "my father's family" comes to interpret the idiom *ḥayyi*. In other words, his family did not belong to this group.[29] David cancels Saul's obligations to him. Saul does not reply. We should point out that David's language repeats Saul's earlier response to Samuel: "But I am only a Benjaminite, from the smallest of the tribes of Israel, and my clan is the least of all the clans of the tribe of Benjamin" (1 Sam 9:21).

Saul had another, younger daughter named Michal, and she loved David. This is the only instance in the Hebrew Bible (except in the book of Song of Songs) that it explicitly says that a woman loved a man. Learning from his first experience with David, Saul sent messengers to convince him

---

28. Tsumura, *First Book of Samuel*, 482.
29. Smith, *Kinship and Marriage*, 36–40; Driver, *Books of Samuel*, 153.

Saul versus David

to marry Michal. The messengers were sent secretly so that David would not know that they came on behalf of the king. Their mission was to flatter David and to convince him that Saul wants him as a son-in-law. Evidently, David needed persuasion in light of Saul's negating his promise to give him Merab in marriage. That is to say, the king did not agree to her marriage and she was married without his consent, but the king still wants him as a son-in-law. David's first reaction is similar to his reaction following Saul's suggestion to marry his oldest daughter Merab. David again mentions his unworthiness, but this time, he adds the fact that he is poor and cannot afford the proper dowry for a princess. For the second time we encounter a reminder that Saul broke his promise to David, since he had promised great riches to the person who will defeat Goliath. As an alternative, Saul set's a new condition; instead of the bridal price, he wanted a hundred Philistines foreskins. Again, Saul was cunning; the true purpose behind the offer was to have David killed at the hands of the Philistines. David, on the other hand, was pleased with the king's proposal, so paid twice and he became the king's son-in-law.

There is a great analogy between the stories of David and Jacob, in particular, between their marriages.[30] Both stories have two daughters with a groom who has to pay a bridal price. Also, in both stories the future father-in-law negated his commitment. The groom had to work twice. In both stories there is a rift between the father-in-law and the future son-in-law, which forces the son-in-law to escape. In both, the daughter deceives her father and helps her husband escape.[31] The *teraphim*, the household idols, play an important role in the deception and trickery in both (Gen 31:34–35; 1 Sam 19:13–17). Michal, like Rachel, renounces allegiance to her father and instead, shows allegiance to her husband. Another common motif is the pursuit; in the first story, Laban chases Jacob and here Saul chases David. Words are exchanged between the pursuer and the escapee that ends peacefully when the two sign a covenant invoking God as a Judge.

KILLING DAVID

Saul's plan to kill David by the hands of the Philistines failed. Saul did not give up, and devised a new plan. Until now, Saul was thinking about it, but he kept his plan to himself. Now he told his son Jonathan and all his

30. Stoebe, *Das erste Buch Samuelis*, 351; Garsiel, *First Book of Samuel*, 130.
31. Alter, *The Art of Biblical Narrative*, 120.

God's First King

servants about his intentions to kill David. Ironically, he tells his plans to his son, Jonathan, who loved David (1 Sam 18:1, 3; 20:17), and to his courtiers who also supported David (1 Sam 18:22). There are three similar short stories in chapter 19, joined by Saul's desire to kill David.[32] This desire intensifies from one story to the next. In the first, Saul urged Jonathan and all his courtiers to take part in his plan, to help him kill David (1 Sam 19:1). In the second story, Saul sent messengers to David's home to watch him, and to kill him in the morning (1 Sam 19:11). In the third story, Saul sent messengers to bring David from Samuel's home, but instead of capturing David the messengers started to prophesy. Since the messengers failed, Saul went to seize David, but like his messengers, he also started to prophesy which allowed David to escape (1 Sam 19:20-24).

Obviously, there is a great similarity among these three stories. Each tells how Saul attempts to kill David, and how David was saved. In each case David was saved by Saul's inner circle. In the first story it is Jonathan, in the second it is Michal, and in the third it is Samuel. Another similarity is found in the second and third stories where Saul sends messengers to David to kill him. The key word in the first and second stories is "to kill" (vv. 1, 2, 5, 6, 11, 15, 17), which points to Saul's intentions to kill David.

The three stories portray Saul negatively. The king has one goal, killing David, and he will not stop until he has achieved it. The fact that even his son and daughter helped David escape portrays him even more negatively. Saul also appears as capricious. First, he wants to kill David, but his son persuades him not to do so. He took an oath using God's name that David shall not be put to death. He then allowed David to return to his court. But all this goodwill was temporary. Since David continued his success against the Philistines, Saul's hatred and envy intensified. He tried to pin David to the wall, he acted alone, as if to say, he trusted no one. His capricious nature is evident as he broke two promises: one to his son, Jonathan, and the other to God.

As mentioned above, Saul's attempt to pin David to the wall is similar to the episode that took place in the previous chapter (18:10–11). Scholars have claimed duplication of stories, and tried to explain it by claiming the presence of different traditions or sources. Some assert that the first story is secondary because it is unlikely that at such an early stage Saul would try to kill David. However, examination of the biblical narrative shows that

---

32. There is another story where Saul tried to pin David to the wall with his spear but he failed a parallel story is found in 18:10–11.

Saul versus David

the stories are an integral part of the story. David succeeded in smiting the enemy, then a bad spirit seized Saul, and as a result of that, Saul tried to kill David. The first incident took place after he killed Goliath, while in this story it took place after he killed the Philistines. Those are not different traditions originating from one story. On the contrary, the author here wished to portray Saul in a negative light, especially after Saul invited David to his court and promised not to kill him. Instead of rewarding David for his victories, Saul renewed his jealousy and wanted his death.

There is another very interesting, symbolic point. In Saul's third attempt to capture David, the spirit of God seized him, and he prophesied on his way to meet Samuel. Saul stripped off his clothes, and spoke in ecstasy before Samuel.[33] That is why people say: "Is Saul too among the prophets?" (19:24). This story echoes an earlier episode where Samuel anointed Saul. Accordingly, Samuel gave Saul different signs, one of which was that he will encounter a band of prophets and the spirit of God will grip him, and he will prophesy with them. When Samuel's signs were fulfilled the people asked each other "Is Saul among the prophets?" (10:11). But another person said: Thus the proverb arose: "Is Saul too among the prophets?" (10:12). There are two explanations for the origin of this saying, but neither explains the meaning or use. The duplication is a result of different traditions to explain how the proverb was created. But more likely, the duplication has a literary purpose in which the narrator stressed the difference between them. In the first story, Samuel anointed Saul. He met a band of prophets, the spirit of God seized him, he became a different person, and God was with him; he was chosen to lead Israel. In this story, the spirit of God seized Saul again, but it did not help him. Rather, it stopped him, and prevented him from capturing David. In the first story, the people were surprised to find that Saul was among the prophets. In this story, when Saul was already the king, the people were astonished to find that Saul descended from his high status and became like one of the prophets. Mettinger points out that 1 Sam 19:18–24 is: "a reversal of what 10:1–9 says of Saul's endowment with the Spirit. In both cases the Spirit is a divine manifestation. In 10:1–9 it gives Saul strength to carry out his feat and bravery. In 19:18ff. it works in the reverse: it makes Saul helpless and drives him to strip off his clothes the clothes of a king."[34] Not surprisingly it has been

---

33. Saul prophesized before Samuel but there was no connection between the two. Therefore there is no contradiction to what we read in 1 Sam 15:35: "Samuel never saw Saul again to the day of his death."

34. Mettinger, *King and Messiah*, 77.

suggested that the two stories are very old pieces of propaganda from the time of David.[35] One story (19:18–24) being pro-Davidic and anti-Saulide, while the other (10:10–12) being pro-Saulide.

The author tells that Saul stripped his clothes and lay naked all day and night. Radak explained that Saul actually took off his cloth and fell down naked. This happened when he went into a prophetic trance, lost all sensation, and thus was not conscious of what he was doing. Therefore, he stripped off all his garments. Saul's stripping of his clothes is a reverse image of the dressing up of the teraphim in David's clothes (v. 13).[36] Sperling points out that when the biblical writer wants to speak positively about the human anatomy, he usually refers to specific beautiful parts of the body. On the other hand, the Hebrew word naked is found only in negative connotation such as: of fear, humiliation, defeat, and negative sexual activity.[37] Fokkelman states the stripping anticipates Saul's death at the last battle at Mt. Gilboa against the Philistines "and stripped him of his armor" (1 Sam 31:9).[38] Rashi points out that there is no similar use to the term *'ārōm* (naked). Targum Jonathan and Rashi renders: *brsn wnfl*, and in the name of Rabbi Menahem, who heard from an Arab, *brsn* in Arabic means "insane." Targum Jonathan also explains *'ārōm* as naked, but not stripped of his clothes but of his physical senses, to imply he was insane or mad. But the removal of the clothes carried with it symbolism. Saul remained naked, as if the kingdom was taken from him. His clothes, which symbolized his royalty and authority were gone.

RELINQUISHING DAVID

According to chapter 23, David escaped twice from Saul. There were two different groups of people who wanted to give David to Saul. The first were the inhabitants of Keilah that David saved from the Philistines. They were ungrateful people who were afraid of David's presence in their city. Therefore, they were willing to betray David. The second were the Ziphites, who took the initiative, and informed Saul of David's hiding place. There is no reason

---

35. Mommer, "Ist auch Saul," 53–61. Nihan on the other hand sees the stories as late post Dtr that reflect conflicting evaluations of charismatic groups in Persian period. See Nihan, "Saul among the Prophets," 88–118.

36. Edelman, *King Saul*, 151.

37. Sperling, *Original Torah*, 124–25.

38. Fokkelman, *Narrative Art and Poetry*, 285.

Saul versus David

for their actions. Most probably the slaughter of the priests of Nob as well as the destruction of the city that included men, women, children, infants, oxen, asses, and sheep, raised their fear of Saul. Saul accused the people of Nob: "for they are in the league with David; they knew he was running away and they did not inform me" (1 Sam 22:17). The Ziphites, who probably learned about the massacre even though they were members of David's tribe, wanted to show their loyalty to the king, therefore they divulged David's hiding place.

According to the biblical account, the Philistines were raiding Keilah and plundering the threshing floors. The language used is very similar to other expressions in the book of Judges (2:14–16; 6:3). David came to the rescue of the city after God ordered him to do so. Evidently, David wanted to help his own tribesmen in their fight against the Philistines. Keilah is listed among cities of Judah (Josh 15:44); and it was located, during David's time, near the Philistine border. Ironically, it is David who came to save the city and not Saul, the king of Israel. Before taking any actions, David consulted God asking him the same question twice. Abiathar, son of Ahimelech the priest, brought an ephod with him and David used his services. David had to ask the same question twice, in order to encourage his people, and to dispel their fear. Alternatively, the first reply was not clear; it could be interpreted that you will smite the Philistines and save the city, but there is no explicit promise that David would defeat the Philistines. The clear promise was given only in the second response: "for I am going to deliver the Philistines into your hand" (1 Sam 23:4). According to von Rad, this answer is a standard rubric for Holy war.[39]

The significance of these two consultations with God highlighted the difference between Saul and David. David consulted God, while Saul did not. Instead he relies on the collaborators among the people of Keilah. More so, David now has a priest with an ephod at his side, as Saul had previously (1 Sam 14:19, 36). The priest with the ephod could obtain a "yes" or a "no" answer from God. Paradoxically, the priest that is at David's disposal, arrived at his camp as a result of Saul's actions. It was Saul's slaughter of the priests of Nob that brought the priest with the ephod to David's camp. Saul blamed Abiathar's father, Ahimelech, for consulting God for David, now it is Abiathar who helps David. Ironically, the ephod is used now to avert, and prevent Saul from capturing David.

The narrator reports that Saul was informed of David's arrival in Keilah. Based on this information, Saul assembled his army. Saul believed that God

39. Von Rad, *Holy War*, 43–44.

had delivered David into his hands, since David was locked in a city. Saul's wickedness surfaced here again, he is willing to destroy the entire city of Keilah in order to capture and kill David. Meanwhile, David knew that Saul was planning evil against him.[40] At this point David sought divine guidance. The difference between the two is striking, Saul thought that God was with him, because David was within a walled city, David on the other hand inquired of the Lord through a priest who was equipped with an ephod.

> David repeated his question to God as before: "Will the citizens of Keilah deliver me into his hands? Will Saul come down, as your servant has heard!" (1 Sam 23:11); and then: "Will the citizens of Keilah deliver me and my man into Saul's hands?" (v. 12). According to the Talmud: "One does not inquire regarding two matters simultaneously, i.e. he must wait until he receives a response to one query before posing the second. And if he did inquire regarding two matters simultaneously, he is answered only the first. David asked the questions in correct order and was answered in correct order. And once he understood that he had asked in incorrect order, he returned and asked in correct order, as it is stated in the next verse: And David said "Will the leaders of Keilah deliver me and my men into the hand of Saul?" and Hashem said, "They will deliver."[41]

The answer that David received from God highlights the ingratitude of the inhabitants of Keilah. David had just saved this city from looting by the Philistines. David saved them, even though his people feared that his actions would lead to a clash with the Philistines. The inhabitants of Keilah were ready to hand him over—evidently they were more afraid of Saul.

The second episode involves the Ziphites who informed Saul about David's presence in their territory. Since Saul failed in his prior attempt to capture David, this time he acted more carefully. Saul, without precise information, did not want to bring his army. Therefore, he asked the Ziphites to find the hideout that David was using since he was constantly moving from place to place. In contrast to chapter 22, where Saul complained that his own tribesman, the Benjaminites, did not tell him that Jonathan supported David, we find that the Ziphites came to Saul's aid. They arrived at Saul's court and informed him about David's whereabouts. At first glance,

---

40. The verb "knew" (yd') appeared also in similar way where we read that David "knew" that Doeg will inform Saul (1 Sam 22:22). Polzin pointed out that knowledge is a key word in chapters 20–23 one third of the root yd' in 1 Samuel appears in those chapters. See Polzin, *Samuel*, 200.

41. *Yoma* 73b.

Saul versus David

their motivation is not clear; probably they belonged to the Caleb family, and did not approve of David controlling their region (see the story of Nabal). Psalm 54 refers to this incident and the Ziphites are described as ruthless men, unmindful of God (Ps 54:3).

Saul is the main speaker in his conversation with the Ziphites. He appears surprised at their arrival and he blessed them for showing compassion towards him. Saul interprets their support as a result of compassion. Saul is unbalanced, full of self-pity, and insecure. The verb "compassion" in Hebrew is *ḥāmal* this is the same verb that was used in 1 Samuel 15 where Saul was instructed to destroy the Amalekites but instead spared (*ḥamal*) Agag. We have here the reverse situation, in chapter 15 it was Saul who spared the life of the king; here it is the Ziphites who spare Saul's life.[42] Saul repeats his own instruction to the Ziphites "look around and learn," and "go now and prepare" (vv. 22–23). They agree to go search for David among all the clans of Judah. As Radak interpreted, the tribe of Judah was hiding David, while the other tribes would have handed David over to Saul.

By the time the Ziphites returned, David and his entourage were in the wilderness of Maon in the Arabah. It appears that David also had informers who told him about Saul's movements, so he ascended the rock to take refuge. After locating David, Saul's men were closing in on him. Saul and his men were on one side of the mountain, while David and his men where on the other side. When Saul's men were about to kill David, a messenger brought Saul an urgent message regarding a Philistine attack on Judah, resulting in his retreat. This calls to mind the binding of Isaac, where, at last moment, Abraham stops before slaying Isaac when the Angel of God appears. In the Keilah story, David was saved by asking of God, and in the Ziphites story he was saved by a divine messenger.

Rashi explained that the messenger was a real angel sent to save David. The Midrash interprets the Psalmist words: "I said in my haste, 'all men are liars (Ps. 116:11),'" referring to the episode where David was in haste to get away from Saul. When he found himself hemmed in by Saul and his men, he said

> Samuel anointed in vain, and told me, "The Lord has anointed you as a king." Upon this, the Holy One, Blessed be He, retorted, "I shall testify that Samuel is faithful, as it is stated, ... and you call him a liar?" Immediately, an angel came to Saul, saying, "Make haste and go ..." Said Rabbi Judah, "That *malach* was a messenger (not an

42. Edelman, *King Saul*, 190.

angel)." Retorted Rabbi Phinehas, "Was the messenger an advisor, telling Saul to hasten and go to battle the Philistines? It was rather an angel from heaven, "He sent from above and saved me" (Ps. 18.17).[43]

Interestingly, the Midrash explains the name "the rock of the Divisions." Accordingly, Saul's men were divided in their opinions. Some said, "While the son of Jesse is in your hand, let us not turn away from him." Others said, "Israel war is first, for the son of Jesse can be found anytime."[44]

PURSUER AND PURSUED

The story of Saul's pursuit of David in chapter 24 is closely paralleled in chapter 26. Therefore, some posit that they are alternate versions of the same incident.[45] Both stories share common elements.[46] David, the pursued, captured Saul, the pursuer. David's men urged him to kill Saul with God's approval, while in chapter 26 it is Abishai who urged David to do so. David refused his people's advice. Instead, he acted symbolically. In the first story, David cut off the corner of Saul's cloak, in the second; he took the spear and water jar that belonged to Saul. This shows that he could harm Saul. Conversation between Saul and David followed; David stated that he had no bad intentions against Saul. At the end of the conversation, Saul expressed his regrets for his actions against David. Modern scholars such as Polzin[47] and Birch see chapters 24–26 as a "shift from David as one whose life is endangered to David as one who spares life."[48]

In spite of the similarities there are significant discrepancies between the two stories, and it might be that this was the reason for their inclusion in the book of Samuel. In chapter 24, Saul arrived coincidentally to the cave where David and his men hid, Saul went to relieve himself, that is, "to defecate." The Masoretic Text uses the euphemism "to cover his feet."

---

43. *Midr. Pss.* 18.7
44. Ibid.
45. Koch, *Growth*, 142; Klein, *1 Samuel*, 236; Bar-Efrat, *I Samuel*, 328. While McCarter and Edenburg argue that chapter 24 was written on the basis of chapter 26. See McCarter, *1 Samuel*, 385–87; and Edenburg, "How (Not) to Murder a King," 64–85.
46. For a detail description of the similarities between the two accounts see Klein, *1 Samuel*, 236–37.
47. Polzin, *1 Samuel*, 203–15.
48. Birch, "First and Second Books of Samuel," 1157 n155.

Saul versus David

As McCarter pointed out, this was interpreted as mockery of Saul.[49] In contrast, in chapter 26, David knew in advance Saul's location and went straight to his camp. In the first story, David and his men were at the back of the cave, in the dark, therefore, Saul could not see them. Surrounded by his people, he was seemingly secure; on the other hand, David entering the camp was suicidal. In the first episode, Saul arrives at the cave by chance, and so we might say this took David by surprise and therefore he hesitated to kill Saul. In the second episode, David planned his entrance, and his decision not to kill Saul was not impulsive, emotional, nor without proper consideration. On the contrary, David had time for sober reflection, and decided not to kill Saul. Still according to the narrator the two stories stress the fact that the prospect of David killing Saul was not merely circumstantial, but directed from God above; so said David and his men (24:4, 10; 26:8, 23); Saul (20:4, 18); and the narrator (26:12).

The first encounter took place during the day, the second at night. In the first story, David acts alone when he was cutting the corner of Saul's coat. How he cut Saul's robe is not clear, unless Saul took off his robe when he went to relieve himself. In the second story, David is accompanied by Abishai when they took the spear and the water jar from Saul. The story also mentions Ahimelech, the Hittite, whom David consulted before going down to Saul's camp. According to Abramski, this fact added validity to the story, Ahimelech, the Hittite, was like Uriah, the Hittite, one of David's heroes.[50] Abishai words "Let me pin him to the ground with a single thrust of the spear" (26:8) are cruelly to the point. In contrast, in the first story we have a general statement by David's men: "This is the day of which the Lord said to you, 'I will deliver your enemy into your hands" (1 Sam 24:5).[51] Abishai's words are typical for the sons of Zeruiah, who, throughout the Davidic stories, are known as ruthless and bloodthirsty.

Only in 24:21 did Saul admit directly to David that he would reign and that the kingdom would be established by him. Saul already knew about it, since Jonathan said to David: "You are going to be king over Israel and I shall be second to you; and even my father Saul knows this is so" (1 Sam 23:17). In addition, Saul asked David not to destroy his family because in the ancient

---

49. McCarter, *1 Samuel*, 386.

50. Abramski, "שאול ודוד," 58–59.

51. Ackroyd believed that vv. 4b-5 were omitted from their original position and should be after v. 8a. He also raised the possibility that the confusion is a result of combining the two stories in our chapter. See Ackroyd, *First Book of Samuel*, 187–88.

God's First King

times it was common for the new ruler to destroy the family of his predecessor. In comparison, in chapter 26, Saul told David: "May you be blessed, my Son David. You shall achieve, and you shall prevail" (1 Sam 26:25).

There is a vast difference between David's first address to Saul and his second. The first time he speaks to Saul harshly, invoking divine judgment upon him. David prays that God will punish Saul. He points to Saul's irrational pursuit. He speaks of himself unsympathetically, not worthy to be chased. In his second address to Saul, he spoke to him with reverence and kindness. Joseph Kara explained that the first time David suspected Saul of intentional treachery, thus he rebuked him while demonstrating his innocence. As a result, Saul admitted that the kingdom would be established in David's hands. After hearing Saul, David was convinced that Saul would stop pursuing him. However, when David learned that Saul resumed his pursuit, he could not believe that it was Saul's initiative. Therefore, he was convinced that God took his free will away and incited Saul against him.[52] Since Saul was not completely to blame, he changed his tone and spoke to him in a gentler manner. However, we should point out that David completely ignores the fact that Saul showed remorse. Instead, David praises himself for not harming the Lord's anointed. What is conveyed here is the contrast between the weak king and the king to be. David portrays himself as righteous and faithful, typical attributes of a king.

There is a difference between Saul's reactions to David's accusations in the two stories. In the first story Saul asks David: "Is this your voice, my son David?" (v. 17). Saul calls David "my son" in response to David calling him "my father" (v. 11). He speaks to him compassionately: "You are like a son to me," and immediately he started to cry. He probably cried because he felt guilty and regretted his past actions against David. Alternatively, he realized how close to mortal danger he was, and since David spared his life, Saul cried. By holding up a piece of Saul's cloak, David showed restraint and innocence. He could have taken the king's life, but did not. His holding a piece of his cloak, recalled for Saul how he had held a piece of Samuel's coat. It was then that the prophet told him the kingdom was taken from him and transferred to a worthier man. Saul faced the truth at this juncture and a realty that he could not escape; the worthier man stood before him and for the first time he admitted it.

In the second story, David does not trust Saul anymore, and he keeps his distance from him. Saul turned to David in a similar manner and asked

---

52. See 1 Sam 18:10–12; compare 1 Kgs 22:20–25.

Saul versus David

the same question that he posed before: "Is that your voice, my son David?" (v. 17). By calling him "son" he tried to appease him. This was done after David rebuked Abner for not guarding the king. Dialogue between the two ensued in which David criticized the king for pursuing him and proclaimed his innocence. David hints he will have to leave the Promised Land to worship other gods. Saul answered David by admitting his sins and confessing his errors. By admitting his guilt before his people, Saul tries to reconcile with David in hopes of gaining his trust. Thus, he called him to return promising not to harm him. It is noteworthy that in the first story, Saul did not stress his sin, but instead pointed to David's righteousness. To admit his fault before David and the all people indicates Saul's greatness. Saul takes full responsibility for his actions. This is in direct contrast to the Amalek story, where he tried to blame the people of Israel for his own sin. Unfortunately, it was too late, because now David did not trust him.

In conclusion, what emerges from this description so far is a king who is capricious, moody, and unfailingly trying to kill David. He makes promises to David, to Jonathan, he even swears by God's name, but to no avail, as he breaks his promises, one after the other. He is mean-spirited and willing to sacrifice the happiness of his daughters in order to get rid of David. Yet, David is a loyal servant who comes to the king's aid when he plays the lyre to relieve him from his spells. He fights the king's war and succeeds. Ironically, the one positive thing that the author mentions is Saul's recognition of David's legitimacy. The stories also give justification to David, not only for severing his ties with Saul, but from the kingdom of Israel to settle among the Philistines.[53] In 1 Sam 16:14—2 Samuel 5, which describes the history of David's rise had one purpose; to show why David was the legitimate successor of Saul and why the kingship was taken from Saul. To achieve this goal the pro-Davidic author used comparative structures that portrayed Saul in a negative way and on the other hand, glorified David.

---

53. Abramski, "שאול ודוד," 50.

4

Feuds in the King's Court!

JOSEPHUS'S DESCRIPTION OF SAUL'S destruction of the city of Nob calls the king's action a barbarous crime. He further states:

> while they are private persons they are equitable and moderate, and pursue nothing but what is just, and bend their whole minds and labors that way. But when once they are advanced into power and authority, then they put off all such notions, and, as if they were no other than actors upon a theater, they lay aside their disguised parts and manners, and take up boldness, insolence, and a contempt of both human and Divine laws . . . They raise those to honor indeed who have been at a great deal of pains for them, and after that honor they envy them; and when they have brought them into high dignity, they do not only deprive them of what they had obtained, but also, on that very account, of their lives also, and that on wicked accusations, and such as on account of their extravagant nature, are incredible. They also punish men for their actions, not such as deserve condemnation, but from calumnies and accusations without examination; and this extends not only to such as deserve to be punished, but to as many as they are able to kill. This reflection is openly confirmed to us from the example of Saul, the son of Kish, who was the first king who reigned after our aristocracy and government under the judges were over.[1]

Does this portrayal of Saul reflect the true personality and image of Saul that emerges from the books of Samuel? In order to answer this question we will analyze the complex relationship between Saul and his own family. In addition, we will examine Saul's relations with his courtiers and

1. Josephus, *Ant.* 6.12.7.

Feuds in the King's Court!

warriors to understand the reason for their dissension. We will also look at the relations between Samuel the Prophet and Saul. Samuel rejected Saul as the king of Israel, but in the end, grieved over him. This chapter will help us to gain a different angle to view his personality and ultimately help us understand his seemingly bizarre behavior.

JONATHAN

In spite of the fact that Jonathan is one of the main characters in the book of Samuel, he does not appear alone. Jonathan is always mentioned with his father Saul or with David. From the start, tension exists between Saul and Jonathan.[2] This tension will intensify with David's arrival at Saul's court. In Jonathan's second attack against the Philistine garrison we are told: "but he did not tell his father" (14:1). At first glance, it is possible that Jonathan did not reveal his plans to his father in order to guard the element of surprise. Had he known, Saul probably would not have approved his plan. Another possible explanation holds that Jonathan wanted to glorify himself, not his father. The narrator inserted this piece of information in order to illuminate the tension between father and son. Jonathan repeatedly sides with David, and conceals his relationship with David from his father. In contrast to 14:1 where Jonathan did not inform Saul about his plan, in 19:1 he tells David that his father, Saul, wants to kill him. He again informs David about his father's plans (20:9).

1 Sam 14:1   ul'abiv lo higgid
1 Sam 19:2   wayyagged yehonatan ledawid
1 Sam 20:9   'aggid lak

To highlight the differences between Saul and Jonathan, the narrator compares the two in chapters 13 and 14. Saul commands the military camp at Michmas and Bethel, while Jonathan was at Gibeah. Jonathan assassinated the Philistine prefect, while Saul called and assembled the people in Gilgal. Praise for Jonathan killing the Philistine is given to Saul and not to Jonathan (1 Sam 13:4). Saul failed time after time to inquire of the Lord (13:8–14; 14:18–19). Moreover, a priest had to remind Saul to inquire of God if he should go after the Philistines (14:36–37). In contrast, Jonathan asked for a sign from God (14:9–10) before he attacked the Philistine outpost. Saul is passive. He fears the dwindling numbers of his soldiers, and a Philistine

2. Long, *Reign and Rejection*, 101; Whitelam, *Just King*, 78.

God's First King

attack in Gilgal (13:8–12). Saul camps at Gibeah, he and his six hundred men sit idle (13:15–16; 14:2). Jonathan, on the other hand, is active. In spite of his military disadvantage, he attacked the Philistine's outpost. He believed that it was God's will, and not the number of soldiers, that would determine the outcome of the battle. This thought will be echoed many hundreds of years later by Judah Maccabaeus: "It is easy for many to be delivered into the hands of few. Heaven sees no difference in gaining victory through many or through a few, because victory in war does not lie in the weight of numbers, but rather strength come from Heaven" (1 Macc 3:18–19).

To further demonstrate the gap between father and son, the text says that Saul wanted to kill David, yet on the other hand, Jonathan was *"very fond"* of David (1 Sam 19:1). The narrator used the words *"very fond"* in order to show the disparity between father and son. Indeed, in the previous chapter, Saul's servants told David that the king was *"fond of him,"* but evidently they were not being honest.

Saul informed Jonathan and his courtiers about his plan to kill David. Jonathan went directly to David to inform him about his father's plan. He advised David to hide. This counsel saved David's life. Jonathan acts contrary to his father's wishes; he aids his father's enemy. He also promised David that he would speak on his behalf and keep him informed about what he discovered; in other words, he was David's spy.

At this point, Jonathan tried to mediate between David and Saul. Jonathan is torn between his loyalties. In his plea to save David, we are told that Jonathan spoke well of David. McCarter points to the Amarna archives, where the king of Jerusalem Abdi-Heba requested the Egyptian scribes act as his advocate and "speak good/beautiful words" to the king.[3] McCarter recognizes the political overtones in Jonathan's words; that David has done well, that he acted with the loyalty that he owes his king. Jonathan stressed the fact that David did not sin against his father Saul, thus, his father should not sin against David. Moreover, he mentioned David's great victory against Goliath, in which he risked his life. The words "he took his life in his hands" *vayyaśem 'eth nafešo bekhapo* (1 Sam 19:5), describes David's bravery; this resonates with Jephthah's words "I risked my life *va'aśimah nafeši bekhapi* (Judg 12:3). Because of the victory and because David did not sin, Jonathan admonished his father not to sin by shedding David's blood. Prevention of bloodguilt was very important for any king, in order not to pollute his kingdom with his own sin. For the moment Jonathan succeeds, since Saul

---

3. McCarter, *I Samuel*, 322; *ANET*, 487–89.

Feuds in the King's Court!

swore that he would not harm David. Following this, Jonathan informed David about his conversation with his father, and brought him back to the king's court where David served Saul as before.

The final break between Saul and his son Jonathan occurred at a sacrificial meal. What is not clear however is why, after three escapes recorded in chapter 19, did David returned to Gibeah. More so, what made him think that Saul would expect to see him in his usual place at the king's table? When Saul noticed David's absence, it appears he forgot about his murderous intentions towards David. He thinks that David's absence has to do with ritual uncleanness; therefore, he asked Jonathan why David was absent? On many occasions, Saul's strange behavior was attributed to his madness. However, how can we explain the behavior of Jonathan and David in chapter 20 after knowing that Saul wished to murder David?

Jonathan stood up at the sacrificial meal, yielding his usual place at his father's side to Abner. According to Radak, Jonathan moved because he did not want to sit next to his father since Saul might become angry with him and attempt to strike him. We can see that Jonathan feared his father. To his father's question about David's absence, he answered with a lie that was arranged by David and him. Accordingly, David had to attend a family feast; therefore he asked his permission to leave for Bethlehem. Jonathan used the phrase "let me slip away" to describe David's request. The verb *mlṭ* appears several times to describe David's flight from Saul in the previous chapter (vv. 10, 11, 12, 17, 18).[4] This phrase here is striking since it provoked Saul's anger. In the previous chapter, it described Michal's assistance to help David escape; now his son helps his archenemy. The mention of the sacrifice also contributed to Saul's anger, it reminded Saul of David's rumored anointing by Samuel in a similar situation.[5]

Not surprisingly Saul's reaction was harsh. He called his wife a rebellious woman and said his son was just like his mother. This insult is directed towards Jonathan. By saying that his mother was a perverse rebel, he puts doubt on his mother's qualities that hints that he was not his son. Interestingly, 4QSam[b] and LXX have "son of rebellious maidens," and McCarter accordingly reads "You son of a rebellious servant girl!" Saul accuses Jonathan of forsaking him, being "son of" meant member of the class, but Jonathan forsakes those to whom he owed allegiance.[6] Being a son of a slave

---

4. Edelman, *King Saul*, 159; Fokkelman, *Crossing Fates*, 335.
5. Edelman, *King Saul*, 159.
6. McCarter, *I Samuel*, 343.

God's First King

girl indicates a lower status, while son of a rebellious mother meant that he might be suspected of being a bastard. Alternatively, a rebellious son does not deserve kingship.

Saul is very angry with Jonathan since he sided with his enemy. He united with David, an act that casts a shadow on him and his mother who gave birth to him. This is the opposite of what we read in Proverbs: "A wise son makes his father happy; a fool of a man humiliates his mother" (15:20). His friendship with David was embarrassing, as it was embarrassing to the nakedness of his mother. The Hebrew word *'erwo*, most often refers to genitalia, which seems to suggest that through his disgraceful actions, Jonathan also brought shame to his mother. Saul wanted to help his son inherit the throne, but at the same time accused him of rebellion and siding with the enemy.

Saul tried to speak to his son's conscience by telling him that his kingdom would not be established as long as the son of Jesse is alive. Ironically, his words echo Samuel's warning to him: "the Lord would have established your dynasty over Israel forever. But now your dynasty will not endure" (1 Sam 13:13). He commands Jonathan to bring David to him because he is "a son of death." The Targum translates this "for he is a man deserving death." Saul fears David; he already knows that the throne will go to David and not Jonathan. "Do not be afraid, the hand of my father Saul will never touch you, you are going to be king over Israel, and I shall be second to you; and even my father Saul knows this is so" (1 Sam 23:17).

Jonathan still tried to defend David in spite of his father's harsh words. He asked his father Saul: "Why should he be put to death? What has he done?" (1 Sam 20:32). Jonathan posed two questions that echo David's own words in the beginning of the chapter. This also echoes Jonathan's own words where he declared that David would not die. Jonathan affirms David's innocence.

Saul did not respond directly to Jonathan's questions, rather he fumed at his son. Saul was so consumed with hatred and fear of David that he considered every ally of David as his enemy. His fury was so great that he tried to kill his own son Jonathan. Saul cast his spear at Jonathan to slay him. Jonathan thus finds himself in the same situation that David experienced when Saul tried to kill him twice. Jobling points to the merging of identities and roles played in the portrayal of David and Jonathan in these chapters.[7] Alternatively, Saul brandished the spear in a threatening move, but he really did not have any intention of killing him. According to Josephus, Saul

---

7. Jobling, *Sense of Biblical Narrative*, 14.

Feuds in the King's Court!

was eager to kill him but: "he did not indeed do what he intended, because he was hindered by his friends."[8] It is at this juncture that Jonathan knew without any doubt the true intent of his father. Previously, he tried to convince himself that his father did not have any lethal intentions, but here is the final break between father and son. Jonathan rose from the table with rage, he was so angry with his father that he left without asking permission and without bidding farewell. He was so grieved that he did not eat that day. Jonathan was shocked by his humiliation; his father not only rebuked him in public but also tried to kill him. Some say that Jonathan was more shocked at his father's humiliation of David.[9] Jonathan resented the wrong done to David. We believe, however, that he was angry over his own and David's humiliation. As Klein observed, Jonathan's anger in v. 34 seems righteous while Saul's anger in v. 30 is motivated by fear and envy.[10]

What emerges from the stories about Jonathan are his idealized characteristics in juxtaposition to those of Saul whom God had rejected as king. Jonathan is portrayed as a military hero who fought for freedom from the Philistine oppression. In the second part of the stories, Jonathan becomes a loyal friend of David, the man who becomes king instead of him. In spite of this, Jonathan is not envious of David, but remains friends with him. The stories that stress Jonathan's heroism belong to sources that were written by the supporters of the house of Saul. On the other hand, supporters of David wrote the stories that describe the friendship between Jonathan and David. The pact between David and Jonathan aided David. But did not Jonathan have any ambition to become king of Israel following his father? Moreover, according to the biblical narrative, Jonathan regarded David as Saul's natural successor (1 Sam 20:13–17). It was Morgenstern who raised the possibility that the son-in-law had greater claim to the throne than the son, so a pact between Jonathan and David was sealed.[11] The fact that he was the son-in-law and a mighty warrior made him the natural candidate to succeed Saul.[12] However, this is unlikely since Jonathan was also a great warrior, and was the king's son. More than likely, a sympathetic author who wanted to legitimize David's right to throne composed these stories. Therefore, not surprisingly, we read about the rift and mistrust between Jonathan

---

8. Josephus, *Ant.* 6.11.9.
9. Klein, *1 Samuel*, 209.
10. Ibid.
11. Morgenstern, "David and Jonathan," 322–25.
12. Ibid.

God's First King

and Saul. Both Saul and Jonathan regarded David as the legitimate successor to the throne. Yet, in spite of it all, with all the negatively portrayed relations between Jonathan and Saul, Jonathan did not desert his father. In the final battle on Mount Gilboa, he went and fought with his father against the Philistines, where he and two of his brothers, died with him.

SAUL AND HIS COURTIERS

A conversation Saul had with his courtiers (1 Sam 22:6–8) provides a glimpse into the relationship between them. This exchange reveals his suspicions. He discovers that some of them had a vague knowledge of David's whereabouts. By not divulging this information, he thought they were conspiring against him. Indeed in v. 8 he complained that they did not inform him of the pact between Jonathan and David. Saul does not even mention Jonathan's name. Saul indulged in self-pity while he complained that everyone was against him. No one has concern or sympathy for him. He repeats his denunciation of his son, who not only made a pact with the son of Jesse, but also set an ambush for him. The fact that his son instigated his servant (he refers to David as his servant) to rebel and plan an ambush is disgraceful. Saul stands alone, while by contrast David receives the sympathy and help from the king's son, Jonathan, and his courtiers.

Saul rebuked his courtiers, the Benjaminites from his own tribe. By mentioning that they are Benjaminites, he was appealing to their feelings as his tribesmen. Evidently, Saul picked people from his own tribe for administrative roles. It was not a coincidence that he refers to his tribesmen as 'Benjaminites' (*bene yamini*) and to David 'son of Jesse' (*ben-yišay*), by so doing he wanted to remind them of their allegiance to him. In another words, he tells them that it was their duty and obligation to assist him against David, but instead they are traitors who unite with a man from a foreign clan. His question to his courtiers is full of sarcasm: "Will the son of Jesse give fields and vineyards to every one of you? And will he make all of you captains of thousands or captains of hundreds?" (1 Sam 22:7). Interestingly, Saul's words here echo the words of Samuel describing kingship (8:14, 12).

Does the narrator provide an accurate picture? It is unlikely that Saul's own tribesmen assisted David. We have to remember that Saul gave his tribesmen vineyards and fields, and they served in his army. What could David offer? He was a fugitive on the run. It seems that the author's

Feuds in the King's Court!

sympathies toward David have led him to portray dissension between Saul and his tribesmen. His aim was to describe a capricious king who does not trust his own people. Thus the author continued the theme "that all Israel loved David," in order to show that David was the better man who deserved to replace King Saul.

It was only Doeg the Edomite who presided *over* Saul's officials who reported to Saul, as Radak and the Targum interpreted. Doeg was an Edomite, an outsider who did not belong to Saul's tribe. It is possible that Saul choose him because of his administrative skills that he acquired in his native land of Edom. Ironically, it is an outsider and not a man from his clan that spied for Saul. Doeg reported to Saul that he saw the son of Jesse in Nob with Abimelech, son of Ahitub. Doeg, like Saul, referred to David as the son of Jesse. Accordingly, Abimelech inquired of the Lord on David's behalf, and also gave him provisions as well as Goliath's sword. What Doeg was doing in Nob and why he stopped there we are not told. Therefore, it might be that he was unclean or went there to fulfill a vow. There is also a possibility that since Doeg was chief of the herdsmen he supplied animals from the king's herds for sacrifice at the temple in Nob. His presence at the sanctuary implies that he was a proselyte, or as Radak explains: the term 'Edomite' refers not to race, but to his place of habitation.

It is not clear from the text if, indeed, Abimelech inquired of the Lord. It is believed that Doeg lied, and said this in order to disgrace him, to portray the priest as a traitor. It is also possible that the priest indeed inquired of the Lord, and Doeg brought this incriminating evidence to Saul. Doeg's version, however, increased Saul's suspicion and anger at Abimelech. He fails to mention the important detail that Abimelech was not aware that David escaped, and he behaved innocently helping David. Doeg evidently wanted to appease his master Saul, and he was aware of the hatred that Saul harbored towards David. Doeg wanted to benefit from passing on information to Saul, confirming his belief that the people were against him. To increase Abimelech's guilt and to emphasize it, Doeg employs the phrase *natan lo'* "gave him." Abimelech gave David food and Goliath's sword. Giving David a sword made him dangerous, for he is now armed and posed a threat. But the mentioning of Goliath was difficult to swallow, since it brought back bad memories. On the one hand, it reminded Saul of his inability to deliver Israel from the hand of the Philistines, while on the other, the great victory that David had against Goliath.[13] This was too much for Saul and so he

---

13. Edelman, *King Saul*, 176.

God's First King

summoned the priest Abimelech and all the priests that belonged to his father's house. Saul was so angry that he did not even confirm that Doeg's words were true; from his point of view, everybody was against him.

Saul addressed the priestly family with harsh words and in an unkind tone. In his denunciation, Saul repeated phrases that he and Doeg previously employed. Saul felt that everyone was conspiring against him. Before it was his courtiers and the son of Jesse, now it is the priest and the son of Jesse. He cannot trust anyone anymore; the whole world is against him! According to Fokkelman, the repetitions depict Saul as a man so caught up in his own world he was not interested in the facts as much as ruminating on his own pathology.[14]

Ahimelech rebuts the charges of disloyalty, but Saul ignored Ahimelech's explanations. According to Josephus, Saul remains unmoved, because his fears were so strong he discredited even a truthful plea.[15] Saul was determined from the start to kill Ahimelech and everyone in his father's house. Saul's death sentence: "You shall die, Ahimelech, you and all your father's house" (1 Sam 22:16), echoes his verdict against his own son Jonathan that ironically contrasts his oath to David in 19:6.[16] Saul ordered the guards to slay the priests because they were siding with David. To describe it the narrator used the phrase "for they are in league with David," which means that they assisted him (1 Chr 4:10). They knew that David was on the run but did not inform him. This is the same language that Saul used earlier when he described the failure of his own courtiers (v. 8). One can see Saul's fear surfaced again, he believed that everyone conspired against him, his courtiers and now, the priests of Nob.

The guards disobeyed Saul's order. To describe it, the narrator uses the phrase *lišloḥ 'et yadam* "would not raise a hand," which is a reversal of the usage of the phrase *ki gam yadam 'im dawid* "for they are in league with David." The guards disobeyed Saul because they felt that the death sentence was unjust and sacrilegious. Their refusal points again to their unspoken support of David. The guards' refusal echoes the people's refusal to execute Jonathan in 1 Sam 14:45.[17]

Only an outsider carries out the king's orders. Saul ordered Doeg to kill the priest. As before, Doeg does not disappoint the king, and does what

---

14. Fokkelman, *Crossing Fates*, 386.
15. Josephus, *Ant.* 6.215.
16. Edelman, *King Saul*, 179.
17. Fokkelman, *Crossing Fates*, 404; Polzin, *Samuel*, 199; Edelman, *King Saul*, 179.

Feuds in the King's Court!

he is commanded to do. According to the biblical account, Doeg murdered eighty-five priests (the LXX mentions 305 while Josephus records 385).[18] Josephus specifies that Saul slew not only priests but prophets as well, but the Bible does not mention prophets. The city of Nob was completely destroyed, it was put under a total ban: "men and women, children and infants, oxen, asses, and sheep-[all] to the sword" (1 Sam 22:19). This description is similar to the orders that Saul received to destroy Amalek: "but kill alike men and women, infants and sucklings, oxen and sheep, camels and asses!" (1 Sam 15:3). Saul did not obey God's commands, and thus lost his kingship. Yet, in contrast he carries out the ban against Yahweh's priests.

By murdering the priests of Nob and destroying their city, Saul wanted to send a clear message that he was king. Any resistance would not be tolerated and would face harsh consequences. This message was understood. We read subsequently that the people of Keilah and the Ziphites feared Saul. They did not assist David, but helped Saul. They tried to deliver David into Saul's hands. Evidently, by that time, people recognized Saul as the legitimate king of Israel, and did not want to help a fugitive hide in their territory. By his murderous actions Saul emulated other kings of the ancient world. There was a custom where the king of a new dynasty would murder his predecessor and family in order to secure his throne.[19] Here, he ordered the murder of the leadership of the pre-monarchial era.

The sages, as the reader might recall, portrayed Saul in a favorable light therefore they gave a different interpretation to the murdering of the priest of Nob. Accordingly, David was responsible for offenses committed by Saul:

> R. Judah said in Rab's name: "A man who came on account of Nob. [For] the Holy One, blessed be He had said to David: How long will this crime be hidden in thy hand? Through thee Nob, the city of priests, was massacred; through thee Doeg the Edomite was banished; and through thee Saul and his three sons were slain [i.e., unpunished]: wouldst thou rather thy line to end, or be delivered unto thy enemy's hand?"[20]

More so, the sages also blamed Jonathan instead of Saul: "Had but Jonathan given David two loaves of bread for his travels, Nob, the city of priests

---

18. Josephus, *Ant.* 6.12.6.
19. 1 Kgs 15:29; 16:11.
20. *Sanh.* 95a.

God's First King

would not have been massacred, Doeg the Edomite would not have been destroyed, and Saul and his three sons would not have been slain."[21]

SAUL AND HIS DAUGHTERS

The first time that the reader learns that Saul had a daughter occurs before the battle against Goliath (1 Sam 17:25). King Saul promised the victor his daughter, in addition to riches. However, no further information is given, not even her name. As Hertzberg pointed out, this is a folkloristic common theme.[22] Daughters had no say in virtually anything, and were totally under their father's authority. It is only after David's victory against Goliath that readers learn that Saul had more than one daughter. Accordingly, Saul offered David his elder daughter, Merab, as a wife as the promised reward. However, Saul was dishonest and deceitful, adding a new condition for David to marry his daughter; he would have to perform heroic deeds against the enemies of God. Saul was hoping that David would die at the hand of the Philistines. Saul did not have any intention to give his daughter to David, since he was planning to kill him, and Merab was only bait. Saul used his daughter to advance his own ambitions.

Although Saul used trickery in dealing with David, his request for the bridal price was not unusual. In ancient Israel, the groom paid the bride price to the woman's father. David was poor and unable to pay the bride price for a princess. In the ancient world, the father could indicate the bridal price, thus Saul established the price of one hundred Philistine foreskins. Was David aware that Saul tricked him? We do not know. However, David would later use similar trickery to eliminate Uriah the Hittite.

Saul's double-dealing and trickery is again obvious when we read that Merab had already been given to Adriel, the Meholathite. Adriel, the Meholathite, is mentioned in 2 Sam 21:8 as Adriel the son of Barzillai. Adriel was from the settlement Abel-meholah, which was located in the Trans-Jordan. It appears that by this marriage Saul wanted to strengthen the ties between his kingdom and the settlements in the Trans-Jordan. Merab was only a pawn in Saul's plan, and he was willing to use her to achieve his goals.[23]

---

21. *Sanh.* 104a.
22. Hertzberg, *I & II Samuel*, 151.
23. This episode is missing from LXX^B it is possible that Saul offered Merab to David he refused and only than Michal was offered to him and he agreed.

Feuds in the King's Court!

We read many times about men who loved women in the Bible. Thus, we read about Isaac and Rebecca, Jacob and Rachel, Samson and Delilah, and Elkanah and Hannah. Michal is the only woman in the Bible that states that she loved a man. She loved David but his behavior and deeds do not demonstrate that he loved her. When David left Jonathan they kissed each other and cried. When Michal helped David escape, no kissing or crying is mentioned. More so, David found various times to meet with Jonathan, but not with Michal. When Michal was given to another man, he neither protested nor raised any objections.

Michal, like her brother Jonathan, saved David's life, and helped him to escape from her father. Saul sent messengers to David's house at night with instructions to watch the house and to kill David in the morning. Klein says that the attempt to arrest David "on that night" presumes one refers to the wedding night.[24] However, this is unlikely since a long period had already passed from the time she was given to David. When Samson went to Gaza to stay with a whore, the Gazites set an ambush to capture him in the morning, thinking he would be weaker in the morning (Judg 16:1–3). It is more likely that Saul did not want to kill his son-in-law before his daughter's eyes. There is also the possibility that he wanted to kill him in the morning as a rebel against the kingship as we can find in Jeremiah: "Render just verdicts morning by morning (21:12). The Talmud reads: "But capital charges must be tried by day [and concluded by day]. Whence is this deduced?—R. Shimi b. Ḥiyya said: Scriptures states, *And hang them before Hashem against the sun*."[25] Similarly, Josephus writes: "and commanded that he should be watched till the morning, lest he should get quiet away, that he might come into the judgment hall, and so delivered up, and condemned and slain."[26]

Michal probably noticed the guards. Therefore she went immediately and informed David. The Bible here refers to her as David's wife, and not Saul's daughter as she usually appears. The narrator stresses this in order to tell the reader that her love for her husband surpassed the love for her father. Michal advised David to run away on the same night because her father's messengers would kill him in the morning. The description of how

---

24. Klein, *1 Samuel*, 196. According to McCarter, our story is continuation of 18:27 in the original story David's house was guarded at the wedding night. But this connection was broken because of the addition of other material to the narrative of David's raise to power. See McCarter, *I Samuel*, 325.

25. *Sanh.* 34b.

26. Josephus, *Ant.* 6.11.4.

God's First King

Michal let David down from the window is reminiscent of the Rahab story. Rahab helped Joshua's spies make a similar escape. According to Hertzberg, the house was in the town wall; otherwise the messengers would have captured David.[27] David's thoughts about his escape are described in Psalm 59. The psalm's title is "A *miktam* when Saul sent men to watch his house in order to put him to death" (Ps 59:1). In Psalms, David thanks God and not Michal for delivering him from his enemies, the evildoers, and murderers.

According to the biblical account, Michal took the household idols (*teraphim*) and laid them in the bed with goat's hair to make it look as if David was still in bed. The *teraphim* were probably the size of a human head. The presence of *teraphim* in David's house is not clear, since they are denounced critically in the Hebrew Bible. According to Budde, the existence of the *teraphim* in David's house was only accepted because "the person concerned was the daughter of the rejected Saul."[28] According to Rabbi Joseph Kara, in case one's life is in jeopardy he may consult the *teraphim* in order to know the future. Since Saul's plans were concealed from Michal, she consulted the *teraphim*. It is possible that Michal kept the *teraphim* in the house on account of her barrenness.

When Saul sent his messengers to take David, Michal lied and said that he was sick. Michal did not allow the messengers to enter the house; she was stalling, giving David time to escape. Alternatively, maybe hearing that David was sick, Saul would have mercy on him and spare his life. The messengers believed that David was sick and did not enter the room to check.

Saul, unlike his messengers, was not convinced; clearly he did not trust his own daughter, since he was very suspicious. Therefore, he sent the messengers for a third time. But this time they were to enter the house. Their mission was to examine David to ascertain his illness. If indeed he was very sick, they were instructed to bring him in a bed so that Saul could slay him. On the second trip to David's house, the messengers discovered that they had been totally fooled. Instead of David, they found the *teraphim*. They probably returned to Saul and told him what they had found; however the Bible is silent about the details. Ralbag suggests that the bed was brought to Saul, and only then was the deception discovered. However, it is hard to believe that they would not notice that David was missing.

Turning to Michal, Saul asked her why she tricked him and let his enemy escape. This is the first time that Saul refers to David as his enemy.

27. Hertzberg, *I & II Samuel*, 166.
28. Budde, *Die Bücher Samuel*, 138.

Feuds in the King's Court!

Interestingly, while in chapter 18, the narrator referred to Michal as Saul's daughter, here he mentions only her name. Perhaps the narrator wanted to convey a break in their relationship. Michal answered her father with another lie. She said that David threatened her: "help me or I will kill you." In other words, she emphasizes that she was following David's orders, and was not responsible for his escape. She tries again to gain her father's sympathy and trust by putting the blame on David. Rashi explained it differently: "you delivered me into the hands of a bandit. He drew his sword over me until I allowed him to leave." She blames Saul for giving her hand to David in marriage.[29] Interestingly, Saul's reaction is not mentioned; maybe he was satisfied with his daughter's explanations. Like Jonathan, Michal helped David to escape; she helped her father's enemy. David does not appear again in Saul's court after this.

Following this episode, Michal is not mentioned until a brief note in 1 Sam 25:44 regarding David's marriage to Abigail and Ahinoam. The narrator states that Saul gave Michal, his daughter and David's wife, to Palti son of Laish from Gallim. Saul wanted to break the family ties with David that is why he gave his daughter to another man. But there are two major questions posed by the Talmud and Jewish commentators; how could Saul have placed her into an adulterous union? And how could David have taken Michal back as a wife after she lived with another man? Unfortunately, no satisfactory answers are given. Later we are informed that when Abner approached David suggesting alliance, David stipulated that Michal must be return to him. A message was sent to Ish-bosheth, Saul's other son, demanding her return. In reply to the demand, Ish-bosheth took Michal from her husband and brought her back to David (2 Sam 3:15–16).

David's marriage to Michal had political significance. Morgenstern suggested that the marriage was "*beena*-marriage," where succession to the throne passed through the family. Thus David had the legitimate right to the throne.[30] Morgenstern assumed that there was matriarchy in Israel. However there is no evidence of this. It is more likely that David married Michal because he wanted to gain admission to Saul's court. David's power and support was based mainly in the south, and he needed to expand his base of power. The marriage to Michal solidified and attracted support from the Benjamanites, and established a stronger claim to the throne.

---

29. See also *Midr. Sam.* 22:4.
30. Morgenstern, "*Beena* Marriage," 93.

God's First King

Saul also had his own reasons for Michal's marriage to David. At first glance, it seems odd for Saul to offer his daughters to his adversary. But as the text suggests, this was only a ploy, thinking that the Philistines would kill David. Ishida suggests that the marriages took place before Saul started to mistrust David.[31] Noth argues that Michal's marriage during Saul's lifetime is not historical, but this view is unsustainable.[32]

Michal is mentioned for the last time in 2 Sam 6:16–23, when the ark was brought into Jerusalem. When Michal, Saul's daughter looked and saw David dancing before the ark, she despised him (v. 16). She criticized David for his behavior, and referred to him as riffraff. At this point, we can see that she did not love him anymore. She probably realized that David used her to advance his political ambitions. The fact that she was David's wife is not mentioned here; she is referred to solely as Michal, the daughter of Saul. David rebuked her, and his response was harsh. God had chosen him and rejected her father and her family. The narrator ends this interchange with a note that Michal remained childless until her death.

MILITARY HEROES

First Chronicles 12 cites a list of military heroes who left Saul at Ziklag to join David. This was at the end of Saul's reign when David was aligned with Achish, the king of Gath, who gave him the city of Ziklag (1 Sam 21:10–14; 27:2–12). However, even in an earlier period there were people who identified with David and joined him. It should be remembered that David was very popular, which is evident in the song of the women, "Saul has slain thousands and David his ten thousands!" (1 Sam 18:7; 21:12; 29:5). It is also said that people loved him: "All Israel and Judah loved David, for he marched at their head" (1 Sam 18:16). The fact that people joined David is mentioned in 1 Sam 22:2. Accordingly, a band of distressed and disadvantage people became his followers.[33] Among them also were debtors who were in danger of being sold into slavery by their creditors (2 Kgs 4:1). These people were fugitives, and could easily identify with David. This band of people numbered four hundred, and later the number would grow to six hundred (1 Sam 23:13; 25:13; 27:2).

---

31. Ishida, *Royal Dynasties*, 72.
32. Noth, *History of Israel*, 184, n.1.
33. We read the same about Abimelech (Judg 9:4) and Jephthah (11:3).

Feuds in the King's Court!

The significance of the list of people who joined David is that it includes warriors, not only troubled people. We find warriors from Benjamin (vv. 1–8), Gad (vv. 9–16), Benjamin and Judah (vv. 17–19), and Manasseh (vv. 20–23), all united in their support for David. The mention of warriors from Benjamin is surprising since in 2 Sam 2:12–23, even after Saul's death the Benjaminites remained loyal to Saul's progeny.[34] According to Braun, it is unlikely that a large number of Benjaminites defected to David's camp while Saul was alive.[35] The writer, however, wanted to stress the theme that all Israel supported David. Therefore the first deserters from Saul's own tribe are included and mentioned by name. They were very skilled, ambidextrous warriors. They came from eight different localities in Benjamin. The first two Benjaminites came from Gibeah, Saul's hometown, and center of his kingdom. Based on v. 2 and vv. 17, 30 and 1 Sam 31:3, Malul raises the possibility that David had formed a fifth column while he was in Saul's court, consisting of close relatives. He further speculates that these allies may have played a role in Saul's death.[36]

The second group was from the tribe of Gad. They separated themselves from the Gadites, who supported Saul. The narrator stressed their military strength; they were brave and skilled with shield and lance, especially in close combat. In addition, they are described as having the faces of lions and the speed of gazelles. The metaphor came to indicate the warrior's strength. Gad's ability to fight is mentioned in the blessings of Moses: "Gad lives like a lion; he tears at arm and scalp" (Deut 33:20). Jacob in a farewell speech to his sons says: "Gad shall be raided by raiders, but he shall raid at their heels" (Gen 49:19). To exaggerate their strength the Chronicler wrote that one Gadite could control a hundred enemies. The best of the Gadites could resist a thousand. Evidently, the narrator wanted to stress the fact that the best of the warriors joined David.

There is probably some truth to the fact that the Gadites joined David. David had some ties with the king of Moab; his parents had stayed with that king (1 Sam 22:3). David operated in the vicinity of Moab which was close to the Gadite's territory. The southern part of Gad's territory bordered Moab and it is not clear if it was part of Saul's kingdom.[37] These events took

---

34. According to Knoppers, the authors of Samuel present later fissures in this loyalty; Knoppers, *I Chronicles, 10–29*, 562; Anderson, *2 Samuel*, 51–64.
35. Braun, *1 Chronicles*, 165.
36. Malul, "Was David," 517–45.
37. Bartal, *Saul's Kingship*, 141 (Hebrew).

God's First King

place before David took refuge with the Philistines in Ziklag. David was hiding from Saul in the wilderness (1 Sam 23:14; 24:1; 25:1; 26:1). Thus the Gadites probably joined David when he roamed the hills around En-Gedi (1 Sam 24:1). The eleven warriors who joined David had their names mentioned. These people were very close to David's area of operation. They had heard about him, and it was very easy for them to contact him. David's charismatic character attracted them and they followed him.

Another list of warriors is mentioned in vv. 17–19; there were some Benjaminites and Judahites who came to David's fortress. The Benjaminites were mentioned separately before this, now they are included with Judah as the "two tribes of the south." This is a common feature of the book of Chronicles. We would expect to see the warriors of Judah as David's natural allies, but only an undetermined number appeared. David was troubled by their arrival and worried about their treachery, therefore, he went out to meet them, but he did not invite them into his camp. David's fear reminds us of the situation described in the book of Samuel when he was betrayed on three previous occasions: by Doeg the Edomite (1 Samuel 21, 22) Judahites of Keilah (1 Sam 23:10–12), and the Ziphites (1 Sam 23:19–24; 26:1). All were willing to betray David, and hand him over to Saul. Japhet believes that the Benjaminites were added later on, and only the Judahites were originally on the list.[38] According to her, it is unlikely that the two tribes, Judah and Benjamin, would have the same leader, especially since the Benjaminites troops were already mentioned in vv. 2–8.

David had no clue whether these soldiers came to help or betray him. Therefore, he calls upon God to give judgment claiming that he is innocent of violence. The spirit of God seized Amasai so it was he who said the warriors from Benjamin and Judah supported David. However, David had good reason to be suspicious of Amasai who was the commander of the officers. Amasai is probably identified with Amasa, later on a commander under Absalom and David (2 Sam 17:25; 19:14; 20:10; 1 Chr 2:17).[39] According to 2 Sam 17:25, his father was Ithra the Israelite and his mother was Abigail, the daughter of Nahash. This later name probably is a textual corruption of 2 Sam 17:27, where Abigail is identified as the sister of Joab's mother Zeruiah. According to 1 Chr 2:16–17, these two women were daughters of Jesse and sisters of David.[40] The fact that Amasai was David's

38. Japhet, *I & II Chronicles*, 263–64.
39. Knoppers, *I Chronicles 10–29*, 565; Fowler, *Theophoric*, 356.
40. Nelson, "Amasa," 182.

Feuds in the King's Court!

nephew explains his suspicion towards him. When David escaped to the cave of Adullam, all his brothers and his entire father's house joined him (1 Sam 22:1). Among the people who joined David were the sons of Zeruiah. Amasai, David's nephew, was not among the people who joined him, rather he stayed home and he could do so only if he showed loyalty to Saul. Now when he realized that Saul became weaker and David was gaining power he decided to switch his allegiance. In his last years, Saul was very suspicious of the tribe of Judah, and David tried to gain their support. Amasai was opportunistic and changed his loyalty. Indeed he would do it again in the revolt of Absalom when he supported Absalom against David.

Another person who joined David when he was at Ziklag was Ishmaiah of Gibeon, a leading warrior among "the thirty" (1 Chr 12:4). His name is included among the twenty-three Benjamenites who joined David. The precise meaning of "the thirty" is not clear. It was hypothesized that this is a technical term referring to the king's bodyguards.[41] The relations between the Gibeonites and the Saulides were not always harmonious. Bad blood existed between the two groups (2 Sam 21:1–9). It is speculated that Ishmaiah belonged to the early Hivite population, which harbored hatred towards Saul for killing the Gibeonites. More likely, Ishmaiah was a Benjamenite like the rest of the people mentioned in the list. These people probably had their quarrels with Saul, similar to the feuds that Saul had with his son, daughters and courtiers. They were aware of the rumor that David would inherit Saul's rule, and even of the fact that Jonathan was siding with David. Thus, they seized the moment and shifted their allegiance to the future king. Still, we have to stress the simple fact that very few warriors changed their allegiance. In comparison to the battle against Amalek, Saul's army numbered 200,000 men on foot and 10,000 men of Judah although these numbers are exaggerated. Evidently, the Chronicler who was sympathetic to the house of David and devoted only one chapter to King Saul tried to create the impression that all Israel and Judah loved David and supported him.

SAUL AND SAMUEL

The feud between Saul and Samuel started during the conflict with the Philistines that is described in chapter 13. Saul's fighting with the Philistines is interrupted by the insertion of vv. 7b–15a, which is an account of Samuel's accusations of Saul. Some scholars connect 13:8 and 10:8, Samuel's

---

41. Kennedy, "Ishmaiah," 520.

God's First King

instructions to Saul to await him at Gilgal for seven days.[42] However, there Saul was a young shepherd who was still living in his father house. Here, he is the king of Israel who had already defeated the Ammonites. From reading chapters 13–14 it appears that a mature Saul conducted the wars with a grown son. Still there are several similarities between 10:8 and 13:8–9. Saul is instructed to wait seven days until Samuel comes, the sacrifice of burnt offerings and peace offerings are also mentioned. Tsumura suggests that the reference to 10:8 and 13:8 are not necessarily about the same occurrence. According to him, "people could 'wait on God at Gilgal for seven days' on many occasions."[43] We should also point out that the Hebrew word *yamim* (days) sometimes also means a year (Gen 38:12; 40:4).

Scholars believe that vv. 9–14, which contain Samuel's rebuke of Saul are a late edition that did not belong to the original narrative and are secondary.[44] Some pointed out the duplication that exists in our verses is also in chapter 15. Both involve Saul and Samuel, both took place at Gilgal. Both sections detail a sin that Saul committed and prompted a rebuke by Samuel. The subject of the two stories demonstrates violations of sacral traditions dealing with a holy war. Thus, why does the author tell the story of Saul's rejection twice? The author provides the same reasons in both stories. However, Saul's sin is an integral part of the story and the narrator has created the dissimilarity between the characters of Saul and Jonathan around it. Saul does not trust God, while Jonathan does. Also, the condemnation of Saul's dynasty and the rejection of his rule were two separate subjects. Birch believes that 13:7b–15a and 15:1–34 were written by the same author who gave different reasons for each account of the scenario. In the first account, only Saul's dynasty is discontinued (13:14); while in the second Saul himself is rejected, leading to David's anointing.[45]

Saul is described in an unflattering way. He is under pressure because Samuel did not arrive on time, meanwhile the people started to leave him. Saul is frightened, indecisive, does not act, and is afraid of the Philistines that come to capture him. As a result, he disobeys Samuel; he did not wait for the prophet and offered a sacrifice by himself. Commentators explain Saul's sin in two ways. According to one explanation, he sinned because

---

42. Yonick, "Rejection of Saul," 30–31; Donner, "Basic Elements," 52.

43. Tsumura, *First Book of Samuel*, 341.

44. Wellhausen, *Prolegomena*, 258–60; Miller, "Saul Rise," 157–74; Klein, *1 Samuel*, 123.

45. Birch, *Rise*, 105–8; McCarter, *I Samuel*, 270–71 n4.

Feuds in the King's Court!

he disobeyed Samuel's order to wait for him for seven days. Saul lost his patience and therefore did not wait for the delayed prophet. The second explanation suggests that Saul did not have the authority to sacrifice, which was Samuel's duty, since he was also a priest.

Samuel rebuked Saul for these actions, and then Saul apologized by describing the events that led him to his actions. Interestingly, Samuel did not react to Saul's apologies and explanations. Clearly, the narrator thought that Saul failed because he did not trust in God. He should have avoided military actions and trust in God to deliver him from his enemies. By disobeying Samuel and not waiting for him, Saul disobeyed God and violated the terms of his appointment as king. Kingship required obedience, thus the kingship would no longer belong to Saul's son, but given to another man of God's choosing.

Actually, Saul waited seven days for Samuel. Ironically, Samuel arrived just when Saul was finishing his sacrifice. Thus it seems that Samuel trapped Saul, pushing Saul to his breaking point.[46] From the description of the ensuing events, Saul did what was permissible. Saul was afraid; he was left with no option but to turn to God. Indeed, sacrifices were offered before a holy war (1 Sam 7:9). God's permission was frequently sought (Judg 20:23, 27; 1 Sam 7:9; 14:8–10; 14:37; 23:2, 4; 28:6; 30:7–8; 2 Sam 5:19, 23). The *'olah* sacrifice, which is the whole burned offering or "holocaust," was considered pleasing to Yahweh. According to the medieval exegetes, "a layman is allowed to offer on a high place." Radak claimed that only the disobedience against Samuel and not that he offered a sacrifice was the reason for the divine rebuff. However, Saul's offering of his sacrifice was a cultic function that in the writer's mind belonged to the priests or prophets and not to kings.

As Hertzberg has noted, if someone is in the wrong here it is Samuel, not Saul. According to him, the compiler of the work conveyed to the reader that: "Saul's kingship was perverted right from the beginning; the first king trod a path with which the Lord was not pleased."[47] In this story and in the following chapters, Saul is portrayed as disobedient, impatient, and lacking in faith. The clash between Saul and Samuel was the first between a prophet and a king; it was the beginning of many feuds between kings and prophets.

The second quarrel between Saul and Samuel took place following Saul's failure to carry a total ban against Amalek. Saul spared king Agag and the best of his livestock. This was the last conversation between the

---

46. Amit, *Reading Biblical Narratives*, 77–78.
47. Hertzberg, *I & II Samuel*, 106.

God's First King

two, and it was a long one (1 Sam 15:13–30). Each person spoke six times. Samuel led Saul step by step to admit his guilt. To Samuel's question, what "is this bleating of sheep in my ears, and the lowing of oxen that I hear?" (v. 14), Saul's response is that of a person caught in a lie. He immediately tries to separate himself from the people to save face; he puts the blame on the people. Interestingly, there is a similarity between Saul under interrogation and Adam under interrogation. Each blames his failure on someone else, and each was punished harshly, yet escaped immediate death. According to Radak, Saul still tries to justify the people's actions by claiming that they reserved the best of the animals for sacrifice to God who was with them in the war. When referring to God, he says to Samuel "*your* god." Saul does not speak here of *his* God, but refers here to Samuel's God, and by that, he tries to lighten his own responsibility as the representative of the people.[48]

Samuel's response to Saul was harsh; he told the king to stop, as Rashi explains. He tells him to wait, to let him deliver God's message from the previous night. By mentioning the time, there may be a hint about Saul's death, which he would learn about at night. Samuel uses sarcasm here. He repeats Saul's own words that refer to the period before he was anointed as a king: "But I am only a Benjaminite, from the smallest of the tribe of Israel" (9:21). In other words, Samuel tells Saul that since he was anointed as a king he must take responsibility for his people's actions. Neither humility nor lessening his self-image can remove him from responsibility.[49] Samuel also repeats his instructions concerning the ban on Amalek, whom Saul did not execute. He rebuked Saul for not listening to God. The word "listen" is a key word here and is repeated in the following verses (vv. 20, 22). "Listen" opened the chapter, where Samuel instructed Saul "listen to the Lord's command" (v. 1). Yet, Saul did not listen.

Samuel's unforgiving response in vv. 22–23 is couched in Hebrew poetry and reflects prophetic teachings. Sacrifices are contrasted with obedience; the word *listen* is repeated. Listening to God and obeying his commandments is preferable to sacrifices that are the products of disobedience. Samuel is the first prophet who says that obedience to God is more important than sacrifices. Indeed, the later prophets will stress values such as justice, humility, truth, and peace that are all preferable to sacrifices (Jer 7:21–23).

Like chapter 13, the question of authority is raised here, the authority of the prophet and obeying his commands. On the other hand, Saul thought that he had the authority not to obey the prophet's instructions. Indeed, after

---

48. Tsumura, *First Book of Samuel*, 399.
49. Mauchline, *1 and 2 Samuel*, 124.

Feuds in the King's Court!

his coronation, Saul became more independent and vain as he erected a monument for himself after the victory against Amalek (1 Sam 15:12).[50]

Saul's sin is referred to as rebellion against God. The rebellion is characterized here as apostasy, the use of forbidden forms of divinations and the worship of idols (v. 23). This denies God's authority and acknowledges magical powers distinctly apart from God. This indictment is ironic because Saul fought against the use of magic, and banned it (28:9). It was only in his desperation, the night before his last battle against the Philistines, that he sought a woman who conjured up ghosts. Saul rejected God; therefore, God rejected him. After his sin in Gilgal, Samuel told Saul: "But now your dynasty will not endure" (13:14). In Gilgal, God rejected Saul's dynasty, here he rejected Saul personally, "Yahweh has torn the kingdom of Israel from you today, and he has given it to your neighbor who is better than you" (1 Sam 15:28).

Only after his rejection did Saul confess his sin of disobeying God's command. He explained that he feared the people. In his confession he exposes his own weakness: that he listened to the people instead of listening to God. It is the king's responsibility to lead his people, and not be led by them. Frisch pointed out the similarity between Saul's confessions "take my sin away," (v. 25) and Pharaoh's confession in Exod 10:16–17.[51] In both, a king declares that he had sinned and asks for forgiveness. This suggests that Saul was not sincere because Pharaoh certainly was not truthful, and changed his mind when the plague was withdrawn.

David Sperling pointed out that scholars believe the story of Saul's failure to destroy the Amalekites is based on Deut 25:17–19, a seventh century BCE text.[52] If this is correct, the story of the *ḥerem* is a much later effort, to explain Saul's replacement by David.[53] According to him, Saul is the historical destroyer of Amalek, and he stood behind Moses, the allegorical scourge of Amalek. He believes that writers sympathetic to David and his dynasty distorted the story.[54]

When Samuel turned to leave, refusing to return with Saul to worship Yahweh, Saul grabbed Samuel's robe and tore it. The tearing away of the edge of Samuel's robe is interpreted as an omen, removing the kingdom from Saul. According to the simple interpretation, it was Saul who tore the prophet's robe. In Midrash Aggadah, the Amoraim differ on this point.

50. Bar-Efrat, *I Samuel*, 195.
51. Frisch, "For I Feared," 102–3.
52. Sperling, *Original Torah*, 128.
53. For a different view that the tale is early see Stern, *Biblical Ḥerem*, 165–77.
54. Sperling, *Original Torah*, 128.

God's First King

Some say that Saul tore Samuel's robe, and some say that Samuel tore Saul's robe, thereby giving him this sign that whoever severed the skirt of his robe would reign in his place. This is what Saul said to David on the day that David cut his robe, "I know that you will reign" (24:21).[55] Similarly Ahijah tore Jeroboam's robe as a sign that his kingdom would be divided (1 Kgs 11:29–31). Radak says that Samuel tore his own robe as a sign of mourning for the failure of his "sapling to thrive." While the Malbim explained that when a prophet performs an act to demonstrate his prophecy, that prophecy becomes an irrevocable reality even though the subject repents. We should point out that in the Hebrew Bible the rending of cloth was a sign of mourning for the dead, a custom that still exists today. Ripping Saul's robe signified the end of his kingship and his death. According to Samuel, the kingship was already given to someone else, the rejection was final. Samuel did not tell Saul, however, who the worthier person was, he would tell him that on the eve of his death: "The Lord has torn the kingship out of your hands, and given it to your fellow, to David" (1 Sam 28:17).

Samuel's symbolic act finally prompted Saul to admit his sin, but this time without excuses. Although he sinned, he still asks the prophet to honor him in the presence of the elders so that he would not be disgraced during his lifetime. Saul, in spite of his independent actions remained dependent on Samuel and his support (vv. 25, 27, 30). Samuel, however, criticizes Saul harshly, but shows compassion towards the king and will later grieve for him. As God's messenger, Samuel has to criticize Saul, but on a personal level he felt sorrow for Saul's failure. According to Klein, Samuel's return with Saul was the narrator's way of saying that the sinful king still retained his office for some time, and this kingship was supported by the prophet before the elders and the people of Israel.[56] Finally, the departure of Samuel and Saul to different locations signifies the end of the story. The narrator adds that Samuel never saw Saul until the day of his death; he mourned for Saul and was no longer angry with him. There is an apparent allusion to an approaching meeting of the two that takes place on the eve of Saul's death. God's attitude towards Saul is also mentioned in v. 35, where we have here a repetition of v. 11, where God said that He regretted that He made Saul reign over Israel. However in v. 29 we read: "Moreover, the Glory Israel does not deceive or change His mind, for He is not human that He should

---

55. *Midr. Sam.* 18:15; *Ruth Rabbah* 7:12; *Midr. Pss.* 57:3.
56. Klein, *1 Samuel*, 154.

Feuds in the King's Court!

change His mind." Thus can we say that God, like the Prophet Samuel, also had contradictory views about Saul?

In conclusion, Josephus's description of Saul echoes similar descriptions of ruthless kings from the Greek and the Roman empires. Some of these traits and characteristics are attributed to Saul. His depiction is unflattering as he quarrels with everyone that surrounds him. There is constant tension between him and Jonathan. On one occasion, he even tried to kill him. Saul's daughters, Merab and Michal, were used as pawns against David. Michal, like her brother Jonathan, sided with David by helping him escape from her father. Saul accused the inner circle of courtiers as traitors. In addition, military heroes changed their allegiance and supported David. Samuel clashed with Saul twice. He condemned him for independent sacral action, and for violating the ban against Amalek. This resulted in Samuel announcing Saul's rejection as a king. However, overall, there is exaggeration in those unflattering descriptions of Saul. Jonathan, in spite of his quarrels with his father, went and fought with his father in the last battle on Mount Gilboa and never deserted him. What is not clear is why he gave his royal rights to David. Michal betrayed her father for David's sake because her love for him was true. Her character is tragic. David, like Saul, used Michal in order to advance his political ambitions; he married her because he craved admission to the royal family. David's base of power was mainly in the south, so he sought to extend his support. The marriage to Michal came to solidify and attract support from the Benjaminites and to establish his claim to the throne. It is unlikely that Saul's courtiers aided David because they did not gain anything from this. The number of people who deserted King Saul was small and insignificant from a military point of view. The clashes between Samuel and Saul foreshadow later clashes between the kings of Israel and the prophets. At the center stood the question of the prophetic authority verses royal authority. Saul had many good reasons for his seemingly irrational behavior. Saul was not naïve and understood David's intentions very well. He realized that David's primary goal was to become king. Therefore, not surprisingly, he was angry with his son Jonathan, who easily gave up the throne. Saul wanted his son Jonathan to succeed him. It was the hand of a sympathetic author from the Davidic circle that was responsible for the negative view of Saul. The aim was to portray an unstable king who failed in his relationships with his inner circle, while David had all Israel and Judah that loved him.

5

Saul: The State Builder

SAUL'S CROWNING SIGNIFIED A major transition from theocracy to kingship. Originally, Israel was a federation of twelve tribes bound by a covenant with God, who was the religious authority, the sovereign, and the king of the Israelites. Now, with Saul as king, a new era emerged. Saul became the architect of the Israelite monarchy, and laid its foundation. Still there are scholars who debate the nature of Saul's role in the history of Israel. Alt, for example, sees Saul only as a military commander with internal affairs run by the tribal elders; thus he was not a true king.[1] According to Goldman, "the organization of the kingdom under Saul seems to have been very simple and rudimentary."[2] He believed that Saul was too preoccupied with the Philistine threats and therefore did not lay the foundation for the civic organization of the kingdom. While Miller viewed Saul as opportunistic, extending his influence outside of the tribe of Benjamin, he was not head of a state. He credited him with laying the foundation of administration and military bureaucracy, but not establishing a state religion.[3]

In the following pages we will critically evaluate the textual material and raise questions regarding the early stages of the state under Saul. Did Saul create a new realty as an absolute king with unlimited powers? Did Saul introduce a new administrative and military order that in turn required new taxation, in order to maintain them? Kings in the ancient world were known for grandiose construction projects such as the state capital,

1. Alt, *Essays*, 223–309.
2. Goldman, *Samuel*, xii.
3. Miller and Hayes, *History*, 142–44.

Saul: The State Builder

religious centers, and fortresses; did Saul do this? All of these questions will be addressed. Ultimately we will answer a major question: Did King Saul achieve his mission to transform Israel into a monarchy?

SERVANTS IN THE KING'S COURT

Since Saul was the first king of Israel we might expect to find new terminology for officials in his court. Indeed, the term "servant of the king," which is found in Mesopotamian, Canaanite, and Egyptian sources, is also found in Saul's court.[4] In those traditions, the term was conferred on a wide spectrum of the king's men. It could refer to a variety of functions inside and outside the royal court. The "servant" (*'ebed*) had high status close to the king, so he could be a prince, an army officer, or another minister of the state.[5] In one of Saul's episodes, Doeg the Edomite is known as *'ebed* of Saul, king of Israel (1 Sam 21:8).[6] David is also dubbed *'ebed* of Saul, the king of Israel (1 Sam 29:3); Sacher explains this term as being an officer in Saul's army. The general collective term *'abdi hammelek* appears in reference to officials and functionaries at court. Thus, when a bad spirit seized Saul, his servants looked for a person skilled at playing the lyre (1 Sam 16:15). The servants in Saul's story refer to high-ranking members of Saul's court, which is made clear from other biblical evidence (2 Kgs 22:12 // 2 Chr 34:20; 2 Kgs 25:8). There is also epigraphic evidence that includes seals inscribed with a proper name followed by the title "servant of the king."[7] Those people who were close to the king received land grants that had been confiscated, this practice was also known in Ugarit.[8]

First Samuel 22:6 describes Saul sitting under a tree with all his *'abadav niṣṣabım 'alav*—all his courtiers in attendance upon him. The term here refers to his entire entourage, all of whom belonged to the tribe of Benjamin. Klein raised the possibility that Saul's power base was small because of this.[9] It is more likely that Saul trusted his own kinsmen from the tribe of Benjamin.

---

4. Fox, *Service*, 60–62.
5. Ibid., 62.
6. The JPS translated this as one of Saul's officials.
7. McCarter, *I Samuel*, 158; Sacher, *Service*, 56–60.
8. Mendelsohn, "Samuel's Denunciation," 19–20; Rainey, "Institutions," 95–97.
9. Klein, *1 Samuel*, 224.

God's First King

The servants are described as standing next to Saul, which is typical of people who appear before a king, they are standing and not sitting (1 Kgs 1:28).[10]

Another title that is mentioned among Saul's administrators is the term *niṣṣab*. This mostly appears during Solomon's reign where we read about twelve individuals in charge of a particular geographical region in Israel (1 Kgs 4:7). They were to supply food for the king and his household. The title also refers to a prefect, where it states that Jonathan killed the *neṣib* of the Philistines who was in Geba (1 Sam 13:3). In 1 Sam 22:9 it appears in a verbal form, which describes an official position. It states that Doeg the Edomite was an official of Saul *niṣṣab 'al-'abdi-Ša'ul*. The verb can be interpreted in two ways. Doeg was standing by Saul's courtiers, as the JPS translated, along with Smith.[11] McCarter says that Doeg was presiding over Saul's servants.[12] As Fox points out, the second interpretation better fits Doeg's exercise of power. She compares his actions to the description of the steward of Boaz's estate *haniṣṣab 'al haqqoṣerim* "who was appointed over the reapers" (Ruth 2:5–6).[13] It is possible that Saul chose Doeg who was an Edomite because he held a senior appointment in Edom before he arrived at Saul's court. This set a precedent because during the reign of David and Solomon, they had many administrators of foreign origin. They choose experienced men from the neighboring countries to conduct their administrative affairs.

Doeg also is referred to as Saul's "chief herdsman" (1 Sam 21:8), meaning he was in charge of the king's property and herds. The LXX has "keeper of Saul's mules" as does Josephus.[14] It is possible that in his capacity as "chief herdsman" he supplied animals for sacrifices at the temple in Nob. This interpretation provides a better understanding of his arrival at Nob.

Doeg's role as an executioner in the massacre in Nob led Heinrich Graetz to read *rāṣîm* runners instead of *rō'îm*.[15] This suggestion was adopted by scholars who believe that Doeg led a contingent of runners; the bodyguards of the king who ran in front of his carriage (2 Sam 15:1).[16]

---

10. Indeed, Maimonides in *Hilchot Melachim* says: "They should stand before him and prostrate to the ground." See Maimonides, *Hilchot Melachim*, chapter 2:5.

11. Smith, *Books of Samuel*, 206–7.

12. McCarter, *I Samuel*, 360.

13. Fox, *Service*, 142 n. 254.

14. Josephus, *Ant*. 6.244.

15. Graetz, *History*, 1:91.

16. Nowack, *Richter*, 111; Driver, *Notes*, 175–76; Budde, *Die Bücher Samuel*, 149; Smith, *Books of Samuel*, 200; McCarter, *I Samuel*, 348–49; Klein, *1 Samuel*, 213.

Saul: The State Builder

Alter suggested that Doeg's services in Saul's court "reflects the enlistment of foreign mercenaries in the new royal bureaucracy."[17] However, there is no textual support for this reading based on 1 Sam 22:17. Sacher Fox reads "strongman" as she points to the possible parallel to the Assyrian title "chief of the shepherds" that was held by a court official of the crown prince. Interestingly, he is listed together with different types of guards, including body guards.[18] Indeed, it was Aster who maintained that Doeg's designation of *'bbîr harō'îm* must be understood as a military title based on evidence from Hittite and Akkadian texts.[19] According to him, Doeg's function was similar to titles held by Joab and Benaiah as "commander of the army" (2 Sam 8:16; 20:23; 1 Kgs 4:4). Therefore it is not surprising that Doeg was dealing with a disloyal individual in 1 Samuel 21–22.

Another term that is mentioned in the king's court is the Hebrew term *na'ar*, which means "young man, servant, or retainer."[20] Ziba is called *'ebed* (slave) of the house of Saul (2 Sam 9:2). When he was addressing King David, he referred to himself as *'ebed* (2 Sam 9:2, 11). However, David called him *na'ar Šā'ul* "Saul's steward" (v. 9); this indicates that David regarded Ziba as more than an *'ebed*. In 19:18, Ziba is called *na'ar bet Šā'ul*, "the steward of the house of Saul," and in 2 Sam 16:1 "Mephibosheth's steward." Macdonald pointed out that the two terms were used properly. Ziba is called *na'ar* because of his specific function as personal servant of a great man, at the same time *na'ar* is the *'ebed*, the subject of the king and the royal house.[21] In 2 Sam 9:10, Ziba's duty is to work on Saul's estate and to provide the family with produce. Evidently the term *na'ar* implies the office of a high-ranking steward or superintendent of property of the estate. The fact that Ziba was important is confirmed by the fact that he had fifteen sons and twenty servants (2 Sam 9:10).

TAXATION

Taxation is one of the first signs of a monarchy. States cannot exist in the fullest form if they do not have the power of taxation. The Bible says little about taxation. Ironically, there were foreign states that taxed the Israelites

17. Alter, *David Story*, 132.
18. Fox, *Service*, 281.
19. Aster, "What Was Doeg," 353–61; Tsevat, "Assyriological Notes," 85–86.
20. McCarter, *II Samuel*, 261–62.
21. Macdonald, "Status and Role," 156.

God's First King

(Judg 3:8, 14). The book of Samuel records that the Philistines exploited the Israelites. In the wars between the Israelites and the Philistines, the conquered became slaves of the conquerors (1 Sam 4:9). More so, Goliath in this challenge to the Israelites says: "If he beats me in combat and kills me, we will become your slaves; but if I best him and kill him, you shall be our slaves and serve us" (1 Sam 17:9). The Philistines denied the Israelites arms, therefore, there were no blacksmiths in all the land of Israel. Clearly this was an indirect tax on the Israelites, who were forced to use the Philistines to repair any of their farm equipment, such as plowshares, mattocks, axes, or sickles (1 Sam 13:20). Evidently, this was another reason for the rebellion against the Philistines and the establishment of the monarchy.

A clue to taxation during Saul's period is found in 1 Sam 17:25, where King Saul promised the person who would slay Goliath great riches. He would also give him his daughter and "grant exemption to his father's house in Israel." The Hebrew word ḥopšî, an adjective meaning free, is used in the Hebrew Bible for a person manumitted from slavery (Exod 21:2). Some scholars tried to connect this term with the Akkadian (Amarna, Nuzi, Alalakh) noun ḥupšu and the Ugaritic ḥpt/ḥbt, both refer to a class of people between slaves and landowners.[22] However, it is difficult to apply this meaning to Israel, as there was no class of ḥopšî.[23] Rainey compared it to the Akkadian adjective zaki, where in the Akkadian texts from Ras Shamra it describes an emancipated slave (RS 16.250:21–22); or a soldier, because of his bravery received freedom from the king, who exempted him from service to the palace: "and the king has exempted him from service to the palace; as the Sun-goddess is free, so he is free" (RS 16.269:14–16).[24]

In the Bible the term, ḥopšî, designates the legal status of a free man who is not subjugated to others. The king's laws, which appear in Samuel's speech outlined the rights of the king, stipulate the king's right to take fields, cattle, servants, even sons and daughters (1 Sam 8:11–18). The exemption that Saul promised the victor was release from the early form of taxes.

Another clue for the existence of taxation during Saul's era is the term minḥah. Generally in the Bible the term minḥah means gift. The term is also attested in Arabic manaḥa, "to give loan" also Tigrinya and Geez, to

---

22. Mendelsohn, "Canaanite Term," 36–39; Gray, "Feudalism," 49–55; Lohfink, "ḥopšî," 5:114–18.

23. De Vaux, *Ancient Israel*, 88; Loewenstamm, "חפשי," 3:256–57.

24. Rainey, "Institutions," 104.

Saul: The State Builder

"give someone a cow on loan."[25] A similar interpretation appears in Ugaritc in KTU, 1.2 I, 38 the suffixed *mnḥyk* means "your gifts."[26] Late Egyptian attests *mnḥt* as meaning "gift of homage," but it might be a loanword from Hebrew.[27] In the Bible, the term signifies a gift given as an expression of friendship with respect, and also a tribute in recognition of the donor's subordinate status. In the Joseph story the brothers brought him *minḥah* consisting of balsam, honey, myrrh, pistachios, and almonds (Gen 43:11, 15, 25, 26). Jacob brought his brother Esau *minḥah* in recognition of his subordinate status, and also to appease him (Gen 32:14, 19, 21, 22). Presenting a gift to a king for receiving his favor was customary (2 Kgs 20:12; Isa 39:1; Ps 45:13). Bringing tribute was traditional between rulers and their subordinate states (Judg 3:15; 2 Sam 8:2, 6; 1 Kgs 4:21; 2 Kgs 17:3, 4). A *minḥah* was presented to the new king "all Judah brought tribute *minḥah* to Jehoshaphat" (2 Chr 17:5); it is stated the king had riches and wealth, evidently this tribute added to his wealth. This is the only instance where people brought tribute to their own king. The other instance appears at Saul's coronation at Mizpah, where we read that the useless scoundrels did not bring him *minḥah* (1 Sam 10:27).

In contrast to these scoundrels, Jesse sent Saul bread *leḥem*, a skin of wine, and a kid (1 Sam 16:20). Solomon received daily provisions of *leḥem* that included thirty *kors* of semolina, sixty *kors* of flour, ten fattened oxen, twenty pasture-fed oxen, and one hundred sheep and goats (1 Kgs 5:2). Nehemiah describes the former governors who laid a heavy burden on the people and took bread *leḥem* and wine in the equivalent of forty shekels of silver from them (Neh 5:15). We believe that the gift of *leḥem* that was sent to King Saul by Jesse was an early form of taxation. This taxation became permanent during Saul's reign: therefore, the king promised tax exemption to the person who would defeat Goliath.

ARMY

Israel's enemies, the Canaanites and the Philistines, had professional armies that included infantry and charioteers.[28] That the Israelites suffered defeats

---

25. Fabry, "*minḥâ*," 8:407–8.

26. KTU 1.2 I:38, 7. In KTU 4.91,1 *mnḥ . bd . ybn* means "tribute from the hand of PN," and has no religious connotation. See Fabry, "*minḥâ*," 8:409; KTU 4.91,1, 245.

27. WbÄS, II, 84.

28. There were exceptions were we read about an attempt to have mercenaries.

God's First King

at the hand of the Philistines further justified that they needed a professional army. The army might be small, but it would be trained, effective, and ready for action. The creation of a skilled army was the work of Saul. He started his army by recruiting mercenaries, thus whenever he saw a *mighty* man or any *valiant* man he took him into his service (1 Sam 14:52); these two terms for soldiers are not mentioned in Ugaritic sources. There is a contrast between the technical terms of the Ugarit text and the biblical text of Iron Age Israel. Rainey has suggested that these two terms appear in Israel due to Aramaean influence.[29] The military terminology did not stem from the tribal period; it was Saul who introduced it. Saul knew about the city-state system of professional soldiers, but he preferred men from his own tribe of Benjamin (1 Sam 22:7). Nevertheless, we read that he took men from other Israelites tribes as well, including David from the tribe of Judah (1 Sam 16:18; 18:2). Foreigners such as Doeg the Edomite were also included in his army (1 Sam 21:8; 22:18). Their numbers probably were small because they were mercenaries.

Saul's professional army was called *baḥurim*. When the term *'iš baḥur* appears it is used to designate selected warriors. This is also true when the term appears alone as a collective form. The root *bḥr* often denotes the selection of soldiers (Exod 17:9; Josh 8:3; 1 Sam 13:3,2; 2 Sam 10:9; 17:1; 2 Chr 13:3, 17; 25:5). Saul himself is called *baḥur* and he selected the national army *'iš baḥur*, which he himself led.[30] This army included 3,000 men (1 Sam 24:2; 26:2). The army was divided into three units each numbering 1,000 men (1 Sam 13:2). They were headed by captains of thousands and captains of hundreds (1 Sam 22:7). This selection process was further developed by David (2 Sam 14:3; 26:2). Saul's kinsman Abner commanded the army whether it was the *baḥurim* or the tribal levies, scholarly opinions are divided.[31]

In historical accounts of David's period, a place named *Baḥurim* is mentioned (2 Sam 3:16; 16:5; 17:18; 19:17; 1 Kgs 2:8). The place was in the Benjaminite territory near Jerusalem. Among its inhabitants was Shimei son of Gera, the Benjaminite, who led a revolt against David (2 Sam 19:17; 1 Kgs 2:8). Also mentioned is one of David's "mighty men" Azmaveth (2 Sam

---

Therefore, Abimelek recruited mercenaries (Judg 9:4). Jephthah gathered a band of armed supporters (Judg 11:3).

29. Rainey, "Institutions," 101.

30. Richter suggested that the term means one who is capable of war, inheritance, and marriage. See Richter, *Berufsberichte*, 30.

31. Alt, *Kleine Schriften*, 2:30 n4; Eissfeldt, *Hebrew Kingdom*, 2:41, says that Abner commanded the military levy.

Saul: The State Builder

23:31 = 1 Chr 11:33). There is also a reference to David's spies, Jonathan, and Ahimaaz who hid in the well belonging to a man from *Baḥurim* (2 Sam 17:18). Thus, it is possible that the name of the place *Baḥurim* should be rendered as "warriors' village" and not "young men's village" as it was assumed before.[32] Indeed, this is supported by 1 Sam 22:7, where we read that Saul gave his soldiers ownership of fields and vineyards. The "men chosen out of all Israel" were picked personally by King Saul to serve in his army, they all received fields, one of which was *Baḥurim*.

In addition to establishing a standing army, Saul also established two units of bodyguards. As the new king of Israel, Saul needed protection. Murders of kings in the ancient world were common, and it came to exist among the Israelite kings. Therefore, Saul surrounded himself with two circles of bodyguards. The first and closest group was the *mishma'ath*, meaning "those who obey who answer the call" (1 Sam 22:14; 2 Sam 23:23). This probably referred to "an intimate circle of royal retainers, i.e. a king's bodyguard."[33] They were very close to the king and had to protect him physically.[34] According to Eissfeldt, David came to Saul's army as an experienced soldier and how he gained his experience is not clear.[35] Later on, David would become the leader of Saul's bodyguards (1 Sam 22:14). This position was held by Benaiah, son of Jehoiada in David's court (2 Sam 23:20–33 = 1 Chr 11:22–25).

The second group of bodyguards included the runner's *raṣim* (1 Sam 22:17). A team of runners escorted the royal chariot. From the context of v. 17, it appears that they were Israelites. Their task was to protect the king's royal chariot, and the king's palace. Indeed, when Absalom, and later Adonijah tried to seize the throne they had at their disposal a chariot with fifty runners (2 Sam 15:1; 1 Kgs 1:5). In 1 Kings they are mentioned as guarding the entrance to the royal palace of King Rehoboam (1 Kgs 14:27–28 = 2 Chr 12:10–11). Their guardroom was located at the entrance to the palace, and they carried bronze shields when they escorted the king to the palace. They were also involved in court intrigue, and played a part in the deposition of Athaliah and the enthronement of Joash (2 Kings 11).

---

32. Weisman, "Nature and Background," 450.
33. McCarter, *I Samuel*, 364.
34. While the term *mishma'ath* on the King Mesha Moabite stone inscription refers to a city or state giving allegiance to the king. See "The Moabite Stone" (*ANET*, 320–21).
35. Eissfeldt, *Hebrew Kingdom*, 41.

Weapons

The men who went to battle supplied their own arms, swords, and slings. The people of the tribe of Benjamin were known as experts with the sling. The Philistines had disarmed the Israelites, so therefore in the battle of Michmas, only Saul and Jonathan had swords (1 Sam 13:19–22). In David's eulogy, Saul's shield is mentioned (2 Sam 1:21); while, Jonathan is mentioned as an archer (1 Sam 18:4; 20:20; 2 Sam 1:22). Among the people who joined David at Ziklag were people from the tribe of Benjamin armed with a bow (1 Chr 12:2). We believe that Saul introduced this weapon into the army. It was used in ancient times for hunting and for war. The Philistines used archers (1 Sam 31:3 = 1 Chr 10:3). Since the Philistines disarmed the Israelites, the bow was an answer to the Philistine threat. The bow was made of wood reinforced with twisted sinew or cord, its end was held by a string. The arrowheads could be made from flint or bronze.

Protective gear was also used in Saul's army, therefore we read of the helmet and breastplate. When David went to fight Goliath, Saul gave him his bronze helmet and breastplate (1 Sam 17:38). Goliath also wore a helmet and breastplate of scales (1 Sam 17:5). De Vaux says that it is questionable whether Saul had this equipment for David to try on.[36] However, we believe that Saul had this gear on hand. Saul was probably trying to eliminate any advantage Goliath had, therefore he gave David the same equipment that was at Goliath's disposal. Thus, David received a sword that was rare among the Israelites, only Saul and Jonathan had swords (1 Sam 13:22); afterwards, it became a common weapon as did the helmet and breastplate.

Soldiers Remuneration

Saul established a mercenary army, but how did the King of Israel pay his soldiers for their services? A clue to this question can be found in Saul's rebuke of his courtiers. In an ironic rhetorical question, Saul asks his tribesman "Will Jesse give to them fields and vineyards?" (1 Sam 22:7). In addition, he says that he made them captains of thousands and captains of hundreds. The implication here is that Saul, in return for their loyal services, compensated his soldiers with fields and vineyards, and also elevated their status.[37] Later, when David became a professional military man of Achish,

---

36. De Vaux, *Ancient Israel*, 245.
37. Royal redistribution of fields and vineyards echoes one of the abuses Samuel

Saul: The State Builder

he received the city of Ziklag for his services (1 Sam 27:6). No doubt David distributed this territory among his troops.

In the ancient world, kings bestowed gifts of land on their servants and soldiers for loyal service. Samuel, in his speech against kingship, criticizes the future king for taking the best fields, vineyards, and olive orchards to give to his servants. A similar description is found in ancient documents from Ugarit that read: "From this day Niqmaddu, son of ʿAmmittamru, king of Ugarit, has taken up the estate of Sinarāna in Maʿraba and has given it to Ibri-šarri, his servant, in perpetuity. In the future no one shall take it from the hand of Ibri-šarri forever. (It is) a gift of the king."[38] Similarly, in several Hittite land grant documents from fifteenth and fourteenth centuries BCE we read that a king gave estates and land property to his officials as a reward for services or for ensuring their loyalty.[39]

Still the question remains: where did Saul acquire the land to give to his soldiers? One possibility is that Saul inherited most of his property. We read that Kish, his father, was "a man of substance" (1 Sam 9:1). The phrase means that he was a mighty warrior as were Gideon, Jephthah, and others. However, the phrase also has the meaning of "a man of wealth" as it appears in Ruth 2:1 and 2 Kgs 15:20. Kish was a wealthy man with high social standing. In addition, Saul probably confiscated land from David's family after they escaped from Bethlehem (1 Sam 22:1) on charges of treason. He also probably confiscated the land of the city of Nob, which he destroyed. In addition, he gained the property of people who died without heirs. Wars were a source of fields and vineyards, yet most of Saul's wars were defensive in nature. He expelled the Philistines, but did not conquer the land of the Philistines. The Amalekites, that Saul defeated, had sheep and oxen, but not fields and vineyards, as they were nomadic.[40]

The only people known to have fields and vineyards were the Gibeonites. Based on 2 Sam 4:2 and 21:1-9, we believe that a large part of Saul's crown lands came from the Gibeonites. The story of Saul destroying the Gibeonites does not appear in the first book of Samuel. It is mentioned indirectly during a famine when David inquired of the Lord; Saul putting

---

predicted about kingship (1 Sam 8:14). Samuel also foretold the appointment of people as commanders of thousand and hundreds (1 Sam 8:12).

38. RS 16.247:1-14; Rainey, "Institutions," 97; Mendelsohn, "Samuel's Denunciation," 19-20 n11, 13-15.

39. See Bryce, *Kingdom*, 92 n85.

40. Bartal, *Saul's Kingship*, 116.

God's First King

the Gibeonites to death was the cause of the famine (2 Sam 21:1). The question also appears in the Talmud: "where, however, does Saul put to death the Gibeonites?' The truth is that, as he killed the inhabitants of Nob, the city of the priests who were supplying them with water and food, Scripture regards it as if he himself had killed them."[41]

Saul's animosity towards the Gibeonites was not limited to the city of Gibeon. In 2 Sam 4:1-3, we read about Baanah and Rechab sons of Rimmon the Beerothite who were officers in Ishbaal's army and they were Benjaminites. The city of Beeroth was part of four cities led by Gibeon that made a treaty with Israel. The population was not destroyed during the Israelite conquest, but later the original Gibeonite population fled and was replaced by the Benjaminites. No reason is given in the text for their escape. But it is possible that they left because of Saul's hostility towards Gibeon and other members of the Gibeonite federation.[42]

What was behind the animosity of Saul towards the Gibeonites? Several explanations are given: Saul destroyed the Gibeonites for political reasons, he was unsure of their loyalty. Saul was afraid of collaboration between the Gibeonites and the Philistines. The war with the Philistines during his reign was long lasting. According to Blenkinsopp, after the battle of Aphek (1 Sam 4:1) and the capture of the ark and the destruction of Shiloh (Jer 7:12; 16:6), the Philistines controlled the Shephelah area, the central highlands, and the Gibeonite region. Possibly they established a garrison or a military command post in Gibeon as they did in other locations.[43] The Gibeonites probably played a role in the wars between Israel and the Philistines, and might even have sided with them as David did. Saul was afraid of collaboration between the Philistines and Gibeonites. The strategic location of the Gibeonite cities was catastrophic because it split Saul's kingdom in half. Saul thus destroyed this alien enclave. Saul, unlike David, did not have the political vision to integrate them into his kingdom.[44] Moreover, the Gibeonite cities were situated between the Israelite tribes located in the center and in the south. Eliminating them was inevitable.

That Gibeon was a wealthy city is evident by the winery discovered there. The land around it was suitable for agriculture, and the slopes beyond for vineyards. Large numbers of pots, and forty cellars were discovered.

41. *Yebamoth* 78b.
42. McCarter, *II Samuel*, 127.
43. Blenkinsopp, *Gibeon and Israel*, 62.
44. Blenkinsopp, "Did Saul," 3.

Saul: The State Builder

Each jar in the cellars held forty-five liters of wine. Wine presses also existed. It is believed that the cellars had space for jars containing 25,000 gallons of wine that was exported to other cities.

Examination of the jars pointed to a link between the names inscribed on the handles of these jars, and Saul's genealogies in 1 Chr (8:29–40; 9:35–44).[45] The genealogies point to the settlement of the Benjaminite families in the Gibeonite territory. History of the Ner family and the clan and villages that depended on Gibeon is found in the Chronicles list. Interestingly, the name Nera' is inscribed on the handles. The *aleph* suggests that this is an Aramaicized form of the name Ner, Neriah, Neryo. The name Ner appears as Saul's uncle. We believe that the existence of the Benjaminites in this territory is due to intermarriages with the local population. This is verified in the genealogical list in Chronicles. One of the more interesting names that appear is Maacah. She was the wife of "the father of Gibeon." The name is not an Israelite name, and when it appears as a personal name it refers to a non-Israelite. Thus, we can see that some of the Benjaminites were married to local women.

As we mentioned earlier, Saul had to compensate his soldiers with land in the form of vineyards and fields. He did not trust the Gibeonites because he was not sure of their loyalty. Saul was afraid of collaboration between the Gibeonites and the Philistines. Saul knew about the great wealth and lands that Gibeon, and the other Gibeonite cities possessed. By destroying the Gibeonites he achieved his two goals. He eliminated the threat from the Gibeonites, and could compensate his standing army by giving them the vineyards and fields that belonged to the Gibeonites. Therefore, not surprisingly, we find Israelite names in Gibeonite territory.

CAPITAL

It was suggested that Saul tried to make Gibeon his capital.[46] According to Blenkinsopp, Saul was impressed by its prestige as a religious center, impressive fortifications, hydraulic work, and especially its strategic position. Indeed, archaeological excavations point to a massive city wall, 10.5–11 ft in width, which circled the hill dating from the Iron Age I Period (1200–1000 BCE). In addition, water systems from the Iron Age I to provide water to

---

45. Demsky, "Genealogy of Gibeon," 16–23; Yeivin, "Benjaminite Settlement," 141–54.

46. Schunck, *Benjamin*, 131–38, 171; Edelman, "Did Saulide-Davidic," 77; Kearney, "Role of the Gibeonites," 16.

God's First King

the inhabitants of the city during the time of siege were also discovered. This system is the Pool of Gibeon mentioned in 2 Sam 2:13. A huge round pit, thirty-seven feet round and eighty-two feet deep was found within the ancient site of the city of Gibeon.[47] Blenkinsopp also points to the term *habbamah haggedolah*, which evidently was the large shrine where Solomon went for his inauguration referred to as Gibeon in 1 Kgs 3:4. He also suggests that David went to the Gibeonite sanctuary and "sought the face of Yahweh" before giving the descendants of Saul to the Gibeonites (2 Sam 21:1). It appears that the Gibeonite sanctuary rivaled Jerusalem before the completion of the temple.[48] However, it is unlikely that Saul ever established his capital in Gibeon simply due to the fact that no biblical passage associates Saul directly with Gibeon.

Saul probably established his capital at Gibeah. There are several places with names based on the root *gbʻ*, which in Hebrew means "hill." Therefore we find Geba (1 Sam 14:5); and Gibeah (1 Sam 14:2). In addition, there are longer versions of these names, such as Geba of Benjamin (1 Sam 13:16), Gibeah of Benjamin (1 Sam 13:2), and *Gibeath Haelohim*, the hill of God (1 Sam 10:5). The latter was the place where the Philistine prefect resided, and became one of the strongholds in the highlands (1 Sam 10:5). According to McCarter, *Gibeath Haelohim* is the longer name of Gibeah of Benjamin, Saul's home.[49] Jonathan struck down the Philistine prefect in Geba (1 Sam 13:3), which seems to be Gibeah of Benjamin (1 Sam 13:2). Saul also resided in this city (1 Sam 10:26; 11:4).[50] Gibeah is mentioned in the "rise of David" stories (1 Sam 15:34; 22:6; 23:19; 26:1). After the battle of Michmas, Gibeah became Saul's capital, and was renamed after him as "Gibeah of Saul"(1 Sam 15:34).

Gibeah is identified with the modern site of Tell el-Ful situated 3.5 miles north of Jerusalem. The ancient path from Judah to Mount Ephraim extends along the Tell. This was the main north-south road of central Palestine. Its location was crucial to the Philistine domination of the central hill country. Saul stationed his army at Gibeah that was situated between

---

47. Pritchard, "Water System," 66–75; Pritchard, *Water System of Gibeon*; Pritchard, *Gibeon*, 159–60.

48. Blenkinsopp, "Did Saul," 5.

49. McCarter, *I Samuel*, 182.

50. According to the genealogical lists in 1 Chr 8:29 and 9:35, Saul's ancestral home was at Gibeon.

Saul: The State Builder

the tribes of Benjamin and Ephraim, placing his army in the midst of the Israelite population.[51]

Archaeological excavation in search of Saul's capital at Tell el-Ful revealed some evidence of the pre-fortress period (1200 BCE), which was an early Iron Age settlement.[52] Sometime after its destruction (1100 BCE), a rectangular fortress was built there with corner towers and casemate walls (Level II A). Later this fortress was rebuilt with masonry and better quality workmanship (Level II B). There is no evidence of destruction from period I but abandonment; this is probably connected to the revenge against the Benjaminites that is recorded in Judges 19–20.

Alt and Mazar suggested that it was the Philistines who built the fort, and one of a series of Philistine fortresses built to control the trade routes. Afterwards, Saul, who built fortress II, occupied the place.[53] Saul's successful campaign against the Philistines, and the expulsion of the Philistines from the Benjaminite territory enabled him to establish his capital at Gibeah. From his capital he went to fight against the surrounding enemies (1 Sam 22:6; 23:19). L. A. Sinclair, however, at first suggested that fortress I was built by Saul, and that David may have simply repaired fortress II. Later he changed his theory and accepted Mazar's theory of reconstruction.[54] Recently a new chronology was proposed by Brooks, and according to her, during Period I, Tell el-Ful was a Philistine post. The place was destroyed by fire when Saul was fighting against the Philistines (1 Samuel 13–14) before or around 1100 BCE. Saul captured the place and he rebuilt it with a large tower (Period II, fortress I). After the battle at Gilboa, the tower was destroyed by massive fire. The second fortress (Period II, fortress II) was built following the destruction of the first one, and since the second fortress was very similar to the first, it is believed that the builder was connected to

---

51. There are scholars such as Miller and Arnold who did not accept the identification of Gibeah with Tell el-Ful. They suggest that Gibeah should be identified with Geba, and to the modern village *Jaba'*. However, we should stress that there is no archaeological evidence to support their claims. Recent excavations produced ceramic from the Iron Age II and also from the Persian period, but nothing from the Iron Age I. See Arnold, *Gibeah*, 54, 87–106; Miller, "Geba/Gibeah of Benjamin," 145–66.

52. Albright, *Excavation*; Albright, "New Campaign," 6–12.

53. Alt, *Kleine Schriften*, 2:31 n1; 3:259; Mazar, "גבעת שאול, גבעת בנימין, גבעת."

54. Sinclair, *Archaeological*, 1–52; Sinclair, "Archeological," 52–63. Simlarly according to Demsky, Tell el-Ful was desolate when Saul arrived. He points to archaeological evidence that was gathered by Albright, Sinclair and Lapp. Accordingly, there is no trace of the Philistines presence at Tell el-Ful, the large well built fortress was Saul's work not the Philistines'. See Demsky, "Geba," 29.

God's First King

Saul. According to Brooks, this was either Saul's uncle Abner or Saul's son, Ishbaal, who rebuilt fortress II. Their goal was to move back to Saul's town, since Abner was murdered, fortress II was abandoned.[55]

According to the biblical narrative, however, the seat of government was transferred to Mahanaim, the capital of Gilead. It was done in light of the victory of the Philistines at Mount Gilboa. The territory of Benjamin was too vulnerable to serve as the seat of the new government. The northern tribes, those of East Jordan, were loyal to Saul. This new location of the capital was far away from the Philistine controlled area. Thus, it is unlikely that Abner, or Saul's son, Ishbaal, rebuilt fortress II. Probably as Alt and Mazar suggested, it was Saul who built fortress II. Saul's successful campaign against the Philistines, and the expulsion of the Philistines from the Benjaminite territory enabled Saul to establish his capital at Gibeah.

CULTIC CENTER

Saul established a cultic center in Nob. During his time, Nob held the prestigious position as the chief sanctuary of Yahweh. This occurred after the fall of Shiloh. Priests from the house of Eli settled in Nob. Albright suggested that Saul gathered the surviving Elides, and resettled them at Nob.[56] Nob was located close to Jerusalem, which is attested to in Isa 10:32 where the invader shakes his fist at Jerusalem from Nob. It has been suggested that Nob was on Râs el-Mešarif, a slope of Mt. Scopus within sight of Mount Zion. Another place that was suggested was a slope north of Mount Scopus, Qu'meh. However, this is not within view of Jerusalem. Nob achieved its prominence during Saul's era because it housed the sacred objects and rites there. The ark was probably also brought there. Even the sword of Goliath, the Philistine, was kept at Nob, to commemorate the great victory against the Philistines.

Saul had a personal priest, Ahijah, who accompanied him to the battlefield (1 Sam 14:18). He was the great-grandson of Eli, priest of Shiloh, and was the brother of Ahimelech. Alternatively, scholars pointed out that Ahijah, son of Ahitub, is the same person named Ahimelech, son of Ahitub, the priest of Nob mentioned in chapters 21–22.[57] During the battle of Michmas, Saul ordered the priest to bring the ark to the battlefield to give

55. Brooks, *Saul*, 136.
56. Albright, *Biblical Period*, 50.
57. Mauchline, *1 and 2 Samuel*, 150; Mazar, "Ahimelech," 217; Blenkinsopp, *Gibeon*, 66.

Saul: The State Builder

confidence to the warriors. This is similar to the battle of Aphek when the ark was brought to encourage the Israelites. Saul captured the ark before the battle of Michmas, and after the victory, transferred it to Nob. By moving the ark to Nob, he converted the city into a cultic center. Through the ages, the ark united the Israelites. Saul wanted to unite the Israelite tribes under his leadership, and in order to achieve this he established a new cultic center to host the ark, the most important religious symbol.

Blenkinsopp suggested that the sanctuary of Nob housed the ark.[58] He advanced three main reasons: 1. The priests at Nob came from Shiloh, which is associated with the ark. Abiathar, the son of Abimelech, became David's priest. He was the ark priest therefore his life was spared (1 Kgs 2:26). David appointed him because he planned to bring the ark to Jerusalem in order to strengthen the religious allegiance of Israel. 2. According to 1 Sam 21:5, the sanctuary of Nob contained the "bread of presence." Exodus 25:23–30 [also Lev 24:5] mentions this in conjunction with the ark. 3. The existence of the sword of Goliath and the ephod point to the privileged status of the place as a cultic center. In addition, the ritual of purification before eating the consecrated bread is mentioned in v. 5.[59]

When Saul found out that his established important cultic center had Ahimelech, the priest, assisting David, he ordered the slaughter of all Elide priests. It was only after the destruction of Nob, and the slaughter of its priests, that the ark was moved to Gibeon.

Samuel's actions are puzzling. He did not restore the tabernacle, and did not communicate with the surviving Elides. He is described as judging the people of Israel, and visiting different cultic centers. Among them were Beth-el, Gilgal, and Mizpah. Samuel built a shrine in his city of Ramah. This is probably because Samuel tried to establish his own dynasty. This might explain Saul's motivation for establishing the cultic center at Nob. The choice of Nob strengthened Saul's position against Samuel. Secondly, it also gave him control over the priestly family with its important symbolic meaning. In the Talmud we read: "Now it was: When Eli the priest died, Shiloh was destroyed and they repaired to Nob; when Samuel the Ramathite died, Nob was destroyed and they went to Gibeon."[60]

---

58. Blenkinsopp, *Gibeon*, 65.

59. This brings to mind Uriah who refused to sleep with his wife during a military campaign. This was due to the religious nature of the war and the presence of the ark in the camp.

60. *Zebaḥim* 118b.

God's First King

In addition to building a cultic center, Saul was also a religious leader. Saul was in charge of the covenant with God, thus, he battled idolatry. He never deserted Yahweh for other gods. On the contrary, he banned the use of the ghost and familiar spirit in the land (1 Sam 28:9). His piety to Yahweh is reflected in the name of his son, Jonathan (Hebrew: Yahweh has given). He attributed his victory over the Ammonites to Yahweh (1 Sam 11:13). Van der Toorn pointed out that the way Saul ruled was innovative. According to him: "The god of the head of state was promoted to the rank of national god; . . . Its priesthood, sworn to loyalty, was expected to serve the king's best interests. They became the civil servants of a state religion."[61] According to him, the religion of the Saulide state was born in the army.[62] Thus, on his military campaigns, he did not go anywhere without a priest. More so, Saul decided to fast during the battle, and ordered the death penalty for its violation (1 Sam 14:24; 7:6; 2 Sam 23:16). Before battle he sacrificed (1 Sam 13:9).[63] He prevented the people from eating flesh with blood (1 Sam 14:33-34). As a religious leader, he is instructed by Samuel to enforce the ban against Amalek (1 Sam 15:3). He set up an altar to the Lord (1 Sam 14:35); and interestingly, in *Leviticus Rabbah*, we find that the sages asserted that he was the first to build an altar to Yahweh:

> It is written: So many altars were built by the ancients—Noah, Abraham, Isaac, Jacob, Moses, and Joshua, and you say 'oto heḥel- "he was the first?" The rabbis say: 'oto heḥel means "he was the first of the kings." But Rabbi Yudan said: Because he was prepared to give his life for this matter, Scripture assigned him as much credit as if he himself had been the first to build an altar to the Lord.

We can see that the rabbis agreed that—according to 1 Sam 14:35—Saul was the first to build an altar to Yahweh. But this assertion is problematic because it contradicts the biblical tradition. To resolve this contradiction, the rabbis said that Saul was the first king to build an altar to Yahweh. Rabbi Yudan solved the problem by not accepting the plain sense of the verse. According to him, Saul chronologically was not the first to build an altar to Yahweh, but because of his courage in building it he might have been the first.[64]

61. Van der Toorn, "Saul," 519.
62. Ibid., 528.
63. In Judges 6 Gideon sacrificed a long time before the battle; and in Gibeah they sacrificed only after the second battle (Judg 20:26).
64. For further study on this Midrash see Sperling, *Original Torah*, 130.

Saul: The State Builder

In conclusion, Saul chose a desolate hill location, Gibeath Benjamin, to establish his capital, which he named after himself. Archaeological excavations for the search of Saul's capital point to Tell el-Ful. As the first king with a capital, we find that he had servants who were referred to as *'abdi hammelek*, officials and functionaries at his court. Another term is *na'ar*, which implies an office with a high rank like a steward, or property superintendent of an estate. Another administrator was the "chief herdsman" who was in charge of the king's property and herds. In addition, Saul established a cultic center in Nob. During his time, Nob held the chief sanctuary of Yahweh. Saul was also a religious leader who fought against idolatry, and never deserted Yahweh for other gods. He also created a skilled army. He started his army by recruiting mercenaries, and thus we read that Saul's professional army was called *baḥurim*. We believe that Saul introduced the bow as a new weapon, as well as the first to use protective gear such as the helmet and breastplate. Saul also established two units of bodyguards. The first and closest group is called *mishma'ath*, which means "those who obey who answer the call." The second group of bodyguards included the runner's *raṣim*. As the new king, Saul was the first to introduce taxes. In his promise to the victor against Goliath he promised the brave soldier and his family would be exempt from taxes and other obligations to the monarch. We believe the gift of *leḥem* was sent to King Saul by Jesse as an early form of taxation. Another clue for the existence of taxation during Saul's reign is the term *minḥah*. In light of all these achievements, Saul was indeed a state builder. He transformed Israel from a loose federation of tribes into a state with a capital, religious center, army, and taxes. Saul laid the foundation for the monarchy that would ultimately be fully developed under David and Solomon.

6

Saul and the "Witch of Endor"

INQUIRING OF THE DEAD parallels inquiring of the Lord in two respects: consulting the oracle and requesting assistance. The former is found in the incident of Saul at Endor (1 Sam 28:4–20). In his distress Saul seeks a woman to bring up the spirit of the dead Samuel, because the Lord has failed to answer him, whether by dreams, by the *Urim ve-Tummim*, or through prophets. The entire incident is set at night: Saul departs the camp after dark and returns before morning (v. 25). According to Ehrlich, this is because witches engage in their magical practices only in the dark. Josephus explained the timing by the king's desire to conceal his absence from his army.[1] Abravanel offered a similar interpretation: "they went at night so that no one would see them and no one in the camp would know that he was gone." Both reasons may be true: darkness was essential for the medium and also for Saul to get away unseen. Another explanation is that the episode's nocturnal setting alludes to the fact that the dead are in darkness (Pss 88:13; 143:3; Job 10:21).

The Midrash describes Saul's adventure as follows:

> Then Saul said to his courtiers, "find me a woman who is a medium" (1 Sam 28:7). R. Simeon ben Levi said: "Whom did Saul resemble? A king who entered a city and said, 'Slaughter all of the roosters in this city.' At night, wanting to leave, he said, 'Is there no rooster here to crow?' They said to him: 'Did you not order us to slaughter them?' Here too Saul destroyed the *'ovot* and *yidde'onim* and then said, 'Find me a medium.'"[2]

---

1. Josephus, *Ant.* 6.14.2.
2. *Yalkut Shimoni*, 2:730.

Saul and the "Witch of Endor"

It is ironic that Saul, who had exterminated the 'ovot and yidde'onim, found himself needing the services of a medium. The very fact of his request reflects his sincere belief that the dead know what will happen in the world of the living.[3]

When the medium sees Samuel rising from the grave she cries out and then rebukes Saul for deceiving her. Readers have long wondered why she did not recognize Saul before Samuel appeared. According to the talmudic sages and traditional commentators, including Rashi and David Kimḥi, the dead rise feet first. Samuel, however, arose in the normal upright posture, out of respect for the king. Seeing this, the woman realized the identity of her visitor.[4] In v. 14 the LXX, evidently based on this midrash, has her telling Saul that she sees *andra orthion* (a man upright) (reflecting a Vorlage of זקף instead of the MT זקן). According to Josephus, it was Samuel himself who revealed Saul's identity.[5] Budde believed that some gesture that Samuel made toward Saul spoiled the latter's incognito.[6]

It is unclear what rites the medium employed to raise Samuel. The midrash reports laconically that "she did what she did, and she said what she said, and raised him."[7] Of course it is possible that she was a fraud, but the Lord worked a miracle, and Samuel really did rise from his grave. When Samuel appears, the woman is taken aback and cries out. Some explain that she knew she had done nothing and was consequently astonished to see a spirit rise up.[8] Several manuscripts of the Septuagint have "the woman saw [i.e., recognized] *Saul* and cried out," instead of the MT "Samuel." Some scholars would adopt this reading. But the emendation seems to be ruled out by Saul's question, "What do you see?" and the woman's response, which describes Samuel's appearance (vv. 13–14).

According to Kaufmann, we are dealing with a method of gaining foreknowledge of the future by getting dead souls to declare what they know.[9] The spirits of the dead are referred to as *'elohim*; as the woman tells Saul, "I see *'elohim* coming up from the earth" (v. 13; cf. Isa 8:19). They have a mantic power to know and reveal what is concealed in the future, a revelation they

---

3. On the other hand, according to Eccl 9:5 the dead know nothing.
4. *Lev. Rab.* 26:7; *Tanḥuma Lev* 21:1; *B. Sanh.* 65b.
5. Josephus, *Ant.* 14.2.333.
6. Budde, *Die Bücher Samuel*, 180.
7. *Lev. Rab.* 26:7.
8. Lewis, *Cults*, 115.
9. Kaufmann, "On the Story," 210 (Hebrew).

God's First King

express in human language just as prophets do. The spirit of the dead recounts what it sees or knows through its mantic power. This is a special form of prophecy, that of the Rephaim.[10] Kaufmann maintains that enchanters worked themselves into an ecstatic state and became mediums. That is, the medium's mind merged with or was taken over by that of the dead person. During the encounter, the medium was in a prophetic trance and had supernatural knowledge. When the woman raised Samuel's spirit, she was imbued with supernatural knowledge that enabled her to recognize Saul.

The problem with Kaufmann's reading is that if the woman was in a trance, how could she suspend it to accuse Saul of deceiving her? Furthermore, according to the biblical narrative the woman served only as an instrument to make the initial connection between Saul and Samuel, who speak directly to each other. She is not a party to the conversation. The implication of v. 21—"the woman came in (or went up [wa-tavo']) to Saul"—is that she was not present during the dialogue of king and prophet, but returned from another room and saw Saul's panicked reaction to the encounter. Kaufmann, however, believes that the entire conversation was conducted by and through the medium.

Another possibility is that it is not the dead person who is raised, but only his shade, which ascends from under the earth and speaks in a chirping voice (Isa 29:4; 8:19). According to this scenario, the medium and the inquirer sat in separate rooms. The medium saw the spirit of the dead in smoke or as a silhouette rising from the earth and translated its chirps into human language. At Endor, however, Samuel appeared in his full form, not as a silhouette or smoke. The woman was startled and then realized that it was only because of Saul that she had been able to raise Samuel. After the two verify that it is indeed Samuel who was brought up by her enchantments, Saul and Samuel converse directly. The woman goes away and returns only at the end of their dialogue.

We have already noted that the woman describes Samuel as 'elohim,[11] meaning a shade or superhuman being, as in Isa 8:19, discussed above. Some scholars, such as Spronk and Lewis, cite various extra-biblical texts as evidence for the use of 'elohim to refer to the dead.[12] One possibility is

10. Ibid.

11. Other instances of 'elohim with a plural adjective are Josh 24:19; Deut 5:23; 1 Sam 17:26, 36.

12. Spronk, *Beatific Afterlife*, 163; Lewis, *Cults*, 49–51, 115. See also Arnold who says that 'elohim "denotes the ancestral dead and not simply a ghost or spirit of the dead." Arnold, "Necromancy," 203.

that the spirit is called *'elohim* because it is the divine part of a human being. Here *Targum Jonathan* renders the word, as often when it cannot refer to God, as "angel": "I saw an angel of the Lord rising up." This meaning is supported by "all *'elohim* bow down to Him" (Ps 97:7). David Kimḥi explains that here *'elohim* means "a great man" (cf. Exod 22:8, 27). This reading is plausible; when Moses hesitates to accept his mission to Egypt and the Lord promises to send his brother Aaron with him, he tells him, "he shall speak for you to the people; and he shall be a mouth for you, and you shall be to him as *'elohim*" (Exod 4:16; cf. Exod 7:1).

As for the plural participle *'olim* "coming up," it agrees in number with *'elohim*, which is a plural form; compare "He is a holy God (*'elohim qedošim hu'*)" (Josh 24:19) and "living God (*'elohim ḥayyim*)" (Deut 5:26; 1 Sam 17:26, 36; Jer 10:10; 23:36). In the next verse, however, the medium describes what she sees in the singular; perhaps the woman saw more than one spirit but Saul asked to speak only with Samuel. Such an interpretation is found in the Talmud: *'olim* implies two: One was Samuel, but [who was] the other? Samuel went and brought Moses with him, saying to him: "Perhaps, God forbid, I am summoned to Judgment: arise with me, for there is nothing that you wrote in the Torah that I did not fulfill."[13]

The Tosafists explain that "although Moses was not of [Samuel's] generation, he said, 'This is how I interpreted the text and what I practiced. Come and bear witness for me, for you too have learned.'"

Hutter offers the interesting suggestion that the location of the ritual and the ritual itself are evidence of Hittite influence. According to him, "gods rising" echoes an ancient Hittite incantation formula for conjuring up underworld gods, which was used by the pre-Israelite residents of Endor.[14] Inquiring of the dead is very similar to consulting with pagan deities, which is why it was banned in Israel. Later, when the denizens of the underworld were no longer considered to be gods, Samuel could be included in the category of *'elohim* without being identified as a god. As Johnston noted, however, a link between Endor and the Hittites is far from certain, and taking the term *'elohim* as denoting both forbidden pagan gods and licit non-divine beings seems to be contradictory.[15] The best interpretation, then, is that mentioned above: the ghost of the dead is the spirit, the divine component of the human being.

13. *Ḥagigah* 4b; *Tanḥuma Lev, Emor* 2.
14. Hutter, "Religionsgeschichtliche," 32–36.
15. Johnston, *Shades*, 146.

God's First King

When the medium raises Samuel, Saul asks her to describe what she sees; the implication is that Saul himself sees nothing. According to the *Tanḥuma* (quoted in *Yalqut Shmuel* 1:28), the medium does not hear what the dead person says, but sees him, whereas the inquirer does not see the shade, but hears its voice. Saul may be in the corner of the room or in the next room and does not see what is happening; this is why he must ask the woman whether it is indeed Samuel who has risen. The woman describes Samuel as "an old man wrapped in a cloak"—apparently the robe that symbolized Samuel's prophetic or judicial status.[16] It may be the robe that Hannah made each year to bring to Samuel when she made her pilgrimage to Shiloh (1 Sam 2:19) or the cloak (it was Samuel's) that was torn in two to symbolize the rift between the Lord and Saul (1 Sam 15:27). The reference to the cloak indicates that the dead in the underworld have the same appearance as they did in the world of the living.[17] In any case, when he hears the woman's description Saul knows that it is indeed Samuel who has risen and consequently bows low out of respect for the prophet.

Saul is committing a grievous sin by inquiring of the dead—a practice that is abhorrent to the Lord (Deut 18:12)—instead of inquiring of the Lord. Raising up a prophet of the Lord by magical means as a way to force the Lord to respond is a detestable action. Samuel's reaction is to rebuke Saul: "Why have you disturbed me (*hirgaztani*) and brought me up?" (1 Sam 28:15). There is a bitter irony here, given that the next day Saul and his sons will join Samuel in the world of the dead.

We will understand Samuel's complaint more clearly if we compare it to Phoenician royal tomb inscriptions: that of Tabnit of Sidon—"Don't, don't open it, and don't disturb (*trgzn*) me, for such a thing would be an abomination to Astarte! But if you do open it and if you do disturb me, may [you] not have any seed among the living under the sun or resting place together with the shades!"[18] A similar description is found on the great sarcophagus of Eshmunazar, discovered near Sidon: "Whoever you are, ruler and (ordinary) man, may he not open this resting place and may he not search in it for anything, for nothing whatever has been placed into it! May he not take the casket in which I am resting, and may he not carry me away from this resting-place to another resting place!" There is also a

---

16. Similarly, King Ahaziah identified the man who met his messengers as Elijah from the leather girdle he wore (2 Kgs 1:8).

17. Isa 14:9; Ezek 32:27; *Sanh.* 90b.

18. "Tabnit of Sidon," in *ANET*, 662.

Saul and the "Witch of Endor"

curse against any ruler or a man who opens the tomb or steals the casket: "May they not have resting place with the shades, may they not be buried in a grave, and may they not have a son and seed to take their place!"[19] A comparison with these inscriptions suggests that Samuel sees Saul's act as desecrating his grave and disturbing his rest, a transgression that is severely punished by Heaven.[20] In fact, Saul has sinned twice, both by inquiring of the dead rather than of God and by disturbing the dead.

The Gemara, by contrast, sees Samuel's reaction as fear of Judgment Day: "Samuel said to Saul, 'Why have you disturbed me and brought me up?' Now if Samuel, the righteous, was afraid of the Judgment, how much more so should we be fearful!"[21] The Jerusalem Talmud is even clearer about Samuel's trepidation. It has Samuel tells Saul, "What is more, I thought that it was the Day of Judgment and I was afraid."[22] On Judgment Day Samuel will be like every other human being. According to the *Midrash Rabba*, Samuel explains his candor to Saul as follows: "When I was with you I was in a false world and you might have heard untrue words from me, for I was afraid of you lest you should kill me, but now that I am in a world of truth you will only hear from me words of truth."[23]

According to the biblical account, when Saul learns that he will fall in battle on the morrow he falls powerless to the ground.[24] Saul collapses both because of the terror inspired by the prophet's words and because he has eaten nothing for a whole day and night. Here the biblical narrator turns the spotlight on the woman, whose merciful and kind nature is revealed when she slaughters her fatted calf to feed Saul.[25] Josephus, too, took note of her positive qualities, despite the fact that biblical law condemned her to death:

> Now it is but just to recommend the generosity of this woman ... She still did not remember to [Saul's] disadvantage that he had condemned her sort of learning, and did not refuse him as a stranger, and one that she had had no acquaintance with; but

19. "Eshmun'azar of Sidon," in *ANET*, 662.

20. The grave should be a place where a person could rest in peace, see Job 3:13–19. Several passages in the Bible insist that the dead cannot be awakened from their sleep (2 Kgs 4:31; Jer 51:39; Job 14:12). For the subject of disturbing the rest of the dead see Hallo, "Disturbing," 183–92.

21. Ḥagigah 4b.

22. J. Ḥagigah. 2a.

23. Lev. Rab. 26:7.

24. The verb *npl* occurs four times in chapter 31 (vv. 1, 4, 5, and 8).

25. On the character of the medium, see Simon, *Reading*, 73–92.

> she had compassion upon him, and comforted him, and exhorted him to do what he was greatly averse to, and offered him the only creature she had, as a poor woman ... It would be well therefore to imitate the [woman's] example and to do kindnesses to all such as are in want and to think that nothing is better, nor more becoming mankind, than such a general beneficence, nor what will sooner render God favorable, and ready to bestow good things upon us.[26]

Saul's punishment was harsh. The talmudic homilists enumerated five transgressions on account of which he died. Although all of them are mentioned in the Saul cycle, the Bible does not allege that they were the reasons for his death. We find in the *Midrash Rabbah*:

> [Saul] was slain because of five sins; as it says, "Saul died for the trespass that he had committed against the Lord" (1 Chr 10:13), because he slew the inhabitants of Nob the city of the priests, because he spared Agag, because he did not obey Samuel: for it says, "Wait seven days until I come to you" (1 Sam 10:8), and he did not do so, and because he inquired of the ghost and the familiar spirit, "and did not seek advice of the Lord; so He had him slain" (1 Chr 10:14).[27]

It is not totally clear how the homilist is counting five transgressions or what the fifth transgression is. Probably the introductory verse, "for the trespass that he had committed against the Lord," is included in the number; the printed editions add the word "and" before "he slew the inhabitants of Nob."[28]

Still the Midrash depicted Saul positively as he accepted his destiny he goes to a war knowing that he and his son will die in the battlefield:

> Abner and Amasa asked him: "What did Samuel say to you?" He answered to them: "He said: 'Tomorrow you will go down to battle and be victorious. Nay, more; your sons will be appointed chiefs.'" He took his three sons and went out to war. At that moment, said Resh Lakish, the Holy one, blessed be He, called the ministering Angles, and said to them: "Come and look at a being whom I have created in My world! Usually if a man goes to a feast he does not take his children with him, fearing the evil eyes; yet this man goes out to battle, and though he knows that he will be killed, he takes his sons with him and faces cheerfully the Attributes of Justice which is overtaking him."[29]

26. Josephus, *Ant.* 6.14.4.

27. *Lev. Rab.* 26:7. See also *Tanḥuma Emor* 2.

28. On the uncertainty of commentators on the Midrash concerning the five transgressions, see Mack, "Three Parables," 5:186 n28.

29. *Lev. Rab.* 26:7.

7

The Last Battle

SAUL'S LIFE WAS ONE of strife and emotion, and even his death overflowed with drama. There are three different accounts of Saul's death. Why we have three accounts and what message do they convey? Saul's death did not signal the end of Saul's dynasty. On the contrary, upon his death, his son, Ish-bosheth, became king. Like his father, Ish-bosheth, was involved in continuous wars with the house of David. Ish-bosheth was dependent on the goodwill and mercy of Abner, the army general. Later, Abner's change of allegiance sealed Ish-bosheth's fate. Ish-bosheth and Abner were both murdered. Was David behind these murders, and was David responsible for Saul's death as some scholars suggest? We will also look at the roll that David played in handing over Saul's seven descendants to the Gibeonites. They were killed because of alleged bloodguilt. Yet, David restored to Mephibosheth his estates, which belonged to his father Saul, as well as offering him a seat at the royal table. So what was behind these opposing gestures and what kind of message was the author trying to convey?

THE DEATH OF SAUL

Saul went to his last battle against the Philistines with the knowledge that he would die: "Tomorrow your sons and you will be with me" (1 Sam 28:19). According to the biblical description, the battle went horribly against Saul. The Vulgate has an interesting interpretation: "and the whole weight of the battle was directed against Saul." In other words, the Philistines noticed the King of Israel and directed their efforts to capture him. Since Saul was severely wounded by the archers he asked his arms bearer to kill him so he would not suffer disgrace at the hands of the Philistines. Radak points to the fact that the text does not suggest that the archers had hit Saul. According to Radak, Saul was in great anguish and distress since he could not escape from the Philistines. The weapon bearer refused to follow Saul's command to kill him because Saul was God's anointed. As a last resort, Saul took the sword and fell on it. In addition to Saul, his three sons and his arms bearer, all of Saul's men died on that day (1 Samuel 31). Interestingly, according to LXX^B Saul was wounded in the belly. In the description of the death of Saul and his sons the MT is similar to LXX^B but adds "indeed all his men" in the list of the slain so does the LXX^{al}.

A second version of the events is found in 2 Samuel 1. On reading the second version, we get the impression that the narrator wanted to remove any signs of heroism or glory from Saul's death. Accordingly, a young Amalekite arrived at David's camp with his clothes torn and dirt on his head. In ancient Israel those were typical signs of mourning, but it is not clear why an Amalekite, a foreigner, displays signs of mourning at the death of Saul. The Amalekite told David about the disastrous outcome of the battle against the Philistines on Mount Gilboa. Many of the troops had fallen and died, among them Saul, and his son, Jonathan. When David asked how he knew that Saul and Jonathan were dead, the Amalekite replied that his presence on the battlefield was accidental. However, in v. 2 we read that he came out of the camp. Evidently, he was attached to Saul's army as a soldier or a camp follower. The Amalekite reported that he saw Saul leaning on his spear. Ironically, it is the same spear with which Saul tried to smite David and Jonathan. It is also the spear that David took from Saul and returned to him. It is believed that Saul was leaning on the spear because he was wounded. Thus he was supporting himself. But this piece of information is for the reader to show the contrast between the stories. In the first account, Saul died by killing himself, and in this account, the Amalekite killed Saul. Ironically, King Saul, who spared the life of the Amalekite King Agag, is now killed by an Amalekite. As previously mentioned, in the first version Saul asked his arms bearer to kill him since he did not want to be killed by the Philistines, and in the second version he asked the Amalekite to kill him because he is in agony and barely alive. The young Amalekite is a foreigner like Doeg the Edomite, who killed the priest of Nob; evidently, the Amalekite was less bothered about killing the King of Israel. The account

The Last Battle

of the Amalekite arrival at David's camp bearing bad news, and of David's interrogating, displays a narrative pattern similar to that of the messenger's report to Eli regarding the Philistine victory at Ebenezer in 1 Sam 4:12–17.[1]

Radak and Ralbag (Rabbi Levi ben Gershom, also known as Gersonides 1248–1344) suggest that the Amalekite story can be combined with the account in 1 Sam 31:3–13 by claiming that Saul did not die after falling on his sword. Saul struggled to rise by leaning on the spear. The arms bearer rushed to a conclusion when he thought that Saul was dead. Alternatively, they accepted the view that the story of the young Amalekite was a fabrication because he wanted to be compensated by David. Modern scholars also share this view.[2]

In the second version, the spotlight is concentrated on David and his reaction to the death of Saul. The Amalekite expected to receive a reward from David, and therefore he brought David Saul's crown and armlet. Then David instructed one of his servants to kill the Amalekite after telling him: "Your blood be on your head! Your own mouth testified against you when you said, 'I put the Lord's anointed to death'" (2 Sam 1:16). David refers to the prohibition against killing the anointed one—the prohibition that prevented David from killing Saul. According to Zakovitch, it was important to the Davidic historian to present Saul's death in such a way that would diminish his glory, and would increase David's stature.[3] It is possible that David himself staged the whole act of Saul's death. Scholars interpreted the existence of the two versions as reflecting two sources. Therefore they assigned the first story to the Saulides and the second to the Davidides.[4]

Josephus tried to solve the discrepancy by reconciling the two accounts:

> As for himself, he fought with great bravery; and when he received so many wounds, that he was not able to bear up nor oppose any longer, and yet was not able to kill himself, he bade his armourbearer draw his sword, and run him through, before the enemy should take him alive. But this armour-bearer not daring to kill his master, he drew his own sword, and placing himself over against its point, he threw himself upon it; and when he could neither run it through him, nor, by leaning against it, make the sword pass through him, he turned him around, and asked a certain young

1. McCarter, *II Samuel*, 58.
2. Ward, "Story of David's Rise," 128–29; Grønbaek, *Die Geschichte*, 218–19; Amit, "שלוש ואריאציות," 97; Anderson, *2 Samuel*, 9–10.
3. Zakovitch, *David*, 67.
4. Amit, "שלוש ואריאציות," 94; McKenzie, *King David*, 104–5, 109.

God's First King

man that stood by who he was; and when he understood that he was an Amalekite, he desired him to force the sword through him, because he was not able to do it, with his own hands, and thereby to procure him such a death as he desired. This young man did accordingly; and he took the golden bracelet that was on Saul's arm, and his royal crown that was on his head, and ran away.[5]

Pseudo-Philo identified the Amalekite as the son of Agag: "And he came to slay him. And Saul said unto him: Before thou kill me, tell me, who art thou? And he said unto him: I am Edab, the son of Agag, king of the Amalekites. And Saul said: Behold, now the words of Samuel are come upon me even as he said: He that shall be born of Agag shall be an offense unto thee."[6]

The third account of Saul's death is found in 1 Chronicles 10. According to Amit, the Chronicler deviated from the parallel story in the book of Samuel in four instances:

1. In Samuel, the narrator stressed that the arms bearer died with Saul and all his people. This came to glorify the King, and to stress the tragedy of his the death with all his people. In contrast, the narrator of the book of Chronicles omits the fact that the arms barrier died with Saul. 2. The book of Chronicles states that: "Thus Saul and his three sons and his entire house died together" (1 Chr 10:6). In other words, the Chronicler stressed the fact that the house of Saul was completely destroyed thus leaving a vacuum and an immediate need to transfer the Kingship (1 Chr 10:14). 3. According to Chronicles, the Philistines impaled Saul's head in the temple of Dagan. This implies that the people of Jabesh buried Saul's headless body with his sons. This description diminishes the heroic actions of the people of Jabesh who removed the bodies of Saul and his sons from the wall of Beth-shan. This mocks Saul whose head was not buried with his body. 4. The book of Chronicles added: "Saul died for the trespass that he had committed against the Lord in not having fulfilled the command of the Lord; moreover, he had consulted a ghost to seek advice of the Lord; so He had him slain and the kingdom transferred to David son of Jesse (1 Chr 10:13–14). According to Chronicles, because of Saul's sins he was punished, and the kingship was transferred to David.[7]

Amit claims rightly that the discrepancies between the stories point to different editorial agendas. In the books of Samuel, the narrator did not want

---

5. Josephus, *Ant.* 6.14.7.
6. *L.A.B* 65.4.
7. Amit, "שלוש ואריאציות," 98.

The Last Battle

to hurt Saul's image. Therefore he describes his death as an end to a life full of struggles, heroism, and suffering. On the other hand, the writer of Chronicles used the story of Saul's death to justify the transfer of kingship from Saul to David. Saul and his household died for the trespass (*m'l*) that he had committed against the Lord by not having fulfilled (*šmr*) the command of the Lord. By using the root *m'l* the narrator reminds us of the Achan episode and creates an association with the story of Saul breaking the ban to destroy the Amalekites (1 Sam 15:3, 8–9, 16; 18:20–21). The verb *šmr* hints at Saul's behavior before the battle of Michmas: "You acted foolishly in not keeping (*šmr*) the commandments . . . because you did not abide (*šmr*) by what the Lord had commanded you" (1 Sam 13:13–14). In addition Saul consulted a ghost for advice, instead of seeking advice from God.[8]

Malul claims that even though David personally did not participate in the war between the Philistines and the Israelites, he was still responsible for the death of Saul and his sons.[9] He based his assumption on the confusing style of 1 Sam 31:3, where the word '*anašim* seems intrusive. He also points to the fact that the archers were not part of the Philistine army. And the Benjaminites were known as archers, and some of them are mentioned as part of David's army in Ziklag. Moreover, the word '*anašim* frequently appears with reference to David's followers. According to him, these people were a fifth column, close relatives of Saul, experts with the bow, who were responsible for Saul's death.

Brooks promoted a similar theory putting the blame on David. Positioning the army at the foot of the mountain was a good tactic, as it allowed Saul to retreat to the mountain. The Philistine chariots could not ascend the slope. However, it appears that the archers attacked Saul and his army from the rear. They were ambushed while retreating. Brooks believes that the archers were David and his men.[10] David and his troops secretly made their way back to Mount Gilboa. David divided them into two groups: the first group consisting of four hundred men returned to Ziklag, while the second group consisting of two hundred went with him to Gilboa.[11] They were behind the Israelite lines and waited for the right moment. When Saul was wounded, David and his warriors wanted to make sure that Saul was dead therefore they approached. At that moment, Saul recognized David, and knowing

8. Ibid, 99; Knoppers, "Israel's First King," 202–3.
9. Malul, "Was David," 517–45.
10. Brooks, *Saul*, 77.
11. Ibid., 113.

God's First King

that he was going to die, pleaded for his life. Brooks changes the order of the events; she transferred Saul's words from 1 Sam 24:22 to Saul's last battle.

The question arises, however: why didn't David kill Saul previously? He had the opportunity twice, and twice he declined. Also he could easily have ordered one of his subordinates to kill Saul (1 Sam 24:4–5; 26:8). Indeed, Abishai even offered to do so (v. 8). According to Brooks, it was safer for David to do it in the turmoil of battle because it would go unnoticed. It is unlikely that he went to war and waited for the right moment to kill Saul when he could have done it much earlier.

In 1 Sam 26:12 we read that when David and Abishai entered Saul's camp: "No one saw or knew or woke up; all remained asleep; a deep sleep from the Lord had fallen upon them."

Saul and three of his sons Jonathan, Abinadab, and Malchi-shua all died in this last battle (1 Sam 31:2, 6, 7, 8, 12). However, in 2 Sam 1:4, only Saul and his son Jonathan died. According to McCarter, the names and numbers of Saul's sons are in doubt.[12] After battling the Philistines with the men of Israel: "on the other side of the valley and on the side of the Jordan saw that the men of Israel had fled . . . they abandoned the towns and fled; the Philistines then came and occupied them" (1 Sam 31:7). With the death of Saul, the Philistines controlled areas north and east of the battlefield. "On the other side of the valley" was the territory north of the plain of Jezreel in the southern reaches of the Galilean hills. "Beyond the Jordan" was probably limited territory. Since Jabesh-gilead and Mahanaim were not included, the latter was the place where Ish-bosheth was made a king (2 Sam 2:8). Evidently, part of Saul's army managed to escape as the Philistines concentrated on capturing Saul. The central highlands to the south are not mentioned, this territory would remain disputed between the house of Saul and the followers of David. According to McKenzie, the location of the battle on mount Gilboa does not make sense historically. Why both armies went so far to fight, thus the setting of the battle seems fictional.[13] However, by capturing the Jezreel Valley the Philistines split the central tribes of Benjamin Ephraim, Mannaseh, and the tribes in the Galilee. Further, by penetrating as far as the Beth-shan Valley and the Jordan Valley they severed the main routes connecting the Israelite tribes on the east and west sides of the Jordan. Capturing the Jezreel Valley and Beth-shan Valley gave

---

12. McCarter, *II Samuel*, 58–59.
13. McKenzie, *King David*, 109.

The Last Battle

the Philistines control over the "Coastal Highway," an important link that connected Mesopotamia and Egypt.

ISH-BOSHETH

The Coronation of Ish-bosheth

Following the defeat on Mount Gilboa, we read about Saul's son, Ish-bosheth. He did not participate in the battle and became the new king. Abner the commander of Saul's army took him and made him king over Israel (2 Sam 2:8–12). The name Ish-bosheth means "Man of Shame."[14] According to Hertzberg, it is possible that the name was intended to denigrate Saul.[15] Here we sense the hand of the sympathetic Davidic author aiming to mock the house of Saul.

The coronation of Ish-bosheth signals the continuation of the war between the house of Saul and the house of David. The two rival camps were led by their military leaders; David's camp by Joab, and the house of Saul by Abner. Here the narrator seems to present an understated David. Evidently, the narrator wanted to remove any misgivings and any hint of bloodshed on David's part. The people of Israel probably suspected that David was involved in the death of Saul and his sons. David was a mercenary in the Philistine army when Saul was fighting against the Philistines. The forces of Achish of Gath, David's overlord, participated in the battle against Saul (1 Sam 29:1–2.). Following Saul's death and the death of his sons, the royal diadem and bracelet were in David's possession. As McCarter pointed out, David was the main beneficiary of Saul death, and the evidence pointed to his involvement. Thus, one of the aims of the author of the Davidic story was to remove any suspicion from David, while demonstrating David's legitimacy and claim to the throne.[16]

Ish-bosheth was crowned with the aid of military forces but without God's approval. He was not acclaimed by the people, and therefore lacked two important conditions for kingship.[17] Abner, the military leader for the house of Saul, demonstrated his loyalty to Saul. In spite of his power and

---

14. For different interpretation for the name Ish-bosheth see McCarter, *II Samuel*, 85–86.
15. Hertzberg, *I & II Samuel*, 249.
16. McCarter, *II Samuel*, 64.
17. Herrmann, *History of Israel*, 145.

God's First King

influence, he did not capture the kingship for himself, but transferred it to Ish-bosheth. In the ancient world people who were close to the royal court often rebelled against their kings and seized the power. This is not true of Abner who displays his loyalty to the house of Saul. Later, when he realized that David was the anointed one, Abner changed his allegiance.

The seat of the kingship was transferred to Mahanaim, the capital of Gilead after the victory of the Philistines at Mount Gilboa. The territory of Benjamin was too vulnerable to serve as the seat of government. The northern tribes of East Jordan were loyal to Saul even after his death. This new capital was far removed from the Philistine area of domination. It is also possible that the place was chosen because of its ancient tradition of holiness. This was the place where Jacob had encountered the angels of God (Gen 32:2–3). Later it became one of the Levitical cities in the territory of Gad (Josh 21:36; 1 Chr 6:65). David used this place as his temporary base during Absalom's revolt (2 Sam 17:24—19:8). Under Solomon, it served as the capital of District VII (1 Kgs 4:14).

As for Ish-bosheth's territory, we read that Abner "made him king over Gilead, the Ashurites, Jezreel, Ephraim, and Benjamin-over all Israel" (2 Sam 2:9). Gilead was the territory of the tribes of Gad and Reuben. The Ashurite territory is mentioned in the Targum as *dybt 'šr*, a place in Galilee, which includes the territory of Asher and Naphtali.[18] Jezreel refers to the valley that separated the Samarian hills from the Galilee. As McCarter points out, it is difficult to accept that after their defeat at Mount Gilboa, the Israelites controlled this entire region.[19] More likely it refers to a city or a district; it was the capital of the Israelite tribe of Issachar.[20] The hill country of Ephraim was home for the tribe of Ephraim and the tribe of Manasseh, and therefore the whole "House of Joseph."[21] As for Benjamin, which was Saul's own tribe, its territory was on the ridge of hills that ran between Jerusalem and Bethel. There is considerable difficulty with the description of his kingdom that states that he was King over all Israel (2 Sam 2:9). This evidently did not include Judah and Simeon. It is more likely that it represents Ish-bosheth's claim to rule all Israel even though he barely

---

18. The Syriac and Vulgate versions translated "the Geshurites," but this is unlikely. During this period it was an established kingdom where David took Maacah, the daughter of Talmai, king of Geshur, as his wife. See Soggin, "Reign of 'ešba'al," 41.

19. McCarter, *II Samuel*, 87.

20. Alt, *Essays on Old Testament*, 161.

21. Ibid.

The Last Battle

ruled his own tribe of Benjamin.[22] Readers will recall that Ish-bosheth's kingship followed the horrendous defeat at Mount Gilboa, and thus sounds more like wishful thinking. More so, examination of the geographical order shows that the author mentioned Gilead then the Galilee, then Jezreel, and finally Ephraim and Manasseh. This is the same geographical order that God showed Moses on the eve of his death: Gilead, Dan, Naphtali, Ephraim and Manasseh, and Judah (Deut 34:3–4).

Clashes with David

That Saul wanted to establish a dynasty is clear from his clashes with David and the events that followed his death. Evidently, the Israelite tribes agreed to Saul's dynasty since there is no recorded objection to the coronation of Ish-bosheth. According to Noth, the Israelites knew from their neighbors that monarchies were hereditary, and beside Saul's son there were no other candidates available.[23] In spite of the defeat at Mount Gilboa and the constant feuds that Saul had with Samuel and David, the people still remained loyal to Ish-bosheth. Most of the people did not desert Saul to support David. It is no surprise, therefore that the feuds between the followers of Saul and David lasted many years after Saul's death. Still, the fact that Ish-bosheth was accepted as a king did not guarantee complete loyalty. During his reign, a few people switched their allegiance to David (2 Sam 3:17–19).

Meanwhile, David had established his kingship at Hebron, the capital of the region. The Calebite clan was living in this territory. Clashes took place between Ish-bosheth's troops under Abner's command, and David's mercenaries under the leadership of Joab (2 Sam 2:12–16). According to Brooks, the skirmishes that she refers to as a "civil war"—were a reaction to David's involvement in the war and outcome of Gilboa.[24] We believe however, that David initiated these skirmishes in the Benjaminite territory. The goal for these encounters was to wipe out Ish-bosheth's power base in the territory of Benjamin.

As the war continued between the house of Saul and the house of David, the Bible describes a famous clash between the servants of Ish-bosheth and David. This occurred at the pool of Gibeon, where twelve warriors from

22. Bright, *History of Israel*, 191.
23. Ibid., 183; Thornton, "Charismatic Kingship," 1–11; Ottosson, *Gilead Tradition*, 200.
24. Brooks, *Saul and the Monarchy*, 142.

God's First King

each side fought against each other. The warriors are called young men *(ne'arîm)*, and, as Albright points out, the Hebrew word means "picked warrior."[25] The idea was to limit the number of casualties. However, this confrontation ended in a draw, as they all slaughtered each other. Because there was no proclaimed victor "a fierce battle ensued that day" (2 Sam 2:17). David did not participate in this battle or in the one that followed. Instead, Joab led his mercenaries. Evidently, the narrator wanted to remove David from the senseless bloodshed that took place. What was the reason for the clash between Ish-bosheth's servants and David's servants? It appears that David tried to extend his rule to the north of Judah. The battle took place in Benjaminite territory that was an integral part of Ish-bosheth's kingdom. Fensham, citing Korošec's work, pointed out that a Hittite king claimed to settle a dispute between himself and his predecessor by warfare.[26] The belief was that the gods decided the outcome of the ordeal, and thus the victor received the favor of the gods. Fensham claims that the same elements of divine will and legitimization of kingship are found in our narrative.[27] Although, the results of this battle were inconclusive, the ensuing battles favored David. Our text does not say that God was with David, but this was stressed several times (1 Sam 16:18; 18:14, 28; 2 Sam 5:10).

Ish-bosheth was the king of Israel for two years (2 Sam 2:10). The famous clash at Gibeon was recorded during this time (2 Sam 2:12–23). However, in 2 Sam 3:1 we read: "The war between the House of Saul and the House of David was long-drawn-out but David kept growing stronger while the House of Saul grew weaker."

At the same time, the Philistines closely monitored these clashes, but did not interfere. This is puzzling, especially after their great victory over Saul. However, David continued as their vassal, and was still obliged to render them military services.[28] The Philistines were practical. They allowed David to become king and to establish a separate Judean monarchy. David's actions served the Philistines' purpose because it split Israel in two and weakened it considerably. The people of Judah probably also welcomed David. He was one of them and he could protect them and mediate between them and the Philistines. Therefore he was anointed at the ancient shrine

---

25. Albright, "Seal of Eliakim," 82; Yadin, "Let The Young Men," 110–16.
26. Fensham, "Battle between," 356–57.
27. Ibid.
28. Noth, *History of Israel*, 183.

of Hebron.²⁹ Evidently, the Philistines hoped to maintain their control over the country by playing the kings against each other.

Only later, when David became King did the Philistines react: "When the Philistines heard that David had been anointed king over Israel, the Philistines marched up in search of David" (2 Sam 5:17). With the unification of Israel and Judah, the Philistines understood the danger that David could pose. The Philistines seized the valley of Rephaim, west of the city-state of Jerusalem with the intent to move southward through Bethlehem to Hebron, David's capital. Their aim was to defeat David and to prevent him from assembling the armies of Israel and Judah.

In addition to the long military war between the house of Saul and the house of David (2 Sam 3:1), David also used diplomacy to weaken Ish-bosheth. David entered into marriage with Maacah, daughter of Talmai, king of Geshur (2 Sam 3:3; 1 Chr 3:2). Marriages between royal houses were common in the ancient world. They helped to cement relations between countries and to promote treaties. David, and later his son Solomon, adopted this practice. David's marriage to the royal family was designed to work against the northern tribes loyal to Ish-bosheth. Thus David became the king's son-in-law, and gained another ally in his battle against Ish-bosheth. This union posed a threat to Ish-bosheth's claim to the Geshurite territory.³⁰ Geshur was located east of the Sea of Galilee close to Ish-bosheth's territory. It placed Ish-bosheth in an inferior strategic position because he was sandwiched between Geshur and Judah.

Another shrewd move by David was an appeal for the support of the people of Jabesh-gilead. David blessed the people of Jabesh-gilead for showing loyalty to Saul by burying him. Since the people of Jabesh were loyal to Saul, David wanted to have the same relationship that Saul had with them. It was one of the main cities of Gilead that belonged to Ish-bosheth's territory. David wished to eliminate any possibility of similar relations between Ish-bosheth and the people of Jabesh. Hillers points out that the Hebrew phrase used by David ('aśa ṭobah "and I too shall establish such a friendship with you") corresponds to the Akkadian ṭabuta epešu, which means "to make friendship by treaty." Hiller adds: "Since treaties did not automatically continue in force when a new king took the throne, it was necessary for David actively to seek a renewal of the pact."³¹ This is

---

29. Bright, *History of Israel*, 191.
30. Malamat, "Aspects of the Foreign Policies," 8.
31. Hillers, "Note on Some Treaty," 47.

God's First King

evident from David's statement: "Saul is dead and I am the king now." In other words, David now wants to assume Saul's place, and become suzerain of Jabesh-Gilead. It is possible at this time that David started to foster a friendship with Nahash, the king of the Ammonites (2 Sam 10:2). David's alliance with the Gehurites in the northern part of the Trans-Jordan, and his alliance with the Ammonites in the central part of the Trans-Jordan, shows his political shrewdness. David's alliances weakened Ish-bosheth, placing constant pressure on his territory.

During the war between the house of Saul and the house of David, Abner was gaining power in the house of Saul (2 Sam 3:1, 6). No detail is given about the war except continued references to strife between the houses of Saul and David, which made him more important and influential than even the king. This in turn led to a feud between Ish-bosheth and Abner. The king accused him of sleeping with Rizpah, daughter of Aia, who was Saul's former concubine. Sleeping with the king's concubine was a declaration that Abner wanted the throne. This custom is attested in the Hebrew Bible: "Absalom lay with his father's concubines, with the full knowledge of all Israel" (2 Sam 16:22). Similarly, after David died, Adonijah claimed his father's concubines to signal his right to succession. According to Tsevat, in Abner's case "the marriage of a former king's wife bestows legitimacy on an aspirant who otherwise has no sufficient claim to the throne."[32]

It is not clear if Abner really slept with the concubine as Ish-bosheth claimed.[33] The LXX^L adds *kai elaben autēn abennēr*, "and Abner took her," and another LXX MS *kai eisēlthen pros autēn abennēr*, "and Abner went in to her." We believe that it is unlikely that Abner, at this point, wanted to seize the kingship. It was Abner who installed Ish-bosheth as king because he was a loyal servant of the house of Saul. If Abner wanted the kingship it was his for the taking as Ish-bosheth was completely dependent on him.

Following Ish-bosheth's rebuke, Abner decided to transfer his allegiance to David. It was not the accusation of sleeping with Rizpah daughter of Aia behind his decision. We believe that the long war with the house of David, which weakened Ish-bosheth, was one of the realistic reasons. In addition, Abner claimed the elders of Israel wished for a long time to have David as king, and thus he insinuated dissatisfaction with Ish-bosheth's rule. Abner also acknowledged that David would deliver Israel from the hand of the Philistines as God's plan. Therefore his claim rested on divine election. Abner

---

32. Tsevat, "Marriage and Monarchical," 241.
33. See Soggin, "The Reign of ʾešbaʿal," 45 n22.

gave a twist to his selfish motivation, which might at first glance be perceived as a treacherous act, so he claimed to implement divine will. This was the beginning of the end for Ish-bosheth's kingship that concludes with his murder.

THE RETURN OF MICHAL

When Abner transferred his allegiance to David he also urged the elders of Israel to do so (2 Sam 3:12–21). Abner wanted to make sure he received a high position under David, and therefore he told David: "I will help you and bring all Israel over to your side" (2 Sam 3:12). Readers will recall that David's constant feuds with Saul were considered rebellious. Moreover, David joined the Philistines in Ziklag. Therefore it was believed he contributed to Saul's downfall. Accordingly, Abner took it upon himself to convince the people of Israel and Benjamin to view David favorably.

Once again we encounter David's political shrewdness. He set as a condition that Michal would be returned to him. This move had one purpose: to ensure his legitimacy to the throne. What is not clear, however, is the role that was played by Ish-bosheth, because the return of Michal meant the end of his rule. More so, the reunion of David and Michal contradicted biblical law: "her first husband, who sent her away, is not permitted to take her again to be his wife after she has been defiled; for that would be abhorrent to the Lord" (Deut 24:1–4). Ben-Barak points to a Mesopotamian code that can explain Michal's repeated marriage. According to her, when a husband is absent from the city by reason of *force majeure* he gives up his wife. The wife becomes a widow after a period of time and may remarry. When the first husband returns, he can reclaim her, and she must be returned to him. According to Ben-Barak, comparison of the Mesopotamian law and biblical narrative shows that identical principles were involved.[34] Upon his return, David, Michal's first husband, claimed her and received her in accordance with this law. This still contradicts the biblical law in Deuteronomy, where it states that the man sends his wife away at his own initiative and afterwards she marries another man. This is contrary to David's case. According to Ben-Barak, the law in Deuteronomy and Jeremiah were not yet in force during David's time.[35] It is noteworthy that David did not send Michal away (and divorce her). It is Saul who gave her to another

---

34. Ben-Barak, "Legal Background," 88.
35. Ibid., 90.

God's First King

man, thus legally she was still his wife and the law in Deuteronomy was not applicable here.

According to Ben-Barak, Ish-bosheth gave Michal to David because David's demand was based on basic law and contemporary customs of society. Not complying with David's demand would tarnish his reputation. He would be the king who undermined the legal foundation of society. He could also be portrayed as not caring about social order and lawfulness in his kingdom.[36] There is a simpler, more logical explanation for his actions. Ish-bosheth was an ineffectual, weak king; the real power was in Abner's hands. Following Abner's harsh response to Ish-bosheth's criticism, it is not surprising we read: "And he could not answer Abner another word, because he feared him" (2 Sam 3:11). The king was not in a position to reject the demand for transferring Michal. Ish-bosheth was realistic. His fear and knowledge that more and more people were siding with the house of David (2 Sam 3:17) prompted his consent. Thus, he was left without any alternative but to comply with the demand to return Michal.

Michal gained nothing by returning to David. She lost the most in this story. When she returned to David we are told that she returned without sons (2 Sam 3:15–16). Later we read: "the king took . . . the five sons that Michal daughter of Saul bore to Adriel son of Barzillai the Meholathite" (2 Sam 21:8). David gave those sons to the Gibeonites who hung them. A textual problem emerges here as the verse refers to Merab and not to Michal. This belief is based on the name of the husband Adriel son of Barzilla, the Meholathite. He was Merab's husband. According to Ben-Barak, the name of the husband is mistaken. It should be Platiel the son of Laish. She adds that "Paltiel" is the Hebrew name, while "Adriel" is the Aramaic name. Both names have the same meaning: "God is my savior." In light of Mesopotamian custom, Ben Barak suggests that Michal bore five sons to her second husband. When she returned to David they remained with their father. Therefore, later in 2 Sam 6:23, we read that Michal has no sons.[37] While, according to the Talmud, Michal reared five boys who were orphans therefore they were called by her name.[38] What lies behind David's demand for Michal was his desire to get the daughter of the former king, not regain

---

36. Ibid., 88.
37. Ibid., 87.
38. *Sanh.* 19b.

The Last Battle

his beloved wife. In other words, David could make sure that Michal would not bear a child to claim the throne after David's death.[39]

For Abner, the condition that David set, the return of Michal meant one thing—the final break with Ish-bosheth together with the transfer of his allegiance to David. Abner agreed to these conditions, but the plan never came to fruition because Abner was murdered at the gate of Hebron on his return from his meeting with David. The plan to transfer Michal backfired; Abner was murdered, as was Ish-bosheth, making David emerge victorious.

THE MURDERS OF ABNER AND ISH-BOSHETH

It seems Joab murdered Abner in vengeance for the murder of his younger brother. There are other motivations to consider as well, such as jealousy and fear of the developing connection between Abner and David. During the secret negotiations between David and Abner, we know that Abner promised to deliver Michal, but what was he to receive in exchange? We believe that Abner offered David his allegiance, and in exchange for that, Abner would become the commander-in-chief of David's army, a post held by Joab. Indeed a similar view is held by Josephus who said that Joab was afraid:

> and that he should himself be put lower, and be deprived of the command of the army; so he took a knavish and a wicked course . . . and but as the truth was, out of his fear of losing his command of the army, and his dignity with the king, and lest he should be deprived of those advantages, and Abner should obtain the first rank in David's court. By these examples any one may learn how many and how great instances of wickedness men will venture upon for the sake of getting money and authority, and that they may not fail of either of them.[40]

David protested his innocence at Abner's funeral: "Both I and my kingdom are forever innocent before the Lord of shedding the blood of Abner son of Ner" (2 Sam 3:28). The language used by David at the funeral sounds like a public declaration of innocence. As he lamented him, David arranged for Abner's burial in Hebron with honors. In the Talmud, we read that David followed the bier because: "This was done only to placate the people. By publicly demonstrating his distress, David sought to show the

39. McKenzie, *King David*, 137; Brooks, *Saul*, 156.
40. Josephus, *Ant.* 7.1.5.

God's First King

people that he was not responsible for Abner's death."[41] It was done in order to preserve peace in the kingdom and to prevent rebellion by those still loyal to Abner. In order to remove suspicion from David, the author of Samuel mentions thrice that Abner left David *unharmed,* in other words, he left him on good terms (vv. 21-23).

The murder of Abner occurred in Hebron, and, as King of Judah, David was responsible for murders that took place in his capital. Therefore David cursed Joab and his father's house for this murder. In the negotiation between Abner and David twenty men accompanied Abner to serve as witnesses. The feast that is mentioned probably refers to the covenant rite. As McCarthy points out, Abner eats at the royal table that is possibly part of the covenant rite, and he departs in *peace,* a covenant word.[42] By killing Abner, Joab broke the alleged covenant and indirectly blamed David. Therefore, David used harsh language in cursing Joab and his house.

Noth believes that it is not likely that David wanted Abner killed. By murdering Abner he would lose the sympathy of many people who were important for the next stage of his career.[43] Noth points out that in 2 Sam 3:37 the writer stated with satisfaction: "That day all the troops and all Israel knew that it was not by the king's will that Abner son of Ner was killed." But this verse in particular casts doubt on David, and it appears there was probably talk, rumors that linked David to the murder of Abner. The Dtr had to insert this verse in order to remove any suspicion from David.

During this period Abner protected Saul's dynasty, and thus David could not fully trust him. David probably promised Abner the leadership of the army. According to Vanderkam, this promise made Abner dangerous if in the future he decided to break his ties with David.[44] David was also aware of the feud that existed between Abner and Joab because he killed the latter's brother, Asahel (2 Sam 2:18-23). He knew that Joab and Abner could not coexist, especially if Abner was promoted over Joab. David negotiated with Abner, but without good intentions. His plan was to lure him in, and then let Joab kill him.[45] Were Joab to kill Abner, one more obstacle in David's march to the throne would be removed.[46] Also his public im-

41. *Sanh.* 20a.
42. McCarthy, "Compact and Kingship," 79.
43. Noth, *History of Israel,* 185.
44. Vanderkam, "Davidic Complicity," 532.
45. Ibid.
46. Brooks, *Saul,* 156-57.

The Last Battle

age would not be tarnished, since Joab would be the murderer. Indeed, at Abner's funeral, David placed the responsibility for the murder on Joab and his family, whom he cursed (2 Sam 3:29). Yet he does not punish them, claiming that although he is the king, he is too weak to do so (2 Sam 3:39). Thus David allowed Joab's crime to go unpunished. Joab was David's right hand man, and David depended on him. He was not sure whether the army would support him if he took action against Joab.

With the murder of Abner, Ish-bosheth was left without power. Hearing the news of the murder we read that "he lost heart"—literally, his hands weakened. Ish-bosheth was murdered in Mahanaim while sleeping during the heat of the day. The two soldiers who murdered him were Rechab and his brother Baanah from Beeroth. Most scholars believe that the inhabitants of Beeroth were forced to leave the city due to their feud with King Saul. The inhabitants of Beeroth thus seized the moment to take revenge on the son of Saul.[47] Alternatively, McCarter points out that the soldiers were Benjaminites, not indigenous Beerothites, and they were officers in Ish-bosheth's army. According to him, they did not act out of revenge, but because of opportunity with the hope of receiving a reward from David.[48] Similarly we read in Josephus:

> ... but was treacherously set upon by the sons of Rimmon, (Baanah and Rechab were their names) and was slain by them; for these being of a family of the Benjamites and of the first rank among them, thought that if they should slay Ishbosheth, they should obtain large presents from David, and be made commanders by him, or, however, should have some other trust committed to them.[49]

The two soldiers brought Ish-bosheth's head to David, expecting praise and reward. According to Vanderkam, here too one may infer that David was behind the murder of Ish-bosheth. But according to him, the brief description does not allow us to conclude that David arranged Ish-bosheth's assassination.[50] In contrast, Halpern points out that the killers are Gibeonites who were David's allies. According to him, "chances are, David commissioned the hit."[51] It is true that this suited David quite well but the

---

47. Noth, *The History of Israel*, 186; Soggin, "Reign of 'ešba'al," 47; Blenkinsopp, *Gibeon*, 36.
48. McCarter, *II Samuel*, 128.
49. Josephus, *Ant.* 7.2.1.
50. Vanderkam, "Davidic Complicity," 534.
51. Halpern, *David's Secret Demons*, 82.

arrival in Hebron of the two murderers bearing Ish-bosheth's head embarrassed David. The murder of Abner had already raised suspicions, and now Ish-bosheth's murder made it appear that David was trying to reach the throne through murder. This could tarnish his image, and so, acting immediately, he ordered both men killed at once in the most severe manner.

David reacted here as he had reacted previously with the Amalekite youth (2 Sam 1:13-16). He ordered the two soldiers killed by hanging, but only after their hands and feet had been cut off. He then ordered the burial of Ish-bosheth's head in Abner's tomb in Hebron. We should point out that when David spoke about the murder of Ish-bosheth he referred to him as an innocent man, not Ish-bosheth the king. This contrasts with his father Saul, whom David called the "Lord's anointed." In other words, he is not describing him as "Yahweh's anointed" or even as king. Evidently, David did not recognize his kingship. Therefore Mabee says: "the crime is not regicide."[52] Ish-bosheth, like his father Saul, was decapitated. In both stories, David punished the murderers. David eulogized Saul, Ish-boshet, and Abner. The author wanted to portray David's acts as righteous by avenging the murders and dealing kindly with the dead.

MEPHIBOSHETH AND SAUL'S REMAINING DESCENDANTS

With the deaths of Saul and Ish-bosheth there was no king in Israel. The path to the throne lay open. Saul's only male descendant was a handicapped son of Jonathan named Mephibosheth, who was unfit to rule. Hertzberg translated the name as "from the mouth of the God of shame."[53] As with Ish-bosheth, the sympathetic Davidic author continued his mockery of the house of Saul by employing derogatory names for Saul's descendants.

Mephibosheth first appears in the middle of the tale of the murder of Ish-bosheth (2 Sam 4:4). Veijola claims that passages mentioning Mephibosheth as Jonathan's son (2 Sam 4:4; 9:3, 6, 7; 21:7) are not authentic. He sees them as an attempt by the redactor to stress David's loyalty to Jonathan.[54] According to him, v. 4 would be more fitting after the account of Ish-bosheth's murder.[55] McCarter views the introduction of Mephibosheth

52. Mabee, "David's Judicial Exoneration," 104.
53. Hertzberg, *I & II Samuel*, 264.
54. Veijola, "David und Meribaal," 352.
55. Ibid., 345.

The Last Battle

at this point as meaningless adding that it interrupts the flow of the narrative unnecessarily.[56] However, as Rashi points out this information appears in the right place: "And Jonathan the son of Saul—the scriptures goes on to recount how the kingdom was taken away from the house of Saul. He and his sons were killed. This one remaining son was killed in bed, and Jonathan's son fell and became lame (hence unfit for the throne)."

The Bible describes Ish-Bosheth's hands as becoming feeble while Mephibosheth was lame. This stresses the infirmities of Saul's descendants, and that there was no suitable heir to the throne. Therefore, following the murder of Ish-Bosheth, the elders of Israel came to David in Hebron and offered him the kingship. David made a covenant with them and he was anointed King. The elders of Israel completed what Abner had started, the transfer of the kingship to David.

The rest of Saul's descendants were killed because of alleged bloodguilt. Saul killed the Gibeonites, and by doing so he violated the treaty with them, which was followed by a famine in the land for three years (2 Sam 21:1–2). The famine could only end if the responsible party was put to death for breaking the oath. This is the only mention of Saul slaughtering the Gibeonites in the Bible. But, as noted above, we believe that Saul expelled the Gibeonites from their land, killing them in order to support his own army. Like many other Israelites, David knew about it and used this in his war against Saul. By claiming to seek justice, David, with the aid of the Gibeonites, removed Saul's family without incurring the bloodguilt himself. In ancient times, it was common practice to eliminate the males of the previous royal family (Judg 9:5; 2 Kgs 10:1–11).[57] David's interests were well served by eliminating the members of Saul's house, and helped secure his position as a king.[58]

Scholars have debated the nature of the covenant between the Israelites and the Gibeonites. Malamat points out parallels to Hittite treaties, but as Whitelam explains there is a "problem of transference of a particular treaty between different political entities."[59] The treaty between the Israelites and Gibeonites in Josh 9 did not form the basis for a claim against the house of Saul. The Gibeonites rejected monetary compensation as reparation. They

---

56. McCarter, *II Samuel*, 128.
57. Whitelam, *Just King*, 113.
58. Mauchline, *1 & 2 Samuel*, 303; Ishida, *Royal Dynasties*, 179.
59. Whitelam, *Just King*, 117; Malamat, "Doctrines of Causality," 1–12.

God's First King

also acknowledged that the option to put to death any man in Israel was not open to them. The only person who could settle their grievance was David.

Scholars point out that the episode of the Gibeonites does not appear in the right chronological order, that is, it does not have a link to what precedes it nor what follows it. Indeed, Ehrlich raises the question why the sons of Saul were punished at the end of David's regime? Moreover, the question that David posed "is there still anyone left of the house of Saul?" and Shimei's accusation in 16:7-8 seem to presuppose 21:1-14 and therefore precedes chapter 9.[60]

Many commentators recognize the connection between chapters 21 and 9. McCarter, for example, suggests Deuteronomistic editing separated chapter 21 from its natural sequel in chapter 9, and transferred it to the materials at the end of David's reign.[61] In contrast, Gunn suggested that chapter 9 is a sequel to chapters 2-4 and not 21:1-14.[62] However, as Brooks suggests, it is more likely that chapter 21:1-14 in addition to 9:1, belong after chapter 4. According to Brooks, the redactor wanted to remove our story about the feuds between David and the house of Saul. In addition, she believes that we have "David attempt to make sure that his successor would be derived from 'David's body' (2 Sam 7:12)."[63] There was growing suspicion regarding David's involvement in the death of Saul, Abner, and Ish-bosheth. Removal of Saul's sons would serve David's political needs. Again, it might have caused increased mistrust among the people. To eliminate growing doubts, the redactor transplanted the story, placing it at the end of David's reign.

David, as we have stressed, was a shrewd politician with the ability to manipulate situations to his advantage. At first the Gibeonites said they had no intentions of killing anyone in Israel: "We have no claim on the life of any other man in Israel" (2 Sam 21:4). In response David repeated his words from v. 3 "What shall I do for you? But this time in v. 4 David adds the words: "Whatever you say I will do for you" (2 Sam 21:4). In other words, David encourages the Gibeonites to tell him explicitly what they want, and he promises to fulfill their request.

The Gibeonites' answer can be divided into two parts. First, they mention Saul's sin (v. 5), and then they mention the suitable punishment by asking for the seven sons of Saul (v. 6). At first they speak about their own massacre,

60. Ehrlich, *Mikrâ Ki-Pheschutô*, 247; Anderson, *2 Samuel*, 247-48.
61. McCarter, *II Samuel*, 263, 443.
62. Gunn, *Story of King David*, 68.
63. Brooks, *Saul*, 59.

The Last Battle

and in the second part they speak about their desire to massacre the sons of Saul. It may be worth noting that the Gibeonites did not mention Saul by name, and referring merely to "the man," thereby expressing their hatred towards him. The Gibeonites asked for the seven sons of Saul, seven being a number that symbolizes completeness. We might have a hint to the oath that was broken by Saul, with the word play with seven (šeba') and oath (š^ebu'â).[64]

David took two sons of Rizpah, daughter of Aiah, and five sons of Michal, and handed them over to the Gibeonites. The Gibeonites hung them. David acts as a just King. If indeed this was the case, it raises the question about his failure to exercise his authority, and failure to bring Joab to justice for the murder of Abner. In addition to murder, Joab also violated the covenant between the king and Abner. David's failure to act meant that bloodguilt was attached to the house of David (1 Kgs 11:5–6).[65] However, as we mentioned, he did not kill Joab because he probably acted on his behalf in the murder of Abner. Similarly, it was the Gibeonites, not David, who killed the sons of Saul. The murders of Abner and the sons of Saul served David's agenda, which was to eliminate the house of Saul and to strengthen the house of David. David knew of the antagonism between the house of Saul and the Gibeonites, and giving them Saul's sons he not only eradicated a potential threat, but also gained another ally against the house of Saul.

The story about Mephibosheth probably followed the episode about the Gibeonites. Since, as we mentioned before, David asked: "Is there anyone still left of the House of Saul with whom I can keep faith for the sake of Jonathan" (2 Sam 9:1). Evidently, Mephibosheth's life was spared because of his physical disability. However, the narrator states that it was because of David's friendship with Jonathan, and the fulfillment of his covenant with Jonathan.[66] Therefore, those estates that belonged to Saul were restored to Mephibosheth, and David offered him a seat at the royal table. Normally this would be considered an honor, but this was another calculated move by David. David wanted to watch Mephibosheth, scout his activities, and this made him a "royal prisoner" in Jerusalem.[67] Mephibosheth was probably fearful in light of the slaughter of Saul's seven sons, because surviving members of an overthrown royal house were usually killed (1 Kgs 15:29; 16:11; 2 Kgs 10:6–7).

---

64. Bar-Efrat, *II Samuel*, 230.
65. Whitelam, *Just King*, 119.
66. Ibid., 146.
67. Miller and Hayes, *History*, 175.

God's First King

The story about Mephibosheth is interrupted again and will reappear later. Ziba, a former servant of the house of Saul and keeper of Mephibosheth's estates, told David that during the uprising against him that his master remained in Jerusalem hoping he would regain his father's kingship (2 Sam 16:3). Based on this testimony and without further examination, David took the estates from Mephibosheth and gave them to Ziba. His actions echo Samuel's words: "He will seize your choice fields, vineyards, and olive groves, and give them to his courtiers" (1 Sam 8:14). It is true that people who rebelled against the king lost their lands, but David passed judgment here without hearing Mephibosheth's version. Only after meeting with David, and telling him that Ziba's accusations were false, did David decide to the divide the land between Ziba and Mephibosheth. However, David did not fully change his deed, since only half of the estate was returned to Mephibosheth. In the Talmud, we find that David was severely punished for this act: "The moment David stated to Mephibosheth that he and Ziba divide the field, a heavenly voice came forth and announced 'Rehoboam and Jeroboam shall divide the kingdom.'"[68]

We also find a debate between Rav and Samuel in the Talmud regarding whose version of the story was true, that of Ziba's or Mephibosheth's.[69] Both Rav and Samuel agree that Mephibosheth's account was correct, yet they debated whether David deserved punishment for believing slander. According to Rav, David was held accountable for not investigating the subject before accepting Ziba's story, while according to Samuel, David could not be blamed for being suspicious of Mephibosheth's loyalty to him.

David's decision in Mephibosheth's case and his pardon of Shimei son of Gera raises some questions as to his inconsistencies in passing judgment. He pardons the blasphemous Shimei while failing to pardon the loyal Mephibosheth. Shimei's insults of David: "Get out, get out, you criminal, you villain!" (2 Sam 16:8); show his resentment and animosity. Shimei blames David for the killing of Saul's descendants, and toppling Saul's dynasty. There were probably many people among the Benjamnites who did not approve of David's kingship. They were willing to join the rebellion against David that was led by his own son Absalom. With the failure of Absalom, they were hoping they would anoint a descendant of the house of Saul. Indeed, Sheba son of Bichri, a Benjaminite, expressed those thoughts: "We have no portion in David, No share in Jesse's son! Every man to his tent,

68. *Sabb.* 56b.
69. Ibid.

The Last Battle

O Israel!" (2 Sam 20:1). Mephibosheth was aware of the wishes of his own tribesmen the Benjaminites, and their disapproval of David. He himself did not forgive David for killing the sons of Saul, and his sarcastic words to David allude to this: "For all the members of my father's family deserved only death from my lord the king" (2 Sam 19:29).

In conclusion there are three accounts of Saul's death. In the first, the narrator glorifies the death of Saul. In the second, the narrator removed any signs of heroism or glory from Saul's death, and instead plays up David, and his reaction to the death of Saul. The idea was to denigrate Saul's death, thus increasing David stature. In the third account, the Chronicler uses the story of Saul's death to justify the transfer of kingship from Saul to David. Saul and his household died for not having fulfilled the command of the Lord.

Following Saul's death, Ish-bosheth became the king of Israel. His reign was characterized by constant battles with the increasingly powerful house of David. Through long war and diplomacy, David weakened Ish-bosheth's power base. David's alliance through marriage with the Gehurites in the northern part of the Trans-Jordan, and his alliance with the Ammonites in the central part of the Trans-Jordan, created constant pressure on Ish-bosheth.

Following Abner's change of allegiance, David demanded the return of Michal; this was to bolster David's legitimacy. It is unlikely that David was behind the death of Saul as some scholars posit, since he could have accomplished this much earlier. Yet, he was behind the death of Abner and Ish-bosheth. On three different occasions, David eulogizes Saul, Ish-bosheth, and Abner. The sense is that the author wanted to whitewash David's actions, and to show that David acted righteously by avenging the murders and dealing kindly with the dead. David also kept his oath to Jonathan. Therefore, it appears he dealt righteously with Mephibosheth, but evidently he kept a close eye on him too. In contrast to Saul who broke the treaty between the Israelites and Gibeonites, David is portrayed as seeking justice on their behalf. David handed the seven sons of Saul to the Gibeonites in order to end the famine. In realty, this act served David well since it removed further legitimate claimants to the throne without incurring bloodguilt. The message it conveys is that David was the legitimate king of Israel meaning he is a righteous person in contrast to the sinful house of Saul.

8

Conclusion

Like the name 'Saul,' which in Hebrew means "the one asked for, or requested," Saul was indeed requested to lay the foundation for the monarchy in Israel. It was Saul who was the first architect of the Israelite monarchy. It was he who set the groundwork for David and the kings that followed. Saul became the first king of Israel since the Israelite leadership could not deal effectively with the Philistine and Ammonite threats. There were, however, other compelling reasons for changes such as moral decline as well as the socioeconomic developments in the Israelite society.

In his capacity as the first king of Israel Saul fought many wars. His goal was to remove the presence of the enemies to protect Israelite territories and to unite the Israelite tribes around his kingdom. In the east, in the Trans-Jordan he fought against the Ammonites, Moabites, Edomites, and the kings of Zobah. In so doing, he expanded the border of his young monarchy. In addition he incorporated the Israelite tribes from the east to his kingdom. In the south, he fought against the Amalekites who raided the territory of Judah; this victory against them added important allies to his kingship, the tribe of Judah. The main foes were the Philistines against whom he fought three major battles and had many skirmishes. The outcome was that he removed their presence from the central hill mountain area. He liberated the land of Judah, thus creating a new reality where he linked his kingdom to Hebron and the northern Negev. This cemented his ties with the tribe of Judah. Saul also tried to create a new reality in the north; but he lost his last battle against the Philistines. Therefore the Philistines again controlled the land of Israel. The only gain that was left from

Conclusion

all of Saul's wars was the territory in the Trans-Jordan where his son was crowned as king after his death.

In chapters 9–15 Saul is presented as shy and modest displaying military strength by defending his people. The description of Saul in 1 Samuel 16–31 is unflattering, we see a king who is capricious, moody, and who constantly tries to kill David. He makes promises swearing by the name of God, but in the end it does no good. On the other hand, David is a loyal servant who comes to the king's aid when he plays the lyre to relieve him from his spells. He fights the king's wars and succeeds. In addition to his fights with David, Saul also quarrels with everyone that surrounds him, this includes his son Jonathan his daughters Merab and Michal, his courtiers and military heroes, and the prophet Samuel. As we pointed out, however, there was exaggeration in these unflattering descriptions of Saul. Moreover, Saul had many good reasons for his unseemly, mad behavior. Saul understood David's intentions very well. He was not naïve, and he realized that David had one important goal, to capture the kingship. Therefore, not surprisingly, he was angry at his inner circle, which included his son Jonathan, who gave up the kingship. Saul wanted his son Jonathan to be his heir to the throne. We believe that it was the hand of a sympathetic author from the Davidic circle that was responsible for all the negativity surrounding Saul's portrayal. The aim was to depict an unstable king who fails in all his relationships, while, on the other hand, David is loved by all Israel and Judah.

Like many other kings in the ancient world, Saul was also a builder. Among his achievements we find the building of a capital city at Gibeath Benjamin, which later he named after himself. In his capacity as a king he established a court that included officials and functionaries. While building the capital Saul also established a cultic center at Nob. Evidently, Saul was a religious leader who fought against idolatry. Ironically Saul, who exterminated the use of ghosts and familiar spirit and fought against idolatry, found himself needing the services of a medium. Saul is the first king who created a standing army in Israel. Saul introduced new weapons and protective gear for his new army. Saul was the first king in Israel who levied taxes in order to finance the building of the capital, the cultic center, as well as the maintenance of the administrative court and the standing army.

The hand of the sympathetic author from the Davidic circle responsible for all the negativity that surrounded Saul is also found in the description of Saul's death. All the elements of heroism and glorification of Saul, which are found in the first version, are omitted. Instead in the second

God's First King

version the narrator highlighted David and his reaction to the death of Saul. In the third version, which is found in the book of Chronicles, the author used the story to justify the transfer of kingship from Saul to David. Saul and his household died for the sins that he had committed against the Lord.

Following the death of Saul, Ish-bosheth became the king of Israel. His period is characterized by continuous battles with the house of David. There was a long military war and with diplomacy, David weakened the power base of Ish-bosheth. In the end, Ish-bosheth was murdered and so was his military chief Abner. The fact that Saul died in a war and Ish-bosheth and Abner were murdered caused suspicion about David's involvement in their deaths. Therefore, to remove this suspicion David eulogizes Saul, Ish-bosheth, and Abner. The sense is that the author wanted to remove any wrongdoing on David's part, thereby conveying that David acted righteously by avenging the murders and in turn dealt kindly with the dead. We can see that from chapter 16 to the end of First Samuel was written by a sympathetic author to the house of David. The author's objective was to glorify and praise David while portraying Saul in a negative light. David is the legitimate king of Israel. He is a righteous person in contrast to the sinful house of Saul. It was only in the book of Esther that the house of Saul was redeemed from its disgraced image. There we read about a Jew by the name of Mordecai son of Jair son of Shimei son of Kish, a Benjaminite who at the end of the story ranked next to the king. Evidently, the negativity towards Saul and the reason for why he lost his kingship troubled the sages. Thus, in spite of their criticism of Saul the sages asked why the monarchy of the house of Saul did not endure because there was no flaw in his family's lineage. Thus Rabbi Shimon ben Yehotzadak explains: "We do not appoint a leader over the community unless he has a box of creeping creatures hanging behind him, so that if he becomes arrogant, we can say to him: 'Turn around and see what is behind you.'"[1]

---

1. *Yoma* 22b.

Bibliography

Abramski, S. "שאול ודוד הנרדפים." *BethM* 100 (1985) 48–68.
Ackroyd, P. R. *The First Book of Samuel*. Cambridge Bible Commentary. Cambridge: Cambridge University Press, 1971.
Albright, W. F. *Excavation and Results at Tell el-Ful (Gibeah of Saul)*. Annual of the American Schools of Oriental Research 4. New Haven: Yale University Press, 1924.
———. "A New Campaign of Excavation at Gibeah of Saul." *BASOR* 52 (1933) 6–12.
———. *The Biblical Period from Abraham to Ezra*. New York: Harper &Row, 1963.
———. "The Seal of Eliakim and the Latest Preëxilic History of Judah with Some Observation on Ezekiel." *JBL* 51 (1932) 77–106.
Alt, A. *Kleine Schriften zur Geschichte des Volkes Israel*. 3 vols. Munich: Beck, 1953–59.
———. "The Formation of the Israelite State in Palestine." In *Essays on Old Testament History and Religion*, 173–237. Translated by R. A. Wilson. Oxford: Blackwell, 1966.
Alter, R. *The Art of Biblical Narrative*. New York: Basic Books, 1981.
———. *The David Story: A Translation with Commentary on 1 and 2 Samuel*. London: Norton, 1999.
Amit, Y. "שלוש ואריאציות על מות שאול." *BethM* 100 (1985) 92–102 (Hebrew).
———. *Reading Biblical Narratives: Literary Criticism and the Hebrew Bible*. Translated by Y. Lotan. Minneapolis: Fortress, 2001.
Anderson, A. A. *2 Samuel*. WBC 11. Waco, TX: Word, 1989.
Arnold, B. T. "Necromancy and Cleromancy in 1 and 2 Samuel." *CBQ* 66 (2004) 199–213.
Arnold, P. M. *Gibeah: The Search for a Biblical City*. JSOTSup 79. Sheffield: JSOT Press, 1990.
Aster, S. Z. "What was Doeg the Edomite's Title? Textual Emendation versus Comparative Approach to 1 Samuel 21:8." *JBL* 122 (2003) 353–61.
Bar-Efrat, S. *I Samuel: Introduction and Commentary*. Jerusalem: Magnes, 1990 (Hebrew).
———. *II Samuel*. Tel Aviv: Am Oved, 1996 (Hebrew).
Bartal, A. *Saul's Kingship*. Tel Aviv: Hakibbutz Hameuchad, 1982 (Hebrew).
Ben-Barak, Z. "Meribaal and the System of Land Grants in Ancient Israel." *Bib* 62 (1981) 73–91.
———. "The Legal Background to the Restoration of Michal to David." In *Telling Queen Michal's Story*, edited by D. J. A. Clines and T. C. Eskenazi, 74–90. JSOTSup 119. Sheffield: JSOT Press, 1991.
Birch, B. C. "The Development of the Tradition of the Anointing of Saul in I Sam 9:1–10:16." *JBL* 90 (1971) 55–68.

Bibliography

———. "The First and Second Books of Samuel: Introduction, Commentary, and Reflections." In *The New Interpreter's Bible*, edited by L. E. Keck et al., 2:947–1383. Nashville: Abingdon, 1998.

———. *The Rise of the Israelite Monarchy: The Growth and Development of I Samuel 7–15*. SBLDS 27. Missoula, MT: Scholars, 1976.

Blenkinsopp, J. "Did Saul Make Gibeon His Capital?" *VT* 24 (1974) 1–7.

Braun, R. *1 Chronicles*. WBC 14. Waco, TX: Word, 1986.

Bright, J. *A History of Israel*. 3rd ed. Philadelphia: Westminster, 1981.

Brooks, S. S. *Saul and the Monarchy: A New Look*. Society for Old Testament Study Series. Burlington, VT: Ashgate, 2005.

Brueggemann, W. *First and Second Samuel*. Interpretation. Louisville: Westminster John Knox, 1990.

Bryce, T. *The Kingdom of the Hittites*. Oxford: Clarendon, 1998. 2nd ed., 2005.

Budde, K. *Die Bücher Richter und Samuel, ihre Quellen und ihr Aufbau*. Giessen: Ricker, 1890.

———. *Die Bücher Samuel*. Kurzer Hand-Commentar zum Alten Testament 8. Tübingen: Mohr/Siebeck, 1902.

Burney, C. F. *The Book of Judges*. New York: Ktav, 1970.

Caquot, A., and R. du Mensil du Buisson. "La second tablette ou 'petite amulette' d'Arslan Tash." *Syria* 48 (1971) 391–406.

Chaney, M. L. "Systemic Study of the Israelite Monarchy." *Semia* 37 (1986) 53–76.

Clines, D. J .A. "X, X Ben Y, Ben Y: Personal Names in Hebrew Narrative Style." *VT* 22 (1972) 266–87.

Cohen, H. R. *Biblical hapax legomena in Light of Akkadian and Ugaritic*. SBLDS 37. Missoula, MT: Scholars, 1978.

Cohen, R. "The Fortress King Solomon Built to Protect His Southern Border." *BAR* 11 (1985) 56–70.

Cross, F. M. "The Ammonite Oppression of the Tribes of Gad and Reuben: Missing Verses from 1 Samuel 11 found in 4QSamuel[a]." In *History, Historiography and Interpretation*, edited by H. Tadmor and M. Weinfeld, 148–58. Jerusalem: Magness, 1984.

Daube, D. *The New Testament and Rabbinic Judaism*. London: Athlone, 1956.

Demsky, A. "The Genealogy of Gibeon (1 Chronicles 9:35–44): Biblical and Epigraphic Considerations." *BASOR* 202 (1971) 16–23.

———. "Geba, Gibeah, and Gibeon-An Historical-Geographic Riddle." *BASOR* 212 (1973) 26–31.

Donner, H. "Basic Elements of the Old Testament Historiography Illustrated by the Saul Traditions." *OTWSA* 24 (1981) 40–54.

Douglas, J. D., and N. Hillyer, editors. *The Illustrated Bible Dictionary*. Leicester, UK: InterVarsity, 1980.

Driver, S. R. *Notes on the Hebrew Text and Topography of the Books of Samuel*. 2nd ed. 1913. Reprinted, Winona Lake, IN: Alpha, 1984.

Edelman, D. V. "Saul." In *ABD* 5 (1992) 989–999.

———. "Saul's Rescue of Jabesh-Gilead (I Samuel 11:1–11): Sorting Story from History." *ZAW* 96 (1984) 195–209.

———. *King Saul in the Historiography of Judah*. JSOTSup 121. Sheffield: Sheffield Academic, 1991.

———. "Did Saulide-Davidic Rivalry Resurface in Early-Persian Yehud?" In *The Land that I Will Show You: Essays on the History and Archaeology of the Ancient Near East*

in Honor of J.Maxwell Miller, edited by J. A. Dearman and M. P. Graham, 69-91. JSOTSup 343. Sheffield: Sheffield Academic, 2001.
Edenburg, C. "How (Not) to Murder a King: Variations on a Theme in I Samuel 24; 26." *SJOT* 12 (1998) 64-85.
Ehrlich, A. B. *Mikrâ Ki-Pheschutô*. New York: Ktav, 1969.
Eissfeldt, O. *Die Komposition der Samuelisbücher*. Leipzig: Hinrichs, 1931.
———. *The Hebrew Kingdom*. Cambridge: Cambridge University Press, 1965.
Elat, M. *Samuel and the Foundation of Kingship in Ancient Israel*. Jerusalem: Magnes, 1998.
Fabry, H. J. "*minḥâ*." In *TDOT* 8 (1997) 407-21.
Faust, A. "Settlement Patterns and State Formation in Southern Samaria and the Archaeology of (a) Saul." In *Saul in Story and Tradition*, edited by C. S. Ehrlich in ooperation with M. C. White, 14-38. FAT 47. Tübingen: Mohr/Siebeck, 2006.
Fensham, F. C. "Did a Treaty between the Israelites and the Kenites Exist?" *BASOR* 175 (1964) 51-4.
———. "The Battle between the Men of Joab and Abner as a Possible Ordeal by Battle?" *VT* (1970) 356-57.
Finkelstein, I. "Arabian Trade and the Socio-Political Conditions in the Negev in the Twelfth-Eleven Centuries B.C.E." *JNES* 47 (1988) 241-52.
———. "The Emergence of the Monarchy in Israel: Environmental and Socio-Political Aspects." *Cathedra* 50 (1988) 3-26.
———. "The Emergence of the Monarchy in Israel: The Environmental and Socio-Economic Aspects." *JSOT* 44 (1989) 43-74.
———. "The Philistines in the Bible: A Late-Monarchic Perspective." *JSOT* 27 (2002) 131-67.
Fleming, D. E. "The Seven-Days Siege of Jericho in Holy War." In *Ki Baruch Hu: Ancient Near Eastern Studies, Biblical and Judaic Studies in Honor of Baruch A. Levine*, edited by R. Chazan et al., 221-28. Winona Lake, IN: Eisenbrauns, 1999.
Fohrer, G. "Die Sage in der Bible." In *Sagen und ihre Deutung*, 59-80. Evangelisches Forum 5. Göttingen: Vandenhoeck & Ruprecht, 1965.
Fokkelman, J. P. *Narrative Art and Poetry in the Books of Samuel*. Vol. 2, *The Crossing Fates (I Sam. 13-31 and II Sam. 1)*. SSN 23. Assen: Van Gorcum, 1986.
Fowler, J. D. *Theophoric Personal Names in Ancient Hebrew*. JSOTSup 49. Sheffield: JSOT Press, 1988.
Fox, N. S. *In the Service of the King: Officialdom in Ancient Israel and Judah*. Monographs of the Hebrew Union College 23. Cincinnati: Hebrew Union College Press, 2000.
Freedman, D. N. Review of *Patterns in the Early Poetry of Israel*, by Stanley Gevirtz." *JBL* 83 (1964) 201-3.
Frick, F. S. *The Formation of the State in Ancient Israel: A Survey of Models and Theories*. Social World of Biblical Antiquity Series 4. Decatur, GA: Almond, 1985.
Frisch, A. "'For I feared the people, and I yielded to them' (I Sam 15, 24): Is Saul's Guilt Attenuated or Intensified?" *ZAW* 108 (1996) 98-104.
Galling, K. "Goliath und seine Rüstung." In *Volume du Congrès Genève 1965*, 150-69. VTsup 15. Leiden: Brill, 1966.
Garsiel, M. "The Dispute Between Samuel and the People on the Question of Appointing King in Israel." *BethM* 87 (1981) 325-43.
———. *The First Book of Samuel: A Literary Study of Comparative Structures, Analogies and Parallels*. Ramat-Gan: Revivim, 1983.

Bibliography

———. "The Book of Samuel: Its Compositions, Structure and Significance as a Historiography Source." *JHS* 10 (2010) 1–42.

———. "The Battle of Michmas: a Historical Literary Study (1 Sam 13–14)." In *Studies in Bible and Exegesis, Arie Toeg in Memoriam*, edited by U. Simon and M. Goshen-Gottstein, 1:15–50. Ramat-Gan: Bar Illan University, 1985.

Gibson, J. C. L., editor. *Canaanite Myths and Legends*. 2nd ed. Edinburgh: T. &T. Clark, 1978.

Givati, M. "משפט המלך ומשפט המלוכה." *BethM* 98 (1984) 220–7 (Hebrew).

Goldman, S. *Samuel*. London: Soncino, 1962.

Gordon, C. H. *Before the Bible: The Common Background of the Greek and Hebrew Civilizations*. London: Collins, 1962.

Gordon C. H., and G. A. Rendsburg. *The Bible and the Ancient Near East*. 4th ed. New York: Norton, 1997.

Gordon, R. P. *1 & 2 Samuel*. Exeter, UK: Paternoster, 1986.

Gottwald, Norman K. *The Tribes of Yahweh: A Sociology of Liberated Israel, 1250–1050*. Maryknoll, NY: Orbis, 1979.

Graetz, H. *History of the Jews*. Edited and translated by Bella Löwy. Philadelphia: Jewish Publication Society of America, 1891–98.

Gray, G. B. *A Critical Introduction to the Old Testament*. New York: Scribners, 1919.

Gray, J. "Feudalism in Ugarit and Early Israel." *ZAW* 54 (1952) 49–55.

Greenspahn, F. E. "An Egyptian Parallel to Judg 17:6 and 21:25." *JBL* 101 (1982) 129–30.

Grønbaek, J. H. *Die Geschichte vom Aufstieg Davids (1. Sam. 15—2. Sam. 5): Tradition und Komposition*. Copenhagen: Prostant apud Munksgaard, 1971.

Gunn, D. M. *The Story of King David: Genre and Interpretation*. JSOTSup 6. Sheffield: JSOT Press, 1978.

Habel, N. "The Form and Significance of the Call Narratives." *ZAW* 77 (1965) 297–323.

Hallo, W. W. "Disturbing the Dead." In *Minhah le-Nahum: Biblical and Other Studies Presented to Nahum Sarna in Honour of His 70th Birthday*, edited by M. Brettler and M. Fishbane, 183–92. JSOTSup 154. Sheffield: JSOT Press, 1993.

Halpern, B. *The Constitution of the Monarchy in Israel*. HSM 25. Chico, CA: Scholars, 1981.

———. *David's Secret Demons: Messiah, Murderer, Traitor, King*. The Bible in Its World. Grand Rapids: Eerdmans, 2001.

Herrmann, S. *A History of Israel in Old Testament Times*. Translated by J. Bowden. Philadelphia: Fortress, 1975.

Hertzberg, H. W. *I & II Samuel: A Commentary*. Translated by J. S. Bowden. Old Testament Library. Philadelphia: Westminster, 1976.

Herzog, Z. "Beer-sheba of the Patriarchs." *BAR* 6 (1980) 12–28.

Hillers, D. R. "A Note on Some Treaty Terminology in the Old Testament." *BASOR* 176 (1964) 46–7.

Hoffner, H. A. "Crossing of the Taurus (1.73)." In *CS* 1 (1997) 184–185.

Hutter, M. "Religionsgeschichtliche Erwägungen zu 'elohim in 1Sam. 28,13." *BN* 21 (1983) 32–36.

Ishida, T. *History and Historical Writings in Ancient Israel: Studies in Biblical Historiography*. SHCANE 16. Leiden: Brill, 1999.

———. *The Royal Dynasties in Ancient Israel: A Study on the Formation and Development of Royal-Dynastic Ideology*. BZAW 142. Berlin: de Gruyter, 1977.

Bibliography

Jagersma, H. *A History of Israel in the Old Testament Period*. Translated by J. Bowden. London: SCM, 1982.
Japhet, S. *I & II Chronicles: A Commentary*. Old Testament Library. Louisville: Westminster John Knox, 1993.
Jastrow, M. *A Dictionary of the Targumim, The Talmud Babli and Jerushalmi, and Midrashic Literature*. New York: Pardes, 1950.
Jobling, D. "Saul's Fall and Jonathan's Rise: Tradition and Redaction in 1 Sam 14:1-46." *JBL* 95 (1976) 367-76.
―――. *The Sense of Biblical Narrative: Three Structural Analyses in the Old Testament (1 Samuel 13-31, Numbers 11-12, 1 Kings 17-18)*. JSOTSup 7. Sheffield: University of Sheffield, 1978.
Johnston, P. S. *Shades of Sheol: Death and Afterlife in the Old Testament*. Downers Grove, IL: InterVarsity, 2002.
Kallai, Z. "The Wars of Saul." In *The Military History of the Land of Israel in Biblical Times*, edited by J. Liver, 135-36. Jerusalem: Maarachoth, 1964 (Hebrew).
Kaufmann, Y. *Toledot ha-'emunah ha-yisre'elit*. 8 vols. Tel Aviv: Bialik Institute & Dvir, 1937-57 (Hebrew).
―――. "On the Story of the Medium." In *Mi-kivshonah shel ha-yetsirah ha-mikra'it: kovets ma'amarim*, 208-215. Tel Aviv: Dvir, 1966 (Hebrew).
Kearney, P. J. "The Role of the Gibeonites in the Deuteronomic History." *CBQ* 35 (1973) 1-19.
Kennedy, J. M."Ishmaiah." In *ABD* 3 (1992) 520.
Kitz, A. M. "The Plural Form of 'ûrîm and tummîm." *JBL* 116 (1997) 401-10.
Klein, R. W. *1 Samuel*. WBC 10. Waco, TX: Word, 1983.
Knoppers, G. N. *I Chronicles 10-29*. AB 12A. New York: Doubleday, 2004.
―――. "Israel's First King 'the Kingdom of Yhwh in the Hands of the Sons of David': The Place of the Saulide Monarchy in the Chronicler's Historiography." In *Saul in Story and Tradition*, edited by C. S. Ehrlich in cooperation with M. C. White, 187-213. FAT 47. Tübingen: Mohr/Siebek, 2006.
Koch, K. *The Growth of the Biblical Tradition*. Translated by S. M. Cupitt. New York: Scribners, 1969.
Kochavi, M. "Rescue in the Biblical Negev." *BAR* 6 (1980) 24-7.
Kooij, A. van der. The Story of David and Goliath: The Early History of Its Text." *ETL* 68 (1992) 118-31.
Kreuzer, S. "Saul—not always—at War." In *Saul in Story and Tradition*, edited by C. S. Ehrlich in cooperation with M. C. White, 39-58. FAT 47. Tübingen: Mohr/Siebek, 2006.
Lambert, W. G. *Babylonian Wisdom Literature*. Oxford: Clarendon, 1960.
Lande, I. *Formelhafte Wendungen der Umgangssprache im Alten Testament*. Leiden: Brill, 1949.
Langdon, S. *Die neubabylonischen Königsinschriften*. VAB 4. Leipzig: Hinrichs, 1912.
Lewis, T. J. *Cults of the Dead in Ancient Israel and Ugarit*. HSM 39. Atlanta: Scholars, 1989.
Lipiński, E. "Nāgîd, der Kronprinz." *VT* 24 (1974) 497-9.
Loewenstamm, S.E. "חפשי." In *EMiqr* 3:256-257.
Lohfink, N. "ḥopšî." In *TDOT* 5 (1986) 114-8.
Long, V. Philips. *The Reign and Rejection of King Saul: A Case for Literary and Theological Coherence*. SBLDS 118. Atlanta: Scholars, 1989.
Luckenbill, D. D. *Ancient Records of Assyria and Babylonia*. 2 vols. Chicago: University of Chicago Press, 1926.

Bibliography

Mabee, C. "Judicial Instrumentality in Ahimelech Story." In *Early Jewish and Christian Exegesis: Studies in Memory of William H. Brownlee*, edited by C. A. Evans and W. F. Stinespring, 17-32. Scholars Press Homage Series 10. Atlanta: Scholars, 1987.

———. "David's Judicial Exoneration." *ZAW* 92 (1980) 89-107.

Macdonald, J. "The Status and Role of the *Na'ar* in Israelite Society." *JNES* 35 (1976) 147-70.

Mack, H. "Three Parables of R. Shimon b. Lakis Concerning King Saul's Inquiry of the Spirits." In *Studies in Bible and Exegesis*, edited by M. Garsiel et al., 5:179-95. Ramat Gan: Bar-Ilan University Press, 2000.

Malamat, A. "Aspects of the Foreign Policies of David and Solomon." *JNES* 22 (1963) 1-17.

———. "Doctrines of Causality in Biblical and Hittite Historiography. A Parallel." *VT* 1955 (5) 1-12.

Malul, M. "Was David Involved in the Death of Saul on the Gilboa Mountain?" *RB* 103 (1996) 517-45.

Mauchline, J. *1 and 2 Samuel*. NCB. Greenwood, SC: Attic, 1971.

Mayer, G. "נזר *nzr*." In *TDOT* 9 (1998) 306-311.

Mazar, B. "גבעת שאול", "גבעת בנימין." In *EMiqr* 2:412-6 (Hebrew).

———. "Ahimelech." In *EMiqr* 1:217-8 (Hebrew).

McCarter, P. K. *I Samuel*. AB 8. Garden City: Doubleday, 1980.

———. *II Samuel*. AB 9. New York: Doubleday, 1984.

McCarthy, D. J. "Compact and Kingship: Stimuli for Hebrew Covenant Thinking." In *Studies in the Period of David and Solomon and Others Essays*, edited by T. Ishida, 75-92. Winona Lake, IN: Eisenbrauns, 1982.

———. "The Symbolism of Blood and Sacrifice." *JBL* 88 (1969) 166-76.

McKenzie, S. L. *King David: A Biography*. Oxford: Oxford University Press, 2000.

Melamed, E. Z. "*Benjamin and Gilead*." *Tarbiz* 5 (1934) 121-25.

Mendelsohn, I. "Samuel's Denunciation of Kingship in Light of Akkadian Document from Ugarit." *BASOR* 143 (1956) 17-22.

———. "The Canaanite Term for 'Free Proletarian.'" *BASOR* 83 (1941) 36-9.

Meshel, Z. "Ḥorvat Ritma-an Iron Age Fortress in the Negev Highlands." *TA* 4 (1977) 110-35.

Mettinger, T. N. D. *King and Messiah: The Civil and Sacral Legitimation of the Israelite Kings*. Coniectanea Biblical: Old Testament Series 8. Gleerup: Lund, 1976.

Milgrom, J. "The Alleged Wave Offering in Israel and the Ancient Near East." *IEJ* 22 (1972) 33-8.

Miller, J. M. "Saul Rise to Power Some Observations Concerning 1 Sam 9:1-10:16; 10:26-11:15 and 13:2-14:46." *CBQ* 36 (1974) 157-74.

———. "Geba/Gibeah of Benjamin." *VT* 25 (1975) 145-66.

Miller, J. M., and J. H. Hayes. *A History of Ancient Israel and Judah*. Philadelphia: Westminster, 1986. 2nd ed., 2006.

Mommer, P. "Ist auch Saul unter den Propheten? Ein Beitrag zu 1 Sam 19,18-24." *BN* 38/39 (1987) 53-61.

Morgenstern, Julian. "David and Jonathan." *JBL* 78 (1959) 322-5.

———. "*Beena* Marriage [Matriarchate] in Ancient Israel and Its Historical Implications." *ZAW* 47 (1929) 91-110.

Na'aman, N. "The Pre-Deuteronomistic Story of King Saul and Its Historical Significance." *CBQ* 54 (1992) 638-58.

———. "Beth-aven, Bethel and the Early Israelite Sanctuaries." *Zeitschrift des deutschen Palstina Verein* 103 (1987) 13–21.

———. "Shaaraim—The Gateway to the Kingdom of Judah." *Journal of Hebrew Scriptures* 8 (2008) 2–5. Online: http://www.jhsonline.org.and http://purl.org/jhs.

Ne'eman, P. "המלכת שאול." *BethM* 30 (1967) 94–110 (Hebrew).

Nelson, R. D. "Amasa." In *ABD* 1 (1992) 182.

Nihan, C. "Saul among the Prophets (1Sam 10:10–12 and 19:18–24): The Reworking of Saul Figure in the Context of the Debate on 'Charismatic Prophecy' in the Persian Era." In *Saul in Story and Tradition*, edited by C. S. Ehrlich in cooperation with M. C. White, 88–118. FAT 47. Tübingen: Mohr/Siebek, 2006.

Noth, M. *Geschichte Israels*. Göttingen: Vandenhoeck & Ruprecht, 1956.

———. *The History of Israel*. 2nd ed. Translated by S. Godman. London: A. & C. Black, 1958.

Nowack, W. *Richter, Ruth u. Bücher Samuelis*. Handkommentar zum Alten Testament. Göttingen: Vandenhoeck & Ruprecht, 1902.

Oded, B. "עמון." In *EMiqr* 6:254–71 (Hebrew).

Ottosson, M. *Gilead Tradition and History*. Lund: Gleerup, 1969.

Paralelle, W., and R. Polzin, "HWQY' and Covenant Institution in Israel." *HTR* 62 (1969) 227–40.

Pardee, D. "The Ba'lu Myth (1.86)." In *CS* 1 (1997) 241–74.

Paul, S.M. "I Samuel 9:7: An Interview Fee." *Bib* 59 (1978) 542–4.

Peden, A. J. *Egyptian Historical Inscription of the Twentieth Dynasty*. Documenta Mundi Aegyptiaca 3. Jonsered: Åströms, 1994.

Pfeiffer, R. H. *Introduction to the Old Testament*. New York: Harper, 1948.

Polzin, R. "On Taking Renewal Seriously: 1 Sam 11:1–15." In *Ascribe to the Lord: Biblical and Other Studies in Memory of Peter C. Craigie*, edited by L. Eslinger and G. Taylor, 493–507. JSOTSup 67. Sheffield: JSOT Press, 1988.

———. *Samuel and the Deuteronomist: 1 Samuel*. San Francisco: Harper &Row, 1989.

Price, B. J. "Secondary State formation: An Explanation Model." In *Origin of the State: The Anthropology of Political Evolution*, edited by R. Cohen and E. R. Service, 161–86. Philadelphia: Institute for the Study of Human Issues, 1978.

Pritchard, J. B., editor. *Ancient Near Eastern Texts Relating to the Old Testament*. 3rd ed. Princeton: Princeton University Press, 1969.

———. *Gibeon, Where the Sun Stood Still*. Princeton: Princeton University Press, 1962.

———. "The Water System at Gibeon." *BA* 19 (1956) 66–75.

———. *The Water System of Gibeon*. University of Pennsylvania Museum Monographs. Philadelphia: University of Pennsylvania, 1961.

Rad, G. von. *Holy War in Ancient Israel*. Translated and edited by M. J. Dawn. 1991. Reprinted, Eugene, OR: Wipf & Stock, 2000.

Rainey, A. F. "Institutions: Family, Civil, and Military." In *Ras Shamra Parallels*, vol. 2, edited by L. R. Fisher, 71–107. Analecta Orientalia 50. Rome: Pontifical Biblical Institute, 1972.

Rainey, A. F., and R. Steven Notley. *The Sacred Bridge: Carta's Atlas of the Biblical World*. Jerusalem: Carta, 2006.

Reviv, H. *From Clan to Monarchy: Israel in the Biblical Period*. Jerusalem: Magens, 1979.

Richter, W. *Die sogenannten vorprophetischen Berufungsberichte*. FRLANT 101. Göttingen: Vandenhoeck & Ruprechts, 1970.

———. "Die nāgîd Formel." *BZ* 9 (1965) 71–84.

Bibliography

Rofé, A. *The Prophetical Stories*. Jerusalem: Magnes, 1982.

———. "נחש מלך בני עמון על פי מגילת שמואל מקמראן." *BethM* 103 (1985) 456–62.

———. "The Battle of David and Goliath: Folklore, Theology, Eschatology." In *Judaic Perspective on Ancient Israel*, edited by J. Neusner et al., 117–51. Philadelphia: Fortress, 1987.

Sawyer, J. "What Was a *Mošiaʿ*?" *VT* 15 (1965) 475–86.

Schmidt, L. *Menschlicher Erfolg und Jahwes Initiative: Studien zu Tradition, Interpretation und Historie in Überlieferungen von Gideon, Saul und David*. WMANT 38. Neukirchen-Vluyn: Neukirchener, 1970.

Schunck, K. D. *Benjamin: Untersuchungen zur Entstehung und Geschichte eines israelitischen Stammes*. BZAW 86. Berlin: Töpelmann, 1963.

Segal, M. Z. *Samuel*. Tell Aviv: Dvir, 1948.

Simon, U. *Reading Prophetic Narratives*. Translated by L. J. Schramm. Indiana Studies in Biblical Literature. Bloomington: Indiana University Press, 1997.

Sinclair, L. A. *An Archaeological Study of Gibeah (Tell el-Ful)*. Annual of the American Schools of Oriental Research 34–35. New Haven: Yale University Press, 1960.

———. "An Archeological Study of Gibeah." *BA* 27 (1964) 52–63.

Smith, H. P. *The Books of Samuel*. ICC. New York: Scribners, 1899.

Smith, W. R. *Kinship and Marriage in Early Arabia*. London: A. & C. Black, 1903.

Soggin, J. A. "The Reign of 'ešbaʿal Son of Saul." In *Old Testament and Oriental Studies*, 31–49. Biblica Orientalia 29. Rome: Biblical Institute Press, 1975.

Sperling, D. *The Original Torah: The Political Intent of the Bible's Writers*. New York: New York University Press, 1998.

Spronk, K. *Beatific Afterlife in Ancient Israel and in the Ancient Near East*. Alter Orient und Altes Testament 219. Neukirchen-Vluyn: Neukirchener, 1986.

Stager, L. E. "The Archaeology of the Family in Ancient Israel." *BASOR* 260 (1985) 1–35.

Stern, P. D. *The Biblical Ḥerem: A Window on Israel's Religion Experience*. Brown Judaic Studies 211. Atlanta: Scholars, 1991.

Stoebe, H. J. *Das erste Buch Samuelis*. Kommentar zum Alten Testament 8/1. Gütersloh: Mohn, 1973.

Thompson, J. A. "The Significance of the Verb *Love* in the David–Jonathan Narrative in 1 Samuel." *VT* 24 (1974) 334–8.

Thornton, T. C. G. "Charismatic Kingship in Israel and Judah." *JTS* 14 (1963) 1–11.

Toorn, K. van der. "Saul and the Rise of Israelite Religion." *VT* 43 (1993) 519–42.

Tov, E. "The Composition of 1 Samuel 16–18 in Light of the Septuagint Version." In *Empirical Models for Biblical Criticism*, edited by J. H. Tigay, 97–103. Philadelphia: University of Pennsylvania Press, 1985.

Tsevat, M. "The Emergence of the Israelite Monarchy: Eli, Samuel, and Saul." In *The Age of the Monarchies: Political History*, 61–75. WHJP 4:1. Edited by A. Malamat and I. Eph'al. Jerusalem: Massada, 1979.

———. "Marriage and Monarchical Legitimacy in Ugarit and Israel." *JSS* 3 (1958) 237–43.

———. "Assyriological Notes the First Book of Samuel." In *Studies in the Bible Presented to M. H. Segal*, edited by J. M. Grintz and J. Liver, 77–86. Jerusalem: Kiryat Sepher, 1964.

Tsumura, D. T. *The First Book of Samuel*. New International Commentary on the Old Testament. Grand Rapids: Eerdmans, 2007.

Ulrich, E. C., Jr. *The Qumran Text of Samuel and Josephus*. HSM 19. Missoula, MT: Scholars, 1978.

Bibliography

Vanderkam, James C. "Davidic Complicity in the Deaths of Abner and Eshbaal: A Historical and Redactional Study." *JBL* 99 (1980) 521-39.
Vaux, R. de. *The Bible and the Ancient Near East.* Translated by D. McHugh. Garden City, NY: Doubleday, 1971.
———. *Ancient Israel: It Life and Institutions.* Translated by J. McHugh. London: Darton, Longman & Todd, 1961.
Veijola, T. "David und Meribaal." *RB* 85 (1978) 338-61.
Ward, R. L. "The Story of David's Rise: A Traditional-Historical Study of I Samuel xvi 14—II Samuel v." Ph.D. diss., Vanderbilt University, 1967.
Weiser, A. *Samuel: Seine geschichtliche Aufgabe und religiöse Bedeutung. Traditionsgeschichtliche Untersuchungen zu 1.Samuel 7-12.* FRLANT 81. Göttingen: Vandenhoeck & Ruprecht, 1962.
———. *The Old Testament: Its Formation and Development.* New York: Association Press, 1961.
Weisman, Z. "The Nature and Background of *bāḥūr* in the Old Testament." *VT* 31 (1981) 441-50.
Wellhausen, J. *Prolegomena to the History of Israel.* Translated by J. S. Black and A. Menzies. Edinburgh: A. & C. Black, 1885.
———. *Israelitische und Jüdische Geschichte.* Berlin: de Gruyter, 1958.
———. *Die Composition des Hexateuchs und der Historischen Bücher des Alten Testament.* Berlin: de Gruyter, 1963.
Whitelam, K. W. *The Just King: Monarchial Authority in Ancient Israel.* JSOTSup 12. Sheffield: JSOT Press, 1979.
Wildberger, H. "Sage and Legende." In *BHH* 3:1641-5.
Willis, J. T. "The Function of Comprehensive Anticipatory Redactional Joints in I Samuel 16-18." *ZAW* 85 (1973) 294-314.
Wilson, R. R. "Prophecy and Ecstasy: A Reexamination." *JBL* 98 (1979) 321-37.
Wiseman, D. J. "Is it Peace?—Covenant and Diplomacy." *VT* 32 (1982) 309-26.
———. "Alalakh." In *Archeology and Old Testament Study*, edited by D. W. Thomas, 119-35. Oxford: Clarendon, 1967.
Yadin, Y. "Goliath's Javelin and the מנור ארגים." *PEQ* 87 (1955) 58-69.
———. "Let the young men, I pray thee, arise and play before us." *JPOS* (1948) 110-6.
Yalkut Shimoni: Midrash al Torah Nevim u-Khetuvim. 2 vols. Jerusalem: Levin-Epshtain, 1966-67.
Yeivin, S. "The Benjaminite Settlement in the Western Part of their Territory." *IEJ* 21 (1971) 141-54.
Yonick, S. S. "The Rejection of Saul: A Study of Sources." *AJBA* 4 (1971) 29-50.
Zakovitch, Y. *David: From Shepherd to Messiah.* Jerusalem: Yad Ben Zvi, 1995.

Scripture Index

HEBREW BIBLE

Genesis

6:6–7	35
15	38
17:6	1
25:15	44
27	2
31:34–35	57
32:2–3	124
32:14	97
32:19	97
32:21	97
32:22	97
36:12	43
38:12	86
39:6	10
40:4	86
43:11	97
49:8–10	51
49:19	83

Exodus

2:2	10
3:7	10
3:9	10
3:10	10
3:11	10, 12
3:12	10
3:15	10
4:1	10
4:10	10
4:12	10
4:16	113
7:1	113
10:16–17	89
15:20	53
17:8	33
17:9	98
17:16	33
18	34
21:2	96
22:8	113
22:27	113
23:6	2
23:8	2
24:1	13
25:23–30	107

Leviticus

8:32	13
24:5	107

Numbers

11:16	13
11:24	13
12:3	17
16:15	8
24:7	34
27:19	13

153

Deuteronomy

5:23	112
5:26	113
10:17	2
16:19	2
18:12	114
20:18	33
24:1–4	129
25:17–19	89
25:19	33
27:25	2
32:30	53
33:20	83
34:3–4	125

Joshua

6	38
7:1	16
8:3	98
9	135
11:4	24
11:21	23
14:14	23
15:24	35
15:33–36	32
15:44	61
18:17	20
21:36	124
23	20
24:19	112, 113

Judges

1:12	28
2:14–16	61
2:14	22
3:8	96
3:9	38
3:13	35
3:14	96
3:15	38, 97
3:27	39
4–5	34
4:3	24
5:4	35
5:14	35
6:3	35, 61
6:14–15	10
6:15	10, 12, 17
6:16	10
6:33	35
6:34	10, 39
7:12	24, 35
7:16	40
7:20	40
7:22	28
8:22–23	7
9:4	82, 98
9:5	135
9:8–15	7
9:23	48
9:43	40
10:4	13
10:6	37, 43
10:9	37
10:11	37, 43
10:12	35, 43
11:3	82, 98
11:29–34	4
11:34	53
12:1–7	4
12:3	70
12:5	35
12:9	13
12:15	35
14:6	16
14:11–13	13
14:19	13, 16
15:14	16
16:1–3	79
16:20	48
16:21	36
17–21	4
19	39
19:30	39
20:16	31
20:23	87
20:26	108
20:27	87
20:31	13
20:39	13
21:12–14	41

1 Samuel

1–7	xiv
2:9	114
2:12–17	2
2:22	2
3:2	2
3:13	2
4:1	102
4:9	96
4:12–17	119
4:12	xv
7:6	108
7:9	87
7:11–14	3
7:14	33, 45
7:17	3
8	xiv
8:1–22	1, 21
8:5	2
8:6	2
8:11–20	52
8:11–18	7, 96
8:11–17	3
8:11	49
8:12	74, 101
8:14	74, 101, 138
8:18	7
8:19	3
8:20	3, 8
9–15	xiii–xiv
9:1f.	18
9:1	101
9:2	xiv, 10
9:7–8	13
9:15–16	12
9:15	10
9:16–17	10
9:16	4, 10
9:20	12, 16
9:21	10, 17, 47, 56, 88
10:1–9	59
10:1	10
10:2	13
10:3–4	13
10:4	13
10:5–7a	10
10:5–6	13
10:5	40, 104
10:6	10, 16
10:7b	10
10:8	85, 86
10:9	16
10:10–12	60
10:11	59
10:12	59
10:16	17
10:17	17
10:19	3
10:22–23	47
10:22	10, 17
10:24	14
10:26	104
10:27	18, 21
11	xvii, 22, 40
11:1–15	19
11:1–11	40
11:4	104
11:6	16
11:8	33
11:12	18, 20, 21
11:13	108
11:14	18
11:15	20
12	1, 8, 21
12:12	3, 4 42
12:13	18
13–14	xvii, 22, 86, 105
13	25, 69, 85, 88
13:1–11	39
13:2–3	41
13:2	8, 26, 33, 104
13:3–4	32
13:3	24, 25, 40, 94, 104
13:4	69
13:7	24
13:7b–15a	85, 86
13:8–14	69
13:8–12	70
13:8–9	86
13:8	85, 86
13:9	108
13:13–14	121

1 Samuel (cont.)

Reference	Pages
13:13	72
13:14	86, 89
13:15–16	70
13:15	33
13:16	104
13:17–18	40
13:19–22	100
13:20	96
13:22	24, 100
13:23	23, 26
14	24–28, 69
14:1	69
14:2	70, 104
14:4	23
14:5	104
14:8–10	87
14:9–10	69
14:18–19	69
14:18	106
14:19	29, 61
14:20	28
14:21	24
14:24–29	16
14:24	108
14:32–35	xv
14:33–34	108
14:35	108
14:36–37	69
14:36	61
14:37	87
14:44–45	34
14:45	76
14:47–48	xvii, 22, 40, 41
14:48	36
14:52	18
15–16	42
15	xvii, 22, 63, 86
15:1–34	86
15:1	88
15:3	77, 108, 121
15:7	36
15:8–9	121
15:9	34
15:11	90
15:12	88
15:13–30	88
15:14	88
15:17	17
15:20	88
15:22–23	88
15:22	88
15:23	88
15:25	89, 90
15:27	90, 114
15:28	51, 89
15:29	90–91
15:30	90
15:34	104
15:35	35, 59, 90
16–31	xiv, 141
16	52
16:7	10, 17
16:11–12	47
16:11	47
16:12	10
16:14—2 Sam 5	67
16:14–23	51
16:14	16
16:15	93
16:18	47, 50, 126
16:19–23	51
16:19	49
16:21	49
16:22	49, 52
16:23	16
17:1—18:4	51
17	xvii, 22, 31, 51
17:1–11	50
17:3–5	14
17:5–7	31
17:5	100
17:9	49–50, 54, 96
17:12–31	50
17:13	14
17:15	52
17:24	32
17:25	54, 78, 84, 96
17:26	113
17:27	54, 84
17:28–29	47
17:32–39	50
17:35	54
17:36	54, 113
17:37	29

Scripture Index

17:38-39	49	19:12	71
17:38	100	19:13-17	57
17:46-47	32	19:13	60
17:46	30, 54	19:14	84
17:49	31	19:15	58
17:50	50	19:17	58, 71
17:51-54	50	19:18-24	59, 60
17:52	4, 33	19:18	71
17:55-58	50	19:20-24	58
17:55	49	19:21	13
17:57	54	19:24	59
17:58	50	20:4	65
18:1-5	51	20:9	69
18:1	55, 58	20:10	84
18:3	58	20:13-17	73
18:4	49, 99, 100	20:17	58
18:5	53, 55	20:18	65
18:7	53, 82	20:30	73
18:10-12	50, 66	20:32	72
18:10-11	58	20:34	73
18:10	16	21-22	95
18:11-12	54	21	84
18:12	55	21:1-9	85, 101
18:14-15	55	21:1	102
18:14	126	21:5	107
18:15	55	21:7	16
18:16	55, 82	21:8	93, 94
18:17	54, 55	21:10-14	82
18:18	56	21:12	82
18:20-21	121	22	62, 84
18:21	55	22:1	85, 101
18:22	58	22:2	82
18:23	17	22:3-4	42
18:25	55	22:3	83
18:27	xvii, 22	22:6-8	74
18:28	55, 126	22:6	93, 104, 105
18:29	55	22:7	74, 100
18:30	xvii, 22	22:8	74, 76
19	71	22:9	94
19:1	55, 58, 69, 70	22:16	76
19:2	58, 69	22:17	61, 95
19:5	20, 58, 70	22:19	77
19:6	58, 76	22:22	62
19:8	xvii, 22	23	60
19:9-10	54	23:1	xvii, 22
19:10	71	23:2	87
19:11	71	23:4	61, 87
19:11	58	23:10-12	84

157

1 Samuel (cont.)

23:11	62	28:17	90
23:12	62	28:19	117
23:13	36, 82	28:20	xvi
23:14	84	28:21	xvi, 112
23:17	65, 72	28:25	110
23:19–24	84	29:1–2	123
23:19	104, 105	29:3	93
23:22–23	63	29:5	82
23:27	xvii, 22	30	35
24–26	64	30:7–8	87
24	64	31	118
24:1	84	31:1	115
24:4–5	122	31:2	41, 122
24:4	65	31:3–13	119
24:4b–5	65	31:3	83, 100, 121
24:5	65	31:4	115
24:8a	65	31:5	115
24:10	65	31:6	122
24:11	66	31:7	122
24:17	66, 67	31:8	115, 122
24:21	65, 90	31:9	60
24:22	122	31:11	41
25:1	84	31:12–13	41
25:2–11	36	31:12	122

2 Samuel

25:13	82		
25:44	81	1	118
26	64–65	1:2–26	35
26:1	36, 84, 104	1:2	118
26:8	65, 122	1:4	122
26:12	65, 122	1:13–16	134
26:23	65	1:16	119
26:25	66	1:20	53
27:2–12	82	1:21	100
27:2	82	1:22	100
27:6	101	2–4	136
27:8	35	2:8–12	123
28–31	xvii, 22	2:8	122
28:4–20	110	2:9	124
28:5	xv	2:10	126
28:6	87	2:12–23	83, 126
28:7	110	2:12–17	28
28:9	88, 108	2:12–16	125
28:13–14	111	2:13	104
28:13	111	2:17	126
28:14	111	2:18–23	132
28:15	xviii, 114	3:1	126–28

Scripture Index

3:3	127	14:3	98
3:6	128	14:25	10
3:11	130	15:1	94, 99
3:12–21	129	16:1	95
3:12	129	16:3	138
3:15–16	81, 130	16:5	98
3:16	98	16:8	138
3:17–19	125	16:18	18
3:17	130	16:22	128
3:21–23	132	17:1	98
3:28	131	17:11	24
3:29	133	17:18	98, 99
3:37	132	17:24—19:8	124
3:39	133	17:25	84
4	136	17:27	84
4:1–3	102	19:14	84
4:2	101	19:17	98
4:4	134	19:18	95
5:8	28	19:29	139
5:10	126	20:1	138–39
5:17	127	20:10	84
5:19	87	20:23	95
5:23	87	21:1–14	136
6:16–23	82	21:1–9	85, 101
6:16	82	21:1–2	135
6:23	130	21:1	102, 104
7:12	136	21:3	136
7:18–21	17	21:4	136
8	42	21:5	136
8:2	42, 97	21:6	136
8:3–5	42	21:7	134
8:3	44	21:8	56, 78, 130
8:6	97	21:19	31
8:12–14	42	23:13	13
8:12	35	23:16	108
8:16	95	23:18	13
9	136	23:20–33	99
9:1	136, 137	23:23	99
9:2	95	23:24	31
9:3	134	23:31	98–99
9:6	134	26:2	98
9:7	134		
9:9	95		

1 Kings

9:10	95
9:11	95
10:1	128
10:2	42
10:9	98

1–2	xiii
1:5	99
1:6	2
1:25	18

159

1 Kings (cont.)

1:28	94
1:32–39	14
1:33–35	11
1:34	18
1:38–40	11
1:39	14, 18
2:8	98
2:26	107
3:4	104
3:7	17
4:4	95
4:7	94
4:14	124
4:21	97
5:1	18
5:2	97
11:4	2
11:5–6	137
11:29–31	90
11:29	14
13:7	13
14:3	11, 13
14:27–28	99
15:29	77, 137
16:11	77, 137
18:45–46	13
22:20–25	66

2 Kings

1:8	114
3:4	18
3:15	16
3:19	13
3:25	13
4:1	82
4:31	115
4:42	11
5:15	13
8:8–9	13
9:10	14
9:13	14
10:1–11	135
10:6–7	137
11	99
11:12	14, 18
11:14	14
15:20	101
17:3–4	18
17:3	97
17:4	97
20:12	97
22:12	93
25:7	36
25:8	93

Isaiah

1:25	44
8:19	111, 112
10:32	106
14:9	114
29:4	112
39:1	97

Jeremiah

1:5–6	15
7:12	102
7:21–23	88
10:10	113
16:6	102
21:12	79
23:36	113
48–49	42
51:39	115

Ezekiel

32:27	114
38:12	44

Hosea

3:4–5	6
3:5	6
8:4	6, 20
8:10	6
9:15	20
13:10–11	6

Amos

7:12	11

Jonah

1:1–5	54

Scripture Index

Micah

3:5	11

Zechariah

9:9	10–11

Psalms

7:1	xvi
18:17	64
45:13	97
54	63
54:3	63
59	80
59:1	80
78:59–72	xiii
83:7	44
88:13	110
89:20–39	xiii
91:7	53
97:7	113
116:11	63
143:3	110

Job

3:13–19	115
7:14	48
10:21	110
14:12	115

Proverbs

14:10	51
15:20	72

Ruth

2:1	101
2:5–6	94

Ecclesiastes

9:5	111

Esther

2:7	10

1 Chronicles

2:16–17	84
2:17	84
3:2	127
4:10	76
4:34–44	44
5:10	44
5:18–22	44
5:19	44
6:65	124
8:29–40	103
8:29	104
9:35–44	103
9:35	104
10	120
10:3	100
10:6	120
10:13–14	120
10:13	116
10:14	116, 120
11:6	28, 31
11:22–29	99
11:26	31
11:33	99
12	82
12:1–8	83
12:2–8	84
12:2	31, 83, 100
12:4	85
12:9–16	83
12:17–19	83, 84
12:17	83
12:30	83
20:5	31
29:22	19

2 Chronicles

12:10–11	99
13:3	98
13:17	98
17:5	97
24:5	19
24:12	19
25:5	98
26:14	31
34:20	93

161

God's First King

APOCRYPHA

1 Maccabees   Psalm 151
3:18–19   70   31, 47–48

~

NEW TESTAMENT

John
1:29–34   12
6:15   17

www.ingramcontent.com/pod-product-compliance
Lightning Source LLC
Chambersburg PA
CBHW030113170426
43198CB00009B/602